ABOVE TOP SECRET

UNCOVER THE MYSTERIES OF THE DIGITAL AGE

BY JIM MARRS

disinformation

Grateful acknowledgment goes to Nick Redfern and Thomas Ruffner, who contributed significantly to this work, as well as the dedicated Above Top Secret management team of Bill Irvine, Mark Allin, Simon Gray and Stephen Melzer, along with the ATS members whose comments are included here.

Published by:

The Disinformation Company Ltd.
163 Third Avenue, Suite 108
New York, NY 10003
Tel.: +1.212.691.1605
Fax: +1.212.691.1606
www.disinfo.com

Library of Congress Control Number: 2008938945
ISBN: 978-1-934708-09-5

Designed by Greg Stadnyk
Printed in the United States of America

Distributed in the U.S. and Canada by:
Consortium Book Sales and Distribution
34 Thirteenth Avenue NE, Suite 101
Minneapolis MN 55413-1007
Tel.: +1.800.283.3572
www.cbsd.com

Distributed in the United Kingdom and Eire by:
Turnaround Publisher Services Ltd.
Unit 3, Olympia Trading Estate
Coburg Road
London, N22 6TZ
Tel.: +44.(0)20.8829.3000
Fax: +44.(0)20.8881.5088
www.turnaround-uk.com

Distributed in Australia by:
Tower Books
Unit 2/17 Rodborough Road
Frenchs Forest NSW 2086
Tel.: +61.2.9975.5566 Fax: +61.2.9975.5599 Email: info@towerbooks.com.au

Attention colleges and universities, corporations and other organizations: Quantity discounts are available on bulk purchases of this book for educational training purposes, fund-raising, or gift giving. Special books, booklets, or book excerpts can also be created to fit your specific needs. For information contact Marketing Department of The Disinformation Company Ltd.

10 9 8 7 6 5 4 3 2 1

JIM MARRS

ABOVE TOP SECRET

UNCOVER THE MYSTERIES OF THE DIGITAL AGE

UFOS, ALIENS, 9/11, NWO,
POLICE STATE, CONSPIRACIES,
COVER UPS, AND MUCH MORE
"THEY" DON'T WANT YOU TO KNOW ABOUT

ATS
abovetopsecret.com
deny ignorance

CONTENTS

conspiracy theorist *n.*

con•spir•a•cy the•o•rist [kʌn n-*spir*-uh-see *thee*-er-ist]

Someone who postulates on the idea that many important geopolitical events or economic and societal trends are the products of secret plots that are generally unknown to the public at large.

FOREWORD

The last century witnessed the rise of what is popularly known as the "conspiracy theorist," a subculture of like-minded people who have become concerned that major contemporary and historical events were not caused by "what we've been told" through mainstream media or our history books. Often misunderstood as "those crazy conspiracy nuts," these people are passionately concerned about society, have a deep affection for their country, and are driven by a strong sense of ethics and justice.

The tipping point that can inspire someone to begin asking the questions that will transform them into a conspiracy theorist are as diverse as the conspiracies they theorize about. Some have looked as far back as the time leading up to World War I and have noticed the oddities surrounding the assassination of Archduke Ferdinand. Many have become doubtful of the official story surrounding the events in Roswell, New Mexico in 1947 and the resulting broad spectrum of UFO cover-up questions. The rise of the Federal Reserve and contemporary economic troubles have provided a fountain spring of stimuli for questions related to financial conspiracies. In fact, if you've ever watched the evening news and wondered to yourself, "that can't be right," you have taken your first tentative step into the world of conspiracy theory.

For years, conspiracy theorists belonged to a soft-spoken subculture relegated to perusing a limited selection of small-press books in the dark, unvisited corners of bookstores, searching out hard-to-find independent newspapers, and mail-order VHS tapes of difficult-to-watch production quality. Even with the relatively robust categories of UFO-conspiracy aficionados and JFK assassination theorists, it was difficult to fathom how many of "us" there really were. Then came the Internet, and everything changed.

Starting first via uncertain voices on early bulletin board systems in the 1980s, conspiracy theorists from an abundance of diverse topic areas found each other online. As additional channels for collaboration grew through IRC, Usenet, and CompuServe, more and more like-minded people with troubling questions found answers in their online conversations. The advent of the web and ubiquitous easy Internet access sparked a startling societal explosion that brought conspiracy theories from the dark corners of bookstores to the forefront of popular culture. In fact, the wildly popular phrase of 2007, "Don't taze me bro," was a plea from a conspiracy theorist that exploded into the pop-culture lexicon because of the Internet.

Today, the web has given birth to what is nothing short of a renaissance of conspiracy theory. The zero-cost of entry and easy access to blogging has inspired a significant portion of the "blogosphere" to focus on a myriad of conspiracy topics. For better or worse, untold millions of pages examine hundreds of variations on thousands of conspiracy theories. Some are superlative examples of relentless research, others push the speculative envelope with magnificence, and many more are dubious flights of fancy. But no matter the accuracy or veracity of these millions of thoughts, the sheer volume bears witness to the tremendous number of people with provocative questions in search of answers.

The evolution of the Internet has given birth to another cultural phenomenon, one that has its roots in the core essence of how the medium was birthed. While the technological underpinnings were created via a military mandate, the users of the Internet directed its evolution as a culture of collaboration, driven by the ethics of sharing. Despite all the billions of dollars invested in e-commerce and Internet advertising, the essence of the medium is driven by the share-and-share-alike ideology of its users. From hyperlinking to Facebook, every important advance in core online usefulness has its roots in the need for the users to share information, and nowhere has the urge to learn through sharing been more readily apparent than in the birth of online communities devoted to conspiracy theories.

AboveTopSecret.com began in 1997 as the hobby of an inquisitive teenager named Simon Gray of Swindon, England. Over the years, user demand dictated the inclusion of a discussion board section of the site so that like-minded conspiracy theorists could share information and collaboratively speculate on what they learn. In 2003, the demand imposed on Mr. Gray's original hobby became so great that the site outgrew its humble beginnings and dedicated hardware was urgently required. Over the next four years, demand continued to grow at a pace that required additional investments in technology every nine months on average. The "perfect storm" explosion of Internet accessibility, online conspiracy theory topics, and the urge to share has grown the humble hobby into a stunning Internet phenomenon with over 1.8 million pages of content and nearly two million visits each month, making it the largest and most-popular website dealing with conspiracy theories.

Regular users of AboveTopSecret.com will be eager to tell you that such growth and success is no surprise. The heart and soul of our website is an inspiring social content community that is often referred to as the best in class of any topical genre. Discussion boards, forums and blogs have rightfully earned negative reputations for an often overly free-form environment of juvenile behavior, questionable content, personal attacks, and insults. Five years ago, the users of AboveTopSecret.com decided that they wanted none of that. A motto of "Deny Ignorance" was adopted as a rallying cry that not only spoke to the need to be civil with one another, but also stated the clear desire to understand the truths behind difficult questions. This unique civil environment of AboveTopSecret.com is credited with its rapid rise to success. Participants are able to focus on whatever they feel are important issues and provocative questions, with complete confidence that those responding will do so out of a desire to aid in collaborative learning.

While the civil environment has attracted a humbling number of intelligent people asking important questions, the real magic of AboveTopSecret.com is that it is a true user defined media vehicle. Complete editorial control is in the hands of the "wisdom of the crowds" as more than 1,200 new topics every day are ranked and prioritized by the participants. The staff and management have no ability to influence editorial decisions or the positioning of topics on any of the site's pages (with exception of removing occasional inappropriate items). The result is an ever-evolving ecosystem of content that represents a stream of consciousness from an enormous collaboration of intelligent people who want nothing more than answers that make sense.

No contemporary author is better prepared to provide you with a summary of AboveTopSecret.com's unique and collaborative stream of consciousness than Jim Marrs. He's a superlative writer, a brilliant conspiracy theorist, and most importantly, a firm believer in the notion that "together we are smarter than any one of us." Jim has selected a collection of topics that represent some of the most stunning and imaginative works in recent memory on AboveTopSecret.com. No matter what conspiracy theories hold your interest, there's something for you in this book. And if you don't believe yourself to be a conspiracy theorist now, you're not being honest with yourself. After all, you picked up a book entitled, *Above Top Secret: Uncovering the Mysteries of the Digital Age*, and read the entire foreword.

Jim, I leave our reader in your capable hands.

Enjoy.

Bill Irvine
CEO, The Above Network, LLC
Owners and operators of AboveTopSecret.com

INTRODUCTION

Contrary to an old adage, what you don't know CAN harm you.

One may be the most highly intelligent person in the world, but if he or she is operating on erroneous or incomplete information, a truthful and correct conclusion on any issue is impossible.

Additionally, a person is at a distinct disadvantage when confronted with new and unfamiliar information in any situation. So, you want to know all you can about a wide variety of topics. And none are more fascinating than the subjects being tossed about on the Internet in the Digital Age.

You say you want to know all about those mysteries and conspiracies you hear about but you don't want to spend your life digging through old dusty books or hours surfing the Net?

Here's the book for you.

In one beautifully designed package, compliments of an inspired linkup between AboveTopSecret.com and The Disinformation Company, you can find answers—or at least understand the questions—to such wild topics as "Did John Titor come from the future?" and "Who parked the Moon?"

Some of these sections deal with mysteries that may involve science of which we are not yet aware. In the primitive past, such things would have been called magic. Today, they are more likely to be called extraterrestrial.

Some of the issues here are concerned with conspiracy, a term formerly disparaged by the corporate-controlled mass media. However, since the attacks of September 11, 2001, were obviously the result of someone's conspiracy, the term has been somewhat rehabilitated. My motto—"If it's not an act of God, it's a conspiracy"—still stands. Sure, accidents happen. Cars crash, ships sink and airplanes crash. But if an event is not an accident and more than one person is involved, by the dictionary definition, you have a conspiracy.

Conspiracies are not all bad. If you throw your friend a surprise birthday party, that's a conspiracy, but it's not a bad one. However, if people conspire to break the law or harm someone else, that's certainly not good.

The Internet is chock-full of conspiracies and mysteries. The Net is a conundrum within itself because the upside of the Internet is that everyone and anyone has access to this modern phenomenon. The downside is that everyone and anyone has access. The problem is separating the wheat from the chaff, distinguishing between good information and bad.

How does one find the truth behind any conspiracy? Take a lesson from the great detectives and journalists of the past.

Don't settle for superficial and facile explanations. Dig past the obvious evidence—which can be fabricated or planted—and look for finer facts. Go past the headlines and seek evidence in the small print deep within a news story.

Carefully look at the source of a story. If you read an article about the safeness of nuclear power and note that the story is based on information from the Atomic Industrial Forum, an industry organization promoting the commercial use of nuclear power, you will know that you are not getting both sides of the story. Likewise, a piece raising alarm over land use citing the Earth Liberation Front as its source most probably is not a fair and balanced account of the issue.

Study all sides of an issue. Don't allow partisan politics or an ingrained belief system to influence what you read and hear. Visit www.AboveTopSecret.com, seek out alternative publications and prowl used bookstores for information you may have missed or never knew. And double check all sources. For example, in the case of the JFK assassination, do you believe a politically-motivated commission that concluded Kennedy was shot through the neck or do you believe the official autopsy report and doctors (supported by the hole in his coat and shirt) which stated he was struck in the back below the shoulder blade? Do you trust government pronouncements on the 1947 Roswell crash that have been changed four times or do you believe several hundred fellow citizens who tell a different story? Sometimes the Devil is in the details.

Don't trust polls and statistics; it has been repeatedly proven that these can be manipulated by loaded questions and misleading arithmetic. For example, did you know that 82.4 percent of all statistics are just made up on the spot? See what I mean?

Don't put your trust in media personalities. In Great Britain, they have it right. Instead of "news anchors," media talking heads there are called "presenters," a more appropriate description. Most news presenters are fine folks but let's face it, they "rip and read," that is, they read news stories right off the wires that are placed before them. They simply do not have the time or inclination to verify all the stories they must deal with on a daily basis. Additionally, they rarely have the background knowledge or leniency from management to pass judgment on the truth of any given story. After all, the sins of the corporate-controlled mass media are primarily those of omission rather than commission.

Most importantly, begin to think for yourself rather than putting your trust in persons and pronouncements in the media. This does not mean that any old idea that pops into your head is as valid as those of conventional thinking. Davy Crockett once said, "Be always sure you're right and then go ahead." The key here is to make certain you know what you are talking about. Just because you learned something in Sunday school, public school or from your parents does not necessarily mean that you got correct information.

When you tackle a controversial issue, start out with the fundamental questions that were once taught to beginning journalism students—Who, What, When, Where and Why.

Armed with these basics and hopefully a dash of deductive reasoning, you are now ready to take on the world of mystery and conspiracy.

While the evidence for some of these conspiracies presented here admittedly may be dubious, many have an impressive amount of narrative and documentation to back them up. Study this material carefully. "I don't believe that!" is not a convincing argument.

The cases here have been selected based on the broad appeal they seem to hold for the more than two million monthly visitors to the *Above Top Secret* website, which in 2007 celebrated its tenth anniversary. The material presented here leans toward the conspiratorial because the corporate mass media leans the other way. If you want the "other side," just watch TV. They will tell you there is nothing to any of the topics presented here. They don't want you to see the little man behind the green curtain.

The world of modern America is very much like that portrayed *in The Matrix* movie trilogy. Today, instead of everyone physically hooked up to some machine that runs a virtual reality program through their brains, everyone is wrapped inside an electromagnetic matrix woven by corporate-controlled radio and TV. A close study will reveal that almost everything you read, see or hear is controlled by six multinational corporations. That's a tremendous concentration of power.

While this media matrix cannot (yet) tell you how to think, it can certainly tell you what to think about and to a large extent, how to view both the news and world events. It sets the agenda and usually presents only one viewpoint.

It is not easy to break away from an electronic media that has been conditioning us all since birth. But it can be done.

Deny ignorance. Break loose from the media matrix. Think for yourself. Question authority.

The following mysteries and conspiracies are a good starting point.

Jim Marrs, October 2008

▶ **WAS 9/11 AN INSIDE JOB?**

▽ **WHO**

▶ Certain officials high within the Federal government of the United States.

▽ **WHAT**

▶ Some claim these officials had foreknowledge of the attacks and, at the very least, did nothing to prevent them.

▽ **WHEN**

▶ September 11, 2001, already acknowledged as a turning point in U.S. history.

▽ **WHERE**

▶ Three modern skyscrapers in New York City collapsed following the attacks and the Pentagon in Washington, DC was seriously damaged.

▽ **WHY**

▶ According to the official government account, 19 fanatical Muslim hijackers were bent on destroying America's freedom and democracy, but other factors appear to have been involved.

additional evidence and commentary:
www.abovetopsecret.com/book/911

A November 2007 Scripps Howard News Service poll showed nearly two-thirds of respondents believed that some federal officials had specific warnings of the 9/11 attacks yet did nothing to prevent them.

E ven more dramatically, a September 11, 2006 MSNBC Question of the Day poll asked, "Do you believe any 9/11 conspiracy theories that indicate the U.S. government was involved?" Amazingly, 58 percent answered, "Yes, I believe there is evidence" with only 30 percent voting, "No, that's ridiculous." Eleven percent responded, "I'm not sure." This means 68 percent were at least open to the suggestion that 9/11 was contrived within the U.S. government. A Zogby International poll conducted between August 24 and 26, 2004, on the eve of the Republican National Convention, showed almost one half of New York City residents (49.3 percent) and 41 percent of New York state residents believed that some national leaders "knew in advance that attacks were planned on or around September 11, 2001, and that they consciously failed to act."

These polls indicate that the subject of a 9/11 conspiracy is taken seriously by a majority of the citizens in the United States. This stands in stark contrast to the corporate-controlled mass media that has bombarded the public with its incredulity on this subject. According to the mass media, any questions about 9/11 come only from paranoid conspiracy theorists.

Yet, by early 2008, there were numerous websites dedicated to disseminating information about the 9/11 attacks, which laid the groundwork for the U.S. invasions of Afghanistan and Iraq, the controversial PATRIOT Act, the creation of the Homeland Security Department and other measures including the Military Commissions Act and the Transportation Security Administration.

Architects and Engineers for 9/11 Truth (www.ae911truth.org), Pilots for 9/11 Truth (pilotsfor911truth.org), Scholars for 9/11 Truth (www.911scholars.org)

and www.911truth.org are among the more credible websites.

Despite the prevalence of some far-out theories regarding the events of 9/11, there is obviously a serious issue here that deserves the attention of every concerned citizen. Even a cursory glance over the 9/11 issues provides fodder for any thinking person.

More than a dozen nations tried to warn U.S. authorities that the country was about to be attacked, as documented in my book *The Terror Conspiracy*. Incredibly, such warnings came from members of the Taliban in Afghanistan and even from Fidel Castro in Cuba.

Then there is the issue of war game exercises being conducted on the morning of the attacks. The fact of these exercises was initially denied and accused of being an Internet rumor. But, more than a year after 9/11, National Security Council counter-terrorism chief Richard A. Clarke acknowledged these exercises, which may have played an important role in confusing the U.S. defense systems' response. In his book *Against All Enemies*, Clarke stated that when he first contacted the acting chairman of the Joint Chiefs of Staff, Gen. Richard Meyers, to see if any interceptors had been launched, Meyers responded, "We're in the middle of 'Vigilant Warrior,' a NORAD [North American Aerospace Defense Command] exercise ..." When Lt. Col. Dawne Deskins, a NORAD airborne control and warning officer, received word regarding the hijackings, she immediately thought, "It must be part of the exercise."

Army Sgt. Lauro "LJ" Chevez, who participated in the war games exercises as a member of the U.S. Central Command headquarters staff in Florida, said this was the first military exercise that he had ever participated in that was classified "Top Secret." Chevez dropped several bombshells in his account of that day—he noted that Vice President Dick Cheney had become the first civilian to take command of NORAD only weeks before 9/11; that the war game exercises included a scenario in which a hijacked commercial airliner was crashed into one of the World Trade Center towers ("What are the odds this could happen for real?" Chevez quoted staffers as asking); that false images called "inputs" representing several hijacked aircraft were placed on radar screens creating confusion over what was real; and that a superior officer said that Cheney had issued a "stand down" order to jet interceptors.

By several reliable accounts these war game exercises also included "Northern Vigilance," which sent fighter interceptors deep into Canada and the northern Pacific in response to a Russian exercise in the arctic; "Vigilant Guardian," which may have included scenarios based on a hijacked airplane; "Northern Guardian," another portion of the Vigilant Guardian exercise; and "Tripod II," a biological warfare exercise mentioned by Mayor Rudolph Giuliani that may explain the arrival of FEMA's National Urban Search and Rescue Team in New York the night before the 9/11 attacks. To echo Sgt. Chevez's question, "What are the odds?" The much-touted *9/11 Commission Report* only mentioned these war game exercises in a single footnote.

"If those looking on from inside the Pentagon as 9/11 unfolded believed [the airliners involved were], or might be, part of a counter-terror exercise set for that very morning, it would explain the otherwise incomprehensible delay, almost to the point of paralysis, in effectively scrambling interceptors," noted Barbara Honegger, a military journalist and author of the 1989 book *October Surprise*.

At least seven of the 19 hijackers still named by the FBI turned up alive in the Middle East long after 9/11:

Abdul Aziz al Omari—A Saudi who stated his passport was stolen while traveling through Denver.

Saeed al Ghamdi—A Saudi Airlines pilot who stated he was "shocked and furious" that he had been named as a 9/11 hijacker.

Salem al Hazmi—A Saudi who proclaimed, "I have never been to the United States."

Ahmed al Ghamdi—Named as a hijacker of Flight 93, he said, "I have never even heard of Pennsylvania ..."

Waleed al Shehri—A Saudi pilot who proclaimed his innocence from Morocco.

Abdul Rahman al Omari—A Saudi who declared his innocence at the U.S. Embassy in Jeddah.

Ameer Bukhari—This man died in a plane crash prior to 9/11, according to his brother, who passed a polygraph test.

All of these men's stories were vouched for by the Saudi Arabian embassy and that country's foreign minister. This story was well covered in the European media but has never been mentioned by America's "watchdog" media.

And what of al Qaeda, officially named as the prime suspect behind the attack? This terrorist organization was a creation of the CIA, who had sent Saudis to Afghanistan in the 1980s to combat the Russian incursion. They had renamed it from the older Muslim Brotherhood, a violence-prone group of Muslim radicals that had been taken over by Nazis during World War II. They later were controlled by the CIA, which used this group to train and arm the Kosovo Liberation Army in the 1990s. Robin Cook, Britain's foreign secretary from 1997–2001, has written that al Qaeda is a CIA creation and its name (literally, the base) actually means the CIA computer database of Arab mercenaries and fanatics rather than some physical headquarters.

> **//**If it was so simple as a plane crashing into the building then where are all the damn videos showing the huge airborne object demolishing itself into the side of the Pentagon!? I saw a picture of the roof and there must have been about 10 cameras ... DUHHH!!! **//**
>
> ATS MEMBER COMMENT

Former counter-terrorism chief Richard A. Clarke also confirmed what was initially said to be another Internet rumor—that more than two dozen members of the bin Laden family were allowed to fly across the U.S. during the "no fly" period following 9/11 when Americans were not permitted to fly. "Someone brought to us for approval the decision to let an airplane filled with Saudis, including members of the bin Laden family, leave the country," he told *Vanity Fair*. "So I said, 'Fine, let it happen.'" His statement implies that the decision to allow the bin Ladens to fly came from his superiors.

In June 2006, FBI Chief of Investigative Publicity Rex Tomb confirmed what critics of the official 9/11 story had been saying all along when he stated, "The reason why 9/11 is not mentioned on Osama bin Laden's Most Wanted page is because the FBI has no hard evidence connecting bin Laden to 9/11."

The controversy over what caused the destruction of the World Trade Center towers has raged since the day of 9/11 when CBS News anchor Dan Rather stated that the collapse of the towers looked like they were "deliberately destroyed by well-paced dynamite."

The FBI took charge of the criminal investigation of the WTC destruction while the little-understood Federal Emergency Management Agency (FEMA) took responsibility for determining what happened to cause the collapse. FEMA seemed determined to haul away the evidence, even before a full and impartial investigation could be made. Such premature destruction of evidence was called into question by Bill Manning, editor of the 125-year-old firemen's publication *Fire Engineering,* in its January 2002 issue. "*Fire Engineering* has good reason to believe that the 'official investigation' blessed by FEMA and run by the American Society of Civil Engineers is a half-baked farce that may already have been commandeered by political forces whose primary interests, to put it mildly, lie far afield of full disclosure," wrote Manning.

The official account, backed by several experts, contended that the towers collapsed due to the heat generated by jet fuel from the crashed aircraft, which then caused structural steel to melt or bend causing a sequential collapse of each floor in the 110-story towers. Critics pointed out that "experts" can be hired and that many were beholden to the federal government for contracts and funding. Others questioned how structural steel giving way on one side of the structure could cause an entire tower to collapse both symmetrically and at almost free-fall speed. Others, noting that jet fuel is basically kerosene with a few added ingredients, have asked how it is possible for kerosene-based commercial jet fuel, which burns at about 1,517 degrees Fahrenheit in open air (the WTC fires were diffused and oxygen-starved as evidenced by the dark billowing smoke), melt structural steel with a melting point of approximately 2,750 degrees? Folks with fuel-burning metal heaters or stoves wondered why their appliances don't melt or warp from constant use.

And no one has successfully elicited an answer from failed 2008 presidential candidate and former New York Mayor Rudolph Giuliani as to who told him the towers were going to collapse beforehand. Giuliani told Peter Jennings of ABC News the day of 9/11 that he was manning a temporary command center—he has also never given an explanation for why he did not go to the newly-completed and hardened command center in WTC Building 7 which collapsed later that day—when someone came in and told him they must evacuate as the towers were going to come down. Obviously, it is necessary to learn who warned him of the towers' collapse, how they knew of this, and why the first responders in the towers were not given that same warning. At one campaign event, when a person tried to ask this question, he was arrested and hauled away.

Considering the fact that no other steel-reinforced building in the history of the world ever collapsed due solely to fire, it is no wonder controversy continues over what brought down the Twin Towers.

Then there is the Salomon Brothers Building, better known as WTC Building 7, a 47-story steel and glass modern skyscraper that dropped symmetrically into its own foundation at about 5:25 p.m. on September 11, 2001. Although airplanes did not hit Building 7, it dropped neatly between the Verizon Building and the U.S. Post Office, neither of which suffered critical damage. FEMA's *WTC Building Performance Study*, issued in May 2002, could only report, "[WTC 7's] loss of structural integrity was likely a result of weakening caused by fires on the 5th to 7th floors. The specifics of the fires in WTC 7 and how they caused the building to collapse remain unknown at this time ... the best hypothesis has only a low probability of occurrence." In other words, this is mere speculation and that speculation is not likely true.

To add to the mystery of Building 7, it has now been established that the BBC announced the collapse of the structure more than 20 minutes before it occurred. Incredibly, as the BBC presenter tells of the building's collapse, it is visible, still standing behind her. There are also videos on the Internet depicting New York firemen moving away from the building while shouting to bystanders that it was about to fall and at least one person claimed to have heard a countdown before the building dropped.

This evidence of foreknowledge only substantiates the remarks of building owner Larry Silverstein, who in September 2002, during a PBS documentary entitled *America Rebuilds*, stated: "I remember getting a call from the, er, fire department commander, telling me that they were not sure they were going to be able to contain the fire, and I said, 'We've had such terrible loss of life, maybe the smartest thing to do is pull it.' And they made that decision to pull and we watched the building collapse." To "pull" a building is acknowledged as industry slang for a controlled demolition. Years after Silverstein's statement, a spokesperson for Silverstein Properties said he meant, "pull the firemen out of Building 7." This explanation was unacceptable to knowledgeable 9/11 researchers as all firemen were withdrawn from Building 7 before 10 a.m. that morning.

How did President George W. Bush's 9/11 Commission explain the collapse of Building 7? They didn't. They didn't bother to mention it on any page of their 567-page report, so willingly accepted as the final word by the corporate mass media.

That same mass media, if not the American public, appears to have largely forgotten two important stories connected with the 9/11 attacks: the subsequent attacks by anthrax spores that infected 23 persons killing five; and the short-selling of certain stocks which evinced foreknowledge of the 9/11 events.

The reason for dropping mention of the anthrax attack is clear. In the immediate aftermath of the biological attacks, an unnamed CIA source told Britain's *Guardian* newspaper, "They aren't making this stuff in caves in Afghanistan. This is prima facie evidence of the involvement of a state intelligence agency." By 2008, it was clearly established that the mailed toxin was a very concentrated electro-magnetized, silica-laced strain of anthrax traceable to the secret military bio-chemical weapons lab at Fort Detrick, MD. It could only have come from the heart of America's military.

One of the anthrax letters carried the phrase "Allah is great," which left the impression that the attacks were Muslim inspired. In October, 2001, Senator John McCain set the tone for the run up to the 2003 invasion when he told David Letterman's audience the anthrax may have been a "second phase" of the 9/11 attacks and may have come from Iraq.

Once it was determined that the anthrax was genetically identified as being the *Ames* strain, which is a weaponized version developed in American military laboratories, media interest waned. About 10 grams of anthrax was used in the attacks, an amount that experts testified would be virtually impossible to steal from government labs considering the stringent security measures employed there.

The targets of the anthrax attacks were Democratic congressmen, Thomas Daschle and Patrick Leahy and their staffs along with some media outlets. Both men were voicing opposition to the pending vote on the PATRIOT Act. These attacks were believed by some to have terrorized Congress into hastily signing into law this act, which according to Rep. Ron Paul and others, legislators did not have time to read.

By mid-2008, no one had been convicted in the anthrax attacks but military biological warfare budgets had been increased to more than 20 times higher than before the attacks.

One 2002 suspect in what the Associated Press described as "one of the most bizarre unsolved crimes in FBI history," was Steven J. Hatfill, a government scientist involved with biological research, who was publicly named as a "person of interest" by the bureau. Both Hatfill and his friends were relentlessly tailed by agents. Finally, in June, 2008, the Justice Department exonerated Hatfill, who received a $5.8 million settlement for his harassment. Friends termed Hatfill "a poster boy for abuses of the PATRIOT Act."

By August, 2008, government interest turned to Bruce Ivins, a Fort Detrick scientist who, as a top expert on the military use of anthrax, had been a member of the government team investigating the 2001 attacks. Conveniently for anyone seeking to halt any investigation into the truth of this case, it was reported that Ivins committed suicide just after Justice Department had decided to file capital murder charges against him in connection with the 9/11 anthrax attacks.

Despite descriptions from family members, neighbors and co-workers that Ivins was a church-going family man incapable of such a dastardly deed as the 2001 attacks, the corporate mass media, passing along government pronouncements, depicted Ivins as a homicidal sociopath. It turned out that this description came from Jean C. Duly, an uncredentialed social worker on probation connected to a minor criminal record, who reportedly was in need of funds. An associate of Ivins, anthrax expert Dr. Meryl Nass, commented, "There has been a tremendous amount of innuendo and information put forward that has never been backed up and never been attributed to anyone...I'm very concerned about the whole concept of having significant amounts of information in a criminal case that is classified or that only the Justice Department has access to and whether that precludes justice for people who are ensnared in those cases."

Even as the controversy over Ivin's guilt continued amid further leaked information from the government, Justice officials declared the 2001 anthrax attacks the work of one lone nut, Bruce Ivins, and closed the case hoping to end any further speculation that the anthrax attacks were an inside job.

It was also widely reported in the mass media in the days following the 9/11 attacks that suspicious stock trades implied foreknowledge of the events. Selling stocks short involves having your broker selling shares you don't yet own at a set price to a given buyer, while betting—or perhaps knowing—you can actually acquire them later at a lower price and supply them to the buyer at the set price within a prescribed short time. If you "bet" right, the difference in price is your profit. This procedure is risky and you can lose at this game, but you can also win big, especially if you have foreknowledge of an event that will negatively impact the market. Historically, if substantial short selling precedes a traumatic event, it is considered to be an indication of foreknowledge. Just prior to the 9/11 attacks, there were an unusually high number of "put" options purchased for the stocks of AMR Corp. and UAL Corp., the parent companies of American and United Airlines respectively. A put option gives the bearer the right to sell at a specified price before a certain date. Just like short selling, placing a put option is betting that the stock will fall in price.

Between September 6 and 7, 2001, the Chicago Board of Options Exchange reported 4,744 put options on United Airlines but only 396 call options. On September 10, there were 4,516 put options placed on American Airlines compared to only 748 calls. (Calls reflect the belief that the stock will increase in worth.) American's 6,000 percent jump in put options on the day before the attacks was not matched by any other airlines. If this activity reflected merely an industry-wide slump, there would have been approximately the same amount of put options on every airline, not just American and United, the two companies whose planes were involved in 9/11.

Other questionable stock trades made just prior to 9/11 were reported by Morgan Stanley, which occupied twenty-two floors of the WTC. This firm witnessed the purchase of 2,157 put options during the three trading days before the 9/11 attacks as compared to 27 per day prior to September 6. Merrill Lynch & Co., which also had offices on twenty-two floors of the WTC, had 12,215 one-month put options bought during four trading days prior to 9/11 compared to the normal 252 contracts per day.

There also was an unusually high volume of five-year U.S. Treasury note purchases made just prior to 9/11. The *Wall Street Journal* on October 2, 2001 noted, "Five-year Treasury notes are among the best investments in the event of a world crisis, especially one that hits the U.S."

Although denied by the U.S. government, it is widely known that the CIA uses the PROMIS computer software to routinely monitor stock trades—in real time—as a possible warning sign of a terrorist attack or suspicious economic behavior. We can safely infer that the CIA could have known in virtual real time, from such trading data alone, that the 9/11 attack was imminent and that it would involve two specific airlines. It also follows that they should also have been able to pinpoint the inside traders through the electronic trail.

But if government investigators did indeed track the culprits behind this suspicious stock activity, it was not brought before the public, especially since the probes led to persons connected with the CIA, not Osama bin Laden.

According to the *San Francisco Chronicle*, "[A] source familiar with the United trades identified Deutsche Bank Alex. Brown, the American investment banking arm of German giant Deutsche Bank, as the investment bank used to purchase at least some of these options." Both the International Policy Institute for Counter Terrorism and European investigators tracked the UAL put options to Deutsche Bank Alex. Brown, a firm formed in 1999 when the German bank merged with Alex. Brown, the oldest investment bank in the United States.

Until 1998, the chairman of Alex. Brown was A.B. "Buzzy" Krongard, who on March 26, 2001 was appointed executive director of the CIA. Beginning in 1998, he was counselor to CIA director George Tenet. Krongard is a man with long-standing and close ties to the financial world. Moving up through the ranks of Alex. Brown, Krongard was elected chief executive officer in 1991 and then chairman of the board in 1994. With the merging of Alex. Brown and Bankers Trust Corp. in 1997, Krongard served as vice chairman of the board until joining the CIA. Bankers Trust was acquired by Deutsche Bank in 1999, becoming the single largest bank in Europe. Krongard also served as chairman of the Securities Industry Association. A native of Baltimore, he received degrees from Princeton University and the University of Maryland School of Law and served as an infantry officer in the Marine Corps.

So, the stock activity that indicated foreknowledge of 9/11 could not be traced to Osama bin Laden but to persons connected with the CIA. Within weeks, this incredible story of high-level profiteering based on the short selling of certain stocks dropped off the corporate mass media's radar screen never to be heard from again.

If all this was not strange enough, there are severe problems with the official account of what hit the Pentagon. According to the government, Hani Hanjour, identified as one of the Muslim hijackers of American Flight 77, took control and slammed this Boeing 757 into the west wall of the Pentagon at full throttle. The resulting explosion and fire claimed the lives of the crew and its 64 passengers out of a capacity of 289, as well as 125 persons in the building.

But numerous problems and questions plagued this account from the very beginning. Initially, government reports stated that the plane had struck the Pentagon's lawn before ricocheting into the wall. However, photos posted on the Internet before the end of the day clearly showed an unmarked green lawn with no major air-

// They've got something to hide OBVIOUSLY. That's why the secrecy. That's why the denial. That's why the ridicule. That's why the defamation of character. Let's see debunkers try explaining that away. //

liner debris in sight. The story was changed to state that the Boeing 757 actually had struck the wall dead on, bored its way into the steel-reinforced exterior, the wings and tail folding up to form a torpedo-like missile, then burst into flames so hot that virtually the entire craft was consumed, which accounted for the lack of debris.

Inexplicably, within a few days the FBI stated that all the passengers on Flight 77 had been identified by their fingerprints. There was no explanation of how fingerprints were obtained from the crash, which reportedly involved a fire so hot it melted an entire airplane including wheels, jet engines, wings and tail.

Unfortunately for the official account, photos taken of the hole in the Pentagon prior to the wall collapse clearly show a hole no more than 15 x 20 feet in the ground floor with no evidence of wings, engines, or wheel assemblies. A Boeing 757 has a wingspan of 124 feet and a height of 44 feet (that's four stories). The two Rolls

Royce turbofan engines, each weighing nearly 2,000 pounds, would have made their own separate holes in the wall but none are seen. The 757's fuselage, with about a 13-feet diameter, indeed could fit the original hole but it is made entirely from aluminum and would have crumpled up against the steel-supported cement wall of the Pentagon like a beer can.

There was also a major problem with the named pilot. Hani Hanjour, who only one month before 9/11 was not allowed to rent a small Cessna 172 at Freeway Airport in Bowie, MD, because in three tests he could not control the craft and had much difficulty in speaking English.

Plus there is the problem of the air cushion. Any airplane must slow almost to stall speed to land because at flight speed it pushes an air cushion before it making landing impossible. A Boeing 757 traveling at 500 miles per hour would have an air cushion preventing it from getting closer than perhaps 50 or 60 feet from the ground.

This condition was supported by data recording information released by the government in 2006.

According to Pilotsfor911truth.org, the data showed an altitude of 180 feet. "This altitude has been determined to reflect Pressure altitude as set by 29.92 inHg [inches of mercury used to determine barometric pressure] on the altimeter. The actual local pressure for DCA [Ronald Reagan Washington National Airport] at impact time was 30.22 inHg. The error for this discrepancy is 300 feet. Meaning, the actual aircraft altitude was 300 feet higher than indicated at that moment in time. Which means aircraft altitude was 480 feet above sea level (MSL, 75 foot margin for error according to Federal Aviation Regulations)," stated the pilots' site. They added, "The aircraft is too high, even for the official released video of the five frames where you see something cross the Pentagon Lawn at level attitude. The five frames of video captured by the parking gate cam are in direct conflict with the Aircraft Flight Data Recorder information released by the NTSB [National Transportation Safety Board]." Furthermore, the recently-released data shows Flight 77 on a different flight path than stated in the official narrative, one in which it could not have knocked down the streetlight poles so well depicted in that day's photos.

This discrepancy adds weight to the theory that a jumbo jet did fly over the Pentagon, as stated by several witnesses, but did not strike the building, an event apparently seen by no one including some 82 security cameras trained on the structure. The videotapes from the cameras were confiscated by the FBI that day and have never been released to the public with the exception of a few frames that show an explosion at the Pentagon but do not show a large jet plane. The account of raging fire able to disintegrate an entire airplane is disputed by photos of the Pentagon taken that day which depict undamaged wooden tables, plastic computers and even a paper book along with the account of April Gallop, who with her small son (both injured in the explosion) nevertheless climbed to safety unharmed through the hole in the Pentagon's west wall.

Such issues comprise only a short list of the more pertinent and troubling questions about 9/11 that have not been addressed or adequately explained. Evidently, the "watchdog" mass media has been cowed by its corporate masters.

Nor have these and many other questions been answered by any of the official government investigations, including President Bush's handpicked panel, the National Commission on Terrorist Attacks Upon the United States, popularly known as the 9/11 Commission. Bush initially tried to appoint globalist Henry Kissinger to head his commission but was thwarted by public outcry that caused Kissinger to decline the position.

His second choice, the team of political veterans Lee Hamilton and Thomas Kean, later admitted that their investigation was hindered by foot-dragging at the White House and contradictory testimony from both NORAD and the FAA.

The growing 9/11 Truth Movement, joined by many of the victims' families, remains divided in their view of the real conspiracy, sometimes referred to as LIHOP (Let It Happen On Purpose) and MIHOP (Made It Happen On Purpose). The LIHOP argument is that certain individuals within the federal government had foreknowledge of the attacks yet did nothing to prevent them as the attacks furthered their political agenda while the MIHOP supporters took notice of the close relationships between the Bush and bin Laden families, as reported in the Texas media, as well as the role of Saudi Arabia and the CIA in the creation of al Qaeda. They argue that the attacks were actually precipitated by elements within the U.S. government, a suspicion echoed by a near majority of the population in several national polls.

A growing number of Americans are echoing the thoughts of several ATS members, who noticed the government's reticence to deal openly and honestly with 9/11. Another member offered some good guidelines in answering a question about what constitutes a conspiracy theory that most people would accept when he wrote: "An acceptable theory has no agenda, has supporting evidence provided to back it up, and acknowledges generally accepted facts, rather than conveniently ignoring them." In the case of 9/11, this simple maxim should be applied to both sides of the controversies.

The controversy over the truth of the 9/11 attacks undoubtedly will continue for some time. How long it will take before the corporate mass media are allowed to objectively investigate and report on this festering scandal is anybody's guess.

▸IS THE SUPPLY OF OIL PEAKING?

▽ WHO

▸ Those who claim that the world's supply of oil has peaked and is now in decline.

▽ WHAT

▸ If the supply of oil has peaked, we can look for higher prices and worldwide turmoil.

▽ WHEN

▸ Now and in the foreseeable future

▽ WHERE

▸ Worldwide

▽ WHY

▸ If the world's supply of petrochemicals indeed faces decline, lifestyles and politics will have to change and new energy sources must be found.

additional evidence and commentary:
www.abovetopsecret.com/book/peakoil

Is the world running out of oil?

Adherents of the notion of "peak oil" say yes.

It is true that all nations are addicted to oil, primarily because the most profitable business on the planet is arms. With the United States as the largest weapons supplier in the world, other nations have followed suit. All war machines run on petroleum, either as fuel or lubricants.

But war machines are only a small part of the picture. Apart from vehicle fuel, oil provides the foundation for civilization. Your plastic computer and TV remote are made from petroleum, as are all plastics, food wrapping, shampoo, garbage bags, clothes softeners, some furniture, most medicines and even water bottles. All of this is delivered to you by the transportation industry, which runs on petroleum fuels.

As outlined by Rep. Tom Udall, a Democrat from New Mexico, the price of petroleum fuel is not the only factor to consider. During congressional peak oil hearings, Udall noted, "Some say that market forces will take care of the peak oil problem. They argue that as we approach or pass the peak of production, the price of oil will increase and alternatives will become more competitive. Following this, consumers will act to replace our need for non-petroleum energy resources. This philosophy is partly true. However, the main problem with this argument is that current U.S. oil prices do not accurately reflect the full social costs of oil consumption. Currently, in the United States, federal and state taxes add up to about 40 cents per gallon of gasoline. A World Resources Institute analysis found that fuel-related costs not covered by drivers are at least twice that much. The current price of oil does not include the full cost of road maintenance, health and environmental costs attributed to air pollution, the financial risks of global warming from increasing carbon dioxide emissions or the threats to national security from importing oil. Because the price of oil is artificially low, significant private investment in alternative technologies that provide a long-term payback does not exist. Until oil and its alternatives compete in a fair market, new technologies will not thrive."

In other words, if basic oil prices rise significantly or there is a shortage, virtually everything you buy will go up in cost.

It has been stated that the world will be consuming nearly 50,000 gallons of oil every second by 2008. And this number will only increase as the world's population continues to grow.

> **// It is a well known fact that Henry Ford originally designed the model-T Ford to run on fuel provided by hemp! Yes hemp. As a potential bio-fuel, hemp can easily provide the energy we as a nation, as a planet, would require. As a renewable resource, it literally cannot be beat. Unlike the much touted corn bio fuels, hemp does not need fertilizers or insecticides as hemp can actually enrich the soil and it is naturally resistant to insects. //**

According to Dr. Colin Campbell, considered by many the world's leading oil expert, humankind has reached "peak oil." Campbell defined peak oil as "the maximum rate of the production of oil in any area under consideration, recognizing that it is a finite natural resource, subject to depletion."

The term "peak" has been coined from the work of American geophysicist Marion King Hubbert, who in 1956 predicted a peak in U.S. oil production by 1970 followed by steady decline worldwide. Initially, many petroleum experts scoffed at the Hubbert Peak Theory but today it has gained respect even though his projection of reaching worldwide peak oil in 2000 has been moved forward to 2010.

According to the U.S. Department of Energy, the United States, as opposed to other nations, uses about two-thirds of all oil use for transportation, one-fifth goes to industrial uses while the remainder goes to electric energy production, both residential and commercial.

Some experts claim the only spare oil production capacity left in the world is in the Organization of the Petroleum Exporting Countries (OPEC), composed primarily of Middle Eastern nations. Peak oil advocates believe that non-OPEC oil production limits have already been reached.

"It's no secret anymore that for every nine barrels of oil we consume, we are only discovering one," reported the *BP* [formerly British Petroleum] *Statistical Review of World Energy*.

"All the easy oil and gas in the world has pretty much been found. Now comes the harder work in finding and producing oil from more challenging environments and work areas," said William J. Cummings, a spokesman for ExxonMobil.

Such "the-sky-is-falling" fears have been criticized by those who note that peak oil has become the pet theory of experts, who are all involved in the oil business. It is apparent that citing a decline in the oil supply provides the rationale for higher prices and more exploration.

But critics of the giant multinational oil companies are not the only ones questioning the idea of peak oil.

Cambridge Energy Research Associates (CERA), composed of energy expert consultants, also questions Hubbert's theory. "Despite his valuable contribution, M. King Hubbert's methodology falls down because it does not consider likely resource growth, application of new technology, basic commercial factors, or the impact of geopolitics on production. His approach does not work in all cases—including on the United States itself—and cannot reliably model a global production outlook. Put more simply, the case for the imminent peak is flawed. As it is, production in 2005 in the Lower 48 in the United States was 66 percent higher than Hubbert projected," stated a 2006 CERA report.

The International Energy Association (IEA) joined such criticism, "The concept of peak oil production and its timing are emotive subjects which raise intense debate. Much rests on the definition of which segment of global oil production is deemed to be at or approaching peak. Certainly our forecast suggests that the non-

OPEC, conventional crude component of global production appears, for now, to have reached an effective plateau, rather than a peak."

Oil sands, also known as tar sands, hold an oily, viscous petroleum that requires treatment before becoming gasoline. Oil sands may represent as much as two-thirds of the world's total petroleum resources, with at least 1.7 trillion barrels in the Canadian Athabasca Oil Sands, and perhaps 1.8 trillion barrels in the Venezuelan Orinoco tar sands—compared to 1.75 trillion barrels of conventional oil worldwide, most of it in Saudi Arabia and other Middle Eastern countries. Between them, the Canadian and Venezuelan deposits contain about 3.6 trillion barrels of oil. That's more than twice as much as the amount of conventional oil.

The Canadian oil sands have been in commercial production since the original Great Canadian Oil Sands (now Suncor) mine began operation in 1967. According to the Royal Dutch Shell 2006 annual report, its Canadian oil sands unit made an after-tax profit of $21.75 per barrel. Canada is the largest supplier of oil to the U.S., with more than a million barrels per day coming from tar sands. At that rate of depletion, the Athabasca Oil Sands should continue to produce for about 1,800 years.

Not only do many people question the Hubbert peak oil theory, but also recently some experts have begun to question the whole concept of "fossil fuel."

In the mid-1800s when the Industrial Age began requiring larger and larger amounts of petroleum, demand brought unprecedented growth to the fledgling oil industry. Scientists were at a loss to explain exactly where oil came from in the first place.

The fact that organic matter was found in the raw petroleum pumped from the ground gave rise to the theory that oil was formed by swamps from the Permian Age settling layer by layer over millennia, compressing vegetation underground until it formed oil.

Austrian geoscientist Dr. Siegfried E. Tischler pointed out, "According to the accepted theory of oil formation, organic matter living in the oceans sinks to the bottom and then decays there ... to form crude oil. While this *might* be happening to some extent in the Black Sea ... there is no present-day example [emphasis in the original] of this happening anywhere on the surface of the Earth."

But it was a 1999 book that threatened everything we thought we knew about oil and its origins.

The book was *The Deep Hot Biosphere* by Dr. Thomas Gold, an Austrian astrophysicist who remained at Cornell University until his death in 2004. The book was an expansion of Gold's 1992 paper presented to the National Academy of Sciences. Dr. Gold was no scientific lightweight. He was a member of the American Academy of Science as well as a member of England's Royal Society.

Briefly, Dr. Gold stated that so-called fossil fuels are actually the product of natural processes deep within the Earth. It is created from underground methane sources, which feed a vast subterranean biosphere of bacteria. These hydrocarbon microbes in turn produce the hydrocarbons of coal, oil, and gas.

Before laughing off Dr. Gold's ideas, remember that the large oil companies use oil-absorbing microbes to clean up tanker spills.

This non-biologic or Abiogenic Theory of Hydrocarbon formation is supported by the fact that some drillers, particularly the Russians, have found hydrocarbons far from traditional sedimentary formations. Conventional oil experts have attempted to explain this anomaly, saying that the oil "migrated," or slipped laterally away from normal sedimentary deposits.

ATS MEMBER COMMENT

//But if we must continue to be dependent upon petroleum and geo-fuels, we have not even begun to tap the available supply. Recently, the RAND think tank announced that shale oil finds in Montana, Wyoming and several other states would provide the United States with petroleum for literally centuries, but if that weren't enough, we always have coal. //

Salt domes were an early and easy source of oil but it is now known that oil may be found in many other geological structures.

In 1986, Dr. Gold advised American and Swedish drilling teams in Sweden who penetrated to a depth of nearly five miles, far beyond sedimentary formations and the possibility of fossils and yet they found petroleum. By 1991, the Siljan Ring site was producing 80 barrels a day. By 1998, Russian drillers had completed 300 producing oil wells in the ring area. Furthermore, the deep Swedish wells produced not only crude oil but also viable bacteria from the depths of the Earth.

Also supporting this theory is the fact that no oil, coal or diamonds have ever been produced in a laboratory based on the conditions of compressed and heated organic matter.

Then there is the matter of tree trunks cutting diagonally through many layers of coal, which according to present theories was produced by vegetation-compressed underground for thousands of years. Over that kind of time, it is obvious that tree trunks would have long since disintegrated.

Dr. Gold determined that coal is produced by the same deep underground abiogenic process that creates oil.

Furthermore, there are the incredible reports that some oil reservoirs are actually refilling. "The phenomenon of petroleum reserves that seem to refill themselves is widely reported, notably in the Middle East and along the U.S. Gulf Coast. I regard these occurrences as strong evidence for the deep-Earth gas theory," said Dr. Gold.

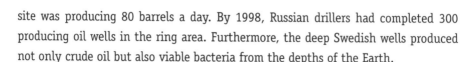

// As an energy source, the United States has coal reserves that could easily supply our nation's energy needs. Yes additional technologies would be required to make the coal based fuels 'cleaner' but, nevertheless, this is certainly a viable energy alternative to petroleum and one that would make the United States energy independent and, in the long run, an energy supplier to the rest of the world. **//**

ATS MEMBER COMMENT

Russian scientists have known for years of the possibility that oil is a by-product of microbes deep within the Earth that are independent from the photosynthesis process of surface vegetation. Western scientists have not bought into this idea, as it would render all of their textbooks and years of schooling obsolete. This is the same hidebound thinking that prevents Egyptologists from accepting the geological evidence that the Great Pyramid was constructed more than 10,000 years ago, long before the arrival of the Egyptian civilization.

"The 'connection' of crude oil with life ..." concluded Dr. Tischler, "is entirely different from what is currently assumed: oil does not form from life, but the hydrocarbons from the inner parts of the globe support life in the deep, hot biosphere!"

A recent study published in *Science* magazine corroborated the idea of oil being produced by natural Earth processes. The lead scientist in this study, Giora Proskurowski of the School of Oceanography at the University of Washington at Seattle, stated that hydrogen-rich fluids were being vented at the bottom of the Atlantic Ocean apparently by abiotic synthesis of hydrocarbons in the mantle of the Earth.

Furthermore, in 2005, NASA officials announced that a probe of Titan, Jupiter's largest moon, showed abundant quantities of Carbon-13 methane of abiotic origin.

If Dr. Gold's theories prove correct—and there is increasing evidence in support of them—then petroleum reserves are much greater than noted in the establishment media. The political impact of such a reversal of thought would be staggering.

After all, it is the specter of worldwide oil shortages that fuels the arguments of such New World Order stalwarts as Al Gore, who wants people to give in to more centralized government programs in the name of conservation and environmentalism.

Obviously, if the theories of Dr. Gold, Dr. Tischler, Russian scientists and others are correct, that oil is a continuing chemical process, which takes place in the Earth's mantle, the theory of "Peak Oil" falls apart.

"Even if it is at this time difficult to produce oil or gas from basement rock in most instances, due to the depth of wells, the discovery of oil welling up from below sedimentary rock frees us from the fossil fuel myth," commented Matt Verdu in a review of Dr. Gold's book. "Reserve calculations for oil and gas fields are based on the false assumption that those resources are fixed pockets of fossil fuel, rather than way stations for oil and gas welling up from below. We can stop cannibalizing each other for oil according to the fossil fuel propaganda, and we should not allow gasoline to be priced as if in blood."

Such cannibalizing was taking place in 2008 with U.S. troops still bogged down in Iraq following the unprovoked 2003 invasion. Saddam Hussein readying a nuclear bomb within six weeks proved totally false, as did the charge of hidden weapons of mass destruction.

After five years if war, it was clear that the reason for U.S. occupation had more to do with oil than with freedom or democracy. In mid-2007, the *New York Times* reported an estimated 100 billion barrels of oil lay under Iraq. With the Saudi Arabian reserves becoming depleted, oil executives looked to Iraq to fill any future gap.

This was all an extension of long-standing U.S. strategy, that is, using cheap imported oil as long as possible while preserving domestic oil for the future in the event of an oil embargo or when higher prices will make recovery more profitable.

Western oil reserves in California and Wyoming, notorious for the Teapot Dome Scandal of the 1920s, are largely unexploited as are reserves in Canada and Alaska.

Numerous domestic wells have been declared "depleted" and remain capped. A "depleted" oil well does not mean there is no oil down the hole. It simply means that it would cost more energy to recover the remaining supply than could be gained from burning it.

Steam injection is one method for invigorating such depleted oil wells. Conventional thinking is that steam injection is not cost effective due to the fact that too much fuel—coal, wood, etc.—must be burned to produce the steam necessary for this process.

However, Dan Foster, who helped pioneer a technology that burns propane and compressed air to produce copious amounts of steam, has proven this a viable means of regaining oil from depleted wells. In 2007, Foster used this method to bring a Texas well producing only a quarter of a barrel of oil a day up to 37 barrels after only six hours of steaming.

All the controversy over the origins of oil does not even address the growing interest in bio-diesel and ethanol, fuels produced from organic materials such as animal fats, soy, grain and corn. Nor does it look back at the fact that Nazi Germany was producing prodigious amounts of synthetic fuel toward the end of World War II, the formulas for which are still held in classified government files.

While the idea of "peak oil" can be called into serious question, this should not be used as a rationale for the continued production of gas-guzzling SUVs or the frivolous use of petroleum because, arguments over the origin and quantity of oil aside, the waste and air pollution being created by the extensive use of petroleum threatens all life on Earth.

▸ WHY DID THE AIR FORCE
CHANGE ITS STORY ON
STEPHENVILLE?

▽ **WHO**

   ▸ The citizens living in the area around Stephenville, Texas.

▽ **WHAT**

   ▸ Hundreds of persons reported sightings of unconventional aerial craft as well as strange multi-colored moving lights in the sky.

▽ **WHEN**

   ▸ Beginning New Years Day, 2008 and continuing well into February.

▽ **WHERE**

   ▸ Residents of Stephenville, Texas, located approximately 70 miles southwest of the Dallas-Fort Worth Metroplex, and surrounding towns including Dublin, Harbin and Selden.

▽ **WHY**

   ▸ U.S. Air Force officials, after initially stating that they had no aircraft in the area of Stephenville, reversed course after two weeks and announced that ten F-16 jets explained the nearly month and a half-long sightings. Many in the public, and even some mainstream news media, have greeted this explanation with disbelief.

additional evidence and commentary:
www.abovetopsecret.com/book/stephenville

Ricky Sorrells lives in an unpretentious home in Dublin, Texas, about eight miles west of Stephenville.

O n New Year's Day, 2008, Sorrells decided to go deer hunting near his home. 2007 had been a wet year in north central Texas and the deer were plentiful. The sun was just setting behind some oak trees near his house when the 37-year-old welder set out carrying a rifle with a 9-power telescopic sight.

"For some reason, I don't know what, I look up and look back down. I don't know what made me look up, but then I realized what I had seen with my eyes and immediately looked back up. There was this thing. It covered from—I could not see the edges in my tree canopy. I couldn't see the front of it. I didn't think about looking behind me to see if I could see an edge that way," Sorrells told a journalist.

Sorrells thought, "What in the world is this?" and after adjusting his rifle's scope, peered through it at the object above him. He estimated the object hung silently a mere 300 feet over his heading, blocking his vision as far as he could see.

"I looked back up there at it and I can see what I would call a 'mirage' coming off of it. It wasn't steam. I don't know really—I've seen it like on a hot highway how the heat waves come up. And this was coming down. I really didn't know what to think. I was not scared, so I dropped my gun. And then I really started noticing how big this thing was. I also noticed that it had these round indentations. They were in a grid pattern all running left to right, and front to back. They were all placed about 40 feet apart. They were deep, like maybe 4 to 6 feet deep into this craft. It basically looked like a piece of sheet iron that had been pressed. I couldn't see any nuts, no bolts, no rivets, no welds, no seams. I was really studying the structure of this trying to get an idea about how it was built ... It is huge! ... While I was looking at this [craft], it drifted to the right by about 100 feet. And I remember looking to my left to see if I could see the edge of this thing. And I could not see the edge of it. I turned back to my right, and I was like, 'Wow, this is crazy!'"

As Sorrells watched with mixed emotions—"What is it? What is it going to do next? Do I need to get out of here?"—the object moved swiftly off and out of sight.

Sorrells could not form a conclusion as to what he had seen but before the end of January, he had sighted the object twice more. "I hope it's our military. I hope we have something that is this advanced. If it's not ours, then we're in trouble. I don't know the capabilities of this thing, to move at such speed that it has, and as big as it is. Does it have the capability of weapons? I don't know. But if they can build this, I'd sure hate to see if they got mad at us! You know what I'm saying?" he said.

But Sorrells' sighting was only the beginning of the activity around Stephenville.

Constable Lee Roy Gaitan, along with his eight-year-old son sighted a red glow in the sky on Jan. 8 that faded and later reappeared. Later he said he saw bright white lights that seemed to "bounce around in the sky" and took off at a "blazing speed."

> **//** I'm really glad that this mass sighting has not fallen through the cracks yet, for I believe this is by far one of the most significant sightings to date. Whether it be extraterrestrial or man made, it is completely extraordinary in every way. **//**
>
> ATS MEMBER COMMENT

In the early morning hours of Feb. 2, Gaitan saw a similar object and this time he was ready with a video camera. "I videotaped it for about 40 minutes. It was an object with red, green, and blue lights. I was on U.S. Hwy. 377 ... looking south towards Dublin. It was about a quarter of the size of a full moon. It was several thousand feet up, maybe 4,500 or 5,000 feet up, I don't know. I zoomed in 168 times and you could see it was round and spinning. Something that could not be seen with the naked eye and you could almost see through it. There was what looked like a pyramid or triangle shape on the inside of the thing."

Early on Feb. 9, Gaitan was in Stephenville looking toward Dublin when he again shot video of a lighted, spinning object. "I videoed for 10 minutes and zoomed in, but it was too far. It was moving, but not real fast. It was spinning and shooting

off colors. I'm fairly certain this thing spins. This time I could not see through it ... we went to County Road 847 and we took several pictures with the new Canon camera we purchased with a special lens. It appeared to be the same thing that was hovering southeast of my house and we never lost sight of it. Then my sister called and they saw it again, too. It headed southwest. Then we lost sight of the first one we'd seen for a little bit and then it reappeared. Then, there was [sic] two of them; one in the southwest sky and one in the northeast sky."

These were not isolated incidents. Many others were beginning to report both huge objects and colorful moving lights in the sky.

Steve Allen of Selden, Texas, southeast of Stephenville, is a pilot and owner of L & S Enterprises and Texas Freight in nearby Glen Rose. On the evening of Tuesday, January 8, he noticed flashing, white lights about 3,500 feet above his home. He told ABC News that the lights formed a rectangle pattern that "spanned about a mile long and a half mile wide and the pattern was headed toward Stephenville at 3,000 miles per hour."

Allen was one of more than 200 area residents who reported seeing yellow, red, blue, and white lights that showed up after sunset. The lights were so bright that witnesses compared them to a welder's torch. Some of the red lights were seen moving together in pairs while red, blue, and yellow lights moved around as if "dancing" with each other. All the lights would then turn to a bright, white light and disappear. Being night, many of the witnesses saw only the bright lights.

Allen said he estimated its size as perhaps a mile long and a half-mile wide, which is why a bunch of the folks there started calling it the "Mother Ship." He also reported seeing two fighter jets he believed were F-16s chasing the object.

> **//**I worked at a major F-16 base for 5 years, where they flew missions every day, and never were there ten in the same place at the same time. They usually went out two or four at a time. This is just fishy, and really is insulting to our intelligence. I'm not saying that it really was a UFO, or claiming to know what happened, but it wasn't ten F-16s. **//**

After more than more than 60 years of tittering and snickering after each belated report of a UFO sighting, the news media, including national and international outlets, actually treated the Stephenville sightings with a modicum of respect.

While there were the usual amount of hucksters and promoters—one "expert" brought forward turned out to be a convicted felon and at least one news photo depicted a city official wearing a green alien mask. On January 15, Bud Kennedy, a columnist for the *Fort Worth Star-Telegram*, echoed the usual media tone by writing, "All I can say is, if space aliens were hovering over Texas last week, then maybe that explains the Cowboys. The Stephenville newspaper, the *Empire-Tribune*, actually broke the story Thursday [Jan. 10]. But as far as I can tell, absolutely nobody in Texas paid attention until after Dallas was knocked out of the football playoffs."

But for the most part the reporting was straightforward and remarkably non-judgmental. A *Washington Post* headline read, "Dozens in Texas Town Report Seeing UFO," while Canada's CBC News reported, "Multiple reports of UFO-like sighting in Texas town." The sightings were even featured on CNN's Larry King Live.

Jim Moore, a contributor to the *Lufkin Daily News* in East Texas, displayed some knowledge of UFO history by writing, "Why do UFOs appear in so many pieces of art that predates the aircraft era? Why do so many texts from ancient times seem to talk about UFO activity? Why are there consistently reliable sightings of gigantic and silent UFOs? I do not know the answers to those questions, but as our X-Files friend, Fox Mulder, told us, 'the truth is out there.'"

When contacted by the *Stephenville Empire-Tribune*, Maj. Karl Lewis, spokesman for the 301st Fighter Wing at the Joint Reserve Base Naval Air Station in Fort Worth, stated "no F-16s or other aircraft from his base were in the area the night of January 8, 2008, when most people reported the light sightings."

Lewis went on to speculate that the sightings were two commercial airliners that momentarily crossed flight paths. This explanation was quickly dismissed since the Stephenville sightings were numerous and took place over a number of days.

Another explanation given was that people had only observed a weather phenomenon known as a parhelion; more commonly called a "sundog." This is a bright spot on the Sun's halo caused by the reflection of sunlight in ice crystals within certain cloud formations and usually seen at sunset. This explanation foundered when it was noted that about half of the Stephenville sightings took place at night, long after the sun had set. Yet another explanation was that the sightings resulted from military flares, the same argument belatedly given following a mass sighting over Phoenix in March 1997. Of course, this explanation failed to match the witness accounts.

ATS MEMBER COMMENT

//Trying to insult the intelligence of ordinary folk in Texas is downright disgusting. Saying nothing at all or denying any involvement would have been more credible in my opinion. This just looks like damage control to me. But very bad damage control indeed. How in the hell can you mistake ten F-16's for a mile-long object? **//**

A Nova Scotia man even proclaimed that the lights were merely military planes guarding President Bush's home in Crawford, Texas, despite the fact that Crawford is about 75 miles southeast of Stephenville and the president was not in residence.

The obvious erroneousness of such explanations prompted a most unusual statement from the government two weeks later in the form of a news release from the 301st Fighter Wing stating they had made a mistake in initially saying no planes were in the area at the time of the sightings. Wing officials said ten F-16 fighters were indeed in the area conducting training flights. Knowledgeable military experts disdained this explanation, stating that at no time would ten F-16s being flying together, short of World War III.

> **//** [After the Air Force stated they were not in contact with the ten F-16s.] You don't make errors like that. How could they not know where a few million dollars' worth of war fighting equipment went? **//**

For a change, even the media were skeptical. A CBS News Dallas-Fort Worth affiliate stated merely, "The mystery of the Stephenville UFOs *might* have been solved." [Emphasis added.]

"In a statement today, a Wing spokesman says they made a mistake and that jets were flying in the Stephenville area that evening. The Air Force no longer investigates UFOs," CBS reported, then added some UFO background:

About 200 UFO sightings are reported each month, mostly in California, Colorado and Texas, according to the Mutual UFO Network [MUFON], which went to the 17,000-resident town of Stephenville to investigate the alleged sightings.

Fourteen percent of Americans polled last year by the Associated Press and Ipsos say they have seen a UFO.

UFO sightings have been reported all over the world for centuries, including the infamous 1897 crash of a cigar-shaped object near the tiny Texas town of Aurora. While some thought it was a hoax, decades later investigators from UFO groups said evidence suggests the disfigured pilot's body buried that day was an alien.

An opinion piece on the editorial page of the normally arch-conservative *Dallas Morning News* was even more pointed in its skepticism stating:

> Something strange happened in the sky over Erath County, and the government's changing story is way fishy.
>
> The Air Force won't come clean. It's impossible to resist that otherworldly conclusion: visitors ... from outer space.
>
> Do they walk among us? How can you tell a space alien from the average computer programmer?

ATS MEMBER COMMENT

// [AF Maj. Karl] Lewis needs to be brought up for court martial because not only has he proven dereliction of duty by not knowing he had ten F-16s on a training exercise from 6 p.m. one evening to 4 a.m. the next morning, but he also has apparently abandoned his post for the past 2 weeks being that nobody could find him for 14 days to let him know of his error. //

> Put away the tinfoil hats, and get serious. The government hid this stuff before. The Air Force once admitted that a "disc" crashed near Roswell, NM, then backed off and came up with a story about a weather balloon. They denied they had spacemen's bodies. (But you can Google up "proof" that they did.) New Mexico's own Gov. Bill Richardson talked about a Roswell cover-up at a presidential debate this year. (Proof on YouTube.) Another ex-candidate, straight-shooting Dennis Kucinich, admits he saw a New Mexico UFO that sent signals to his mind. (More YouTube.)
>
> These guys were running for president. Would they make something up? And why not trust the eyes of the hard-working people around Stephenville? A bunch of them saw the same things in the sky this month: slow-moving, direction-changing, glowing spheroids flying in formation.
>
> Witnesses also saw military jets come in for a peek, but the Air Force first denied they were in the area. But here's that familiar pattern: Officials now

say a whole squadron of F-16s was in the air. Why the shifting story? What did the jets see up there?

Here's the official line: "Operational procedures that can't be released." Swell. People see hovering flying things, and that's all we get? You could get better information from Dick Cheney.

Experience tells us you can't hide the truth forever; it was years before we heard that Roswell spaceship debris was carted off to the Air Force's mysterious Area 51 in Nevada.

Meantime, we swear by Orson Welles that there's no reason to panic here in Texas. If aliens meant us harm, we'd be earthling burgers by now.

> **// Doesn't the military realize this just makes people more suspicious? To say that there were no jets in the area, and now to recant that by saying there was a major training exercise going on is ludicrous. //**
>
> ATS MEMBER COMMENT

But if the citizens of Texas were not panicking, many were pondering what the aerial apparitions might portend. Witness Allen, a Baptist church greeter, told the Associated Press that Texans are curious about the flying lights because "this is the Bible Belt, and everyone is afraid it's the end of times."

But the most amazing—and somewhat disconcerting—account involving the Stephenville sightings came on Dec. 11, 2007, with a prediction by Scottish evangelist Catherine Brown. A member of Gatekeepers Global Ministries in Ayrshire, Scotland, Brown posted to a website the following prediction: "I see Texas ablaze and a stunning star, like the star from the East rising over the land. I hear the Spirit of the Lord saying to: 'Watch for cosmic signs and wonders in Texas.' He said there will be a cosmological phenomenon that scientists cannot explain, and the media will carry as front-line news. People will begin to ask about 'the Light' ... For a period of four months—from Christmas to Easter—there will be a window of opportunity for salvations, signs, healings and wonders in Texas."

Contacted by a newsman in her Scottish home, Brown, who has never been to Texas, said, "I saw this huge light over Texas. It was actually just a short vision. When I saw the news today [about the Stephenville sightings], I thought—how interesting."

The Stephenville sightings were also of interest to Ken Cherry, president of the Texas state chapter of MUFON, who went with an eight-person team to the Stephenville area on Jan. 18 to interview witnesses.

"Normally, we get 15 to 20 [UFO] reports a month, which puts us among the top two or three [states] in the country. With the high number of reporting results we have had in the Stephenville-Brownsville area, this is very significant—over 150 reports. But these aren't all related to an individual sighting at a specific time. These took place at different hours of the day and night, and some even over the last several years," Cherry said. "What we've uncovered is a pattern of UFO sightings at the area. They appear to be related to the same phenomenon. But they're not all at the same time. We consider this to be even more significant because so many people have reported incidents.

"We've eliminated a lot of the known possibilities. Early on in the investigation, we could see that something important was happening, or we wouldn't be devoting so many resources to this event."

Asked his reaction to the Air Force's explanation that jets were training in the area, Cherry said, "Initially [when they denied any involvement], I think they were trying to discredit the witnesses by saying that what they had viewed was an optical illusion. We had witnesses who had accurately described F-16s in the area that were chasing a UFO. I think the new military explanation only reinforces the credibility of our witnesses, [who have] proved to be more reliable than the Air Force, frankly. The idea that they forgot they had an exercise in the area just doesn't hold water. So it appears to have been a cover-up."

//Perhaps the Air Force's changing story is simply a way to subtly acknowledge the reality of the event while at the same time pacifying the people who do not wish to learn of such things? //

At the Jan. 18 meeting with MUFON investigators in the Rotary Club building at Dublin, a small town south of Stephenville where many more witnesses came forward, the number of media people in attendance was startling, said Cherry. There were more than 75 media people in attendance. There were more than 50 witnesses who provided written reports while another 50 simply left contact information because they didn't want to deal with the media. "There was a crowd of about 600 persons in this small town. We caused a traffic jam in this little place," said Cherry. The Dr. Pepper Company provided drinks for the attendees.

// It was only a matter of time before someone injected 'flares' into this Stephenville UFO account. One has to wonder if it's a SOP to eject flares anytime a UFO is reported near an Air Force Base. //

"We now have about 200 reports in our MUFON.com system," added Cherry, "and we have more than a dozen videos and photos submitted but we have eliminated all but a couple. We are still working with these. These look promising but none is from the Jan. 8 sighting."

Cherry said he believed one of reasons so much public attention has been paid to the Stephenville sightings is that "this is middle-class America coming forward, not just some jokers coming out of the woodwork. These witnesses are for the most part, older folks, pillars of the community—pilots, farmers, ranchers, flight attendants, oil field workers, just about every demographic you can think of. Most of them want to remain anonymous. The media has only reported four or five out of the total number of witnesses."

He also said he is aware that there appeared to be an effort to stifle both the reporting and witness testimony in this case. "One of the things they are trying to do is bring these sightings down to the one sighting on Jan. 8 but there were many other sightings over a number of days. The inconsistencies of witness reports can be explained by the fact that they saw different things on different days," said Cherry.

Witness Ricky Sorrells later claimed that someone in the government tried to harass and intimidate him into silence regarding his UFO experience. He said following his experience, military helicopters began low flights around his home scaring his cattle and disturbing his family's sleep.

Sorrells said on January 15, the day after he was interviewed by the Associated Press, a man identifying himself as an Air Force Lt. Colonel called him and asked to come and visit. When Sorrells said he did not want any more visitors, he reported that the man became abusive and said he was not taking "no" for an answer. As the conversation heated up, Sorrells warned his caller not to cross his cattle guard [the entrance to his property] whereupon the caller stated, "So, we have the same caliber weapons as you do but a lot more of them." Sorrells said he then demanded that the Air Force ceased its low-flying helicopter flights over "my air space," to which the man replied that "it was not my air space, it was his."

Following this conversation, the helicopter flights ceased but Sorrells said F-16 fighter jets were still over flying his home.

Sorrells said he felt the phone call was an attempt to intimidate him into silence, especially after a man he knew who was once in the military told him, "You need to shut your mouth about what you saw." Other persons in the Stephenville area also reportedly have been cautioned, in one way or another, to cease talking about their experiences.

> **[The flare theory is untenable] especially since most of north central and central Texas is under a burn ban because of drought conditions. Yes, we got a ton of rain last year but it's all dried up now and some towns won't even let ya have a BBQ. I would think local military bases would know this since they have to live here too, and not endanger their homes or ours by dropping flares.**

Even a local reporter was forced to leave her job as a result of her coverage of the UFOs. Angelia Joiner had been working for the *Stephenville Empire-Tribune* for about 18 months when the lights began appearing overhead. Faithfully following the story, Joiner was able to publish several news stories, which brought her to the attention of the national media.

But by the first week in February, her publisher had had enough. Despite the fact that January 2008 was a record high sales month for the *Empire-Tribune*,

Joiner was told the paper did not want any more stories concerning the UFOs. "It is time to move on," Joiner was told. Faced with compliance or following the story, Joiner gave her notice to the newspaper. But there was no grace period. "This morning they had confiscated my computer and I was told to pack up and get out," Joiner said on Feb. 9. "I'm devastated and still in shock."

"It's funny how one day I was sitting on top of a huge global story and practically the next I'm looking for a job," she added.

Apparently, the Stephenville area has been a hotbed of UFO activity for more than 100 years.

> **//**Perhaps the Swamp gas on Venus flared up and reflected off of space flares making them appear to fly. **//**

Strange objects in the sky are nothing new in the Stephenville area, which boasts sightings going back as far as 1891 when a newspaper story spoke of citizens seeing what could only be described as a burning bale of cotton in the air, which exploded scattering metallic debris imprinted with strange and undecipherable hieroglyphics.

In 1897, six years before the Wright Brothers made the first heavier-than-air flight at Kitty Hawk, NC, the *Dallas Morning News* in its April 19, 1897 edition wrote that farmer C. L. McIlhany of Stephenville along with more than 20 other named citizens had seen a 60-foot-long "aerial monster," described as a large cigar-shaped craft with two immense wheels on either end sitting in his pasture. McIlhany said the craft carried a pilot and engineer financed by "certain capitalists of New York." The crew, who identified themselves as S. E. Tilman and A. E. Dolbear, claimed they were testing the machine and had landed to make repairs. Prophetically, McIlhany was quoted as wondering, "[W]hat you reckon is going to happen when dynamiters get to riding in airships and dropping bombs down on folks and cities? Is this world ready for airships?"

But the most unusual aspect of the recent sightings has been the widespread and largely non-judgmental media coverage. "It's amazing how this has taken on an international profile," remarked MUFON's Cherry. "I've had calls from Japanese and British newspapers."

"The serious attention being given the Stephenville story by the news media, including the national and international media, may mark a turning point in the coverage of UFO incidents which, in turn, may mark a new and more open public perspective," Cherry added.

▸ **DO ROAD SIGNS CONTAIN HIDDEN CODES?**

▽ **WHO**

▶ The United States government, apparently in coordination with state and local governments.

▽ **WHAT**

▶ Highway signage that can double as covert markers for the direction of troops in time of emergency.

▽ **WHEN**

▶ Whenever a "national emergency" is declared, which, according to recent Presidential Directives, can be anything the president decides constitutes an emergency.

▽ **WHERE**

▶ In signs found across the United States and perhaps even in Canada and other NATO nations.

▽ **WHY**

▶ Covert highway signs can facilitate the movement of foreign troops who may not be able to read or understand conventional U.S. signage.

additional evidence and commentary:
www.abovetopsecret.com/book/roadsigns

The next time that friendly road sign points the way to gas or breakfast at Denny's, you might want to consider that in reality it may be a "Tacmar."

Tacmar is a military-style abbreviation for "tactical markings," an easily understood sign allowing military units to quickly locate civilian hospitals, airports, transportation hubs and other important facilities. Such Tacmars, sometimes referred to as "sign codes," seem to be found mainly throughout the United States, although some have been reported in Canada.

Suspicious researchers contend that some road signs contain embedded codes as well and that the U.S. sign system has been covertly altered, changing from a word based system to European-style pictures, images, color codes, and a variety of arrow configurations.

Some who have researched these signs say they are markers that serve as "pointers" to point direction or identify a site or facility to be confiscated and used as a base of operation. These codes reportedly are created by positioning reflective markers in quadrants on the back of such sign. By imagining the rear of the sign vertically divided in half, markers on the left side indicate left while those on the right indicate right. Color codes, basically red and blue, are supposed to indicate the nature of whatever is being pointed out, such as a hospital, airport or support facility.

Some of the signs noticed by researchers don't seem to make sense, such as signs for facilities that don't seem to exist there.

Marking routes and facilities is nothing new. During the 1950s and 1960s, Civil Defense authorities marked designated buildings and sites with signs and symbols to identify shelters and command centers in the event of a nuclear strike. Routes through cities leading to "relocation centers" were marked as disaster corridors for the evacuation of civilians.

Critics claim such signs are in place to facilitate a military takeover of the United States, whether by the imposition of martial law or an invasion by foreign troops, perhaps labeled as United Nations Peacekeepers. These forces would require pre-placed road signs to swiftly locate their objectives.

Debunkers claim such fears are groundless and that the signs, along with

> **// The sign codes and markers are universal codes to bridge language barriers for foreign troops who can't decipher our English road signs and highway visuals. //**

ATS MEMBER COMMENT

stickers on their reverse side, are simply a means of locating lost or stolen signs.

Others pointed out that the U.S. Interstate Highway system was originally a military project designed and built during the Cold War to rapidly move men and materials across the nation in the event of war or a national emergency. Its official name, the Dwight D. Eisenhower National System of Interstate and Defense Highways, reflects the military nature of this system. Interstate highways must conform to several federal requirements, including being capable of 90-mile-per-hour traffic with a mile-long straight stretch of road every few miles, which can serve as an emergency runway for aircraft.

Obviously, in a nation the size and density of the United States, signage is very critical to any military operation. While road maps are always desirable, they may be unavailable or badly out of date.

Many conspiracy scenarios for the coming years have foreign troops—either NATO or UN—occupying portions of the United States. Such troops, many unfamiliar with the English language or our customs, would require universal signage to travel easily. Some researchers believe that this was the real purpose behind the universal signage approved by the United Nations. It goes far beyond merely helping foreigners find the restroom or a place to eat.

Additionally, if the U.S. was attacked by nuclear weapons, producing an electromagnetic pulse capable of knocking out all electricity, GPS location devices would become useless. Pre-placed easily read road signs would become a necessity whether for defense or conquest.

If a military incursion—foreign or domestic—into your town or city seems like paranoia run rampant, consider the experience of the small town of Kingsville, Texas, even prior to 9/11.

Beginning on the night of February 8, 1999, a series of mock battles using live ammunition erupted around the 25,000 inhabitants of the town, located near Corpus Christi. In a military operation named Operation Last Dance, eight black heli-copters roared over the town. One nearly crashed when it hit the top of a telephone pole and started a fire near a home. Soldiers of the elite 160th Special Operations Aviation Regiment, known as the "Night Stalkers," ferried by the choppers, staged an attack on two empty buildings using real explosives and live ammunition. During the action, an abandoned police station was accidentally set on fire and a gas station was badly damaged when one or more helicopters landed on its roof.

Citizens of Kingsville were terrified during the drill as only Police Chief Fe-

lipe Garza and Mayor Phil Esquivel were notified of the attack in advance. Both men refused to give any details of the operation, insisting they had been sworn to secrecy by the military. Only Arthur Rogers, the assistant police chief, would admit to what happened. "The United States Army Special Operations Command was conducting a training exercise in our area," he said but refused to provide any details.

// They're used to track stolen street signs. Someone steals a sign, it shows up sometime later, they run the ID on the back and know exactly where it came from. How hard is that [to understand]? Some cities are using barcodes instead of stickers. Some are using GPS locations... A handful of people really believe our armies (or NATO) are that dense, that they can't read a road map? //

Local emergency management coordinator for FEMA, Tomas Sanchez, was not happy with the frightening attack and the lack of information and warning. Sanchez, a decorated Vietnam veteran with 30 years of service in Naval Intelligence, was asked what the attack was all about. He replied that based on his background and knowledge, the attack was an operational exercise based on a scenario where "martial law has been declared through the Presidential Powers and War Powers Act, and some citizens have refused to give up their weapons. They have taken over two of the buildings in Kingsville. The police cannot handle it. So you call these guys in. They show up and they zap everybody, take all the weapons and let the local PD clean it up."

One resident told a reporter, "This is total BS. If we don't stop it now it's going to get worse." Asked for comment, then Texas Gov. George W. Bush said it was not his job to get involved in the concerns over the Night Stalkers using live ammunition in a civilian area of his state.

The night attack indicated the use of Presidential Decision Directive (PDD) 25, a Top Secret document that apparently authorizes military participation in domestic police situations. Some speculated that PDD 25 may have surreptitiously superceded the 1878 Posse Comitatus Act, which prohibits the use of military forces to police civilians.

The events in Kingsville may date as far back as 1971, when plans were drawn up to merge the military with police and the National Guard (State Guards were gradually eliminated during the past two decades). In that year, Sen. Sam Ervin's Subcommittee on Constitutional Rights discovered that military intelligence had established an intricate surveillance system to spy on hundreds of thousands of

American citizens, mostly anti-war protesters. This plan was code named "Garden Plot." Britt Snider, who worked for the subcommittee, said the plans seemed too vague to get excited about. "We could never find any kind of unifying purpose behind it all," he told a reporter. "It looked like an aimless kind of thing."

Four years later Garden Plot began to come into sharper focus. "[C]ode named 'Cable Splicer' [and] covering California, Oregon, Washington, and Arizona, under the command of the Sixth Army, [it] is a plan that outlines extraordinary military procedures to stamp out unrest in this country," reported Ron Ridenhour and Arthur Lubow in *New Times* magazine. "Developed in a series of California meetings from 1968 to 1972, Cable Splicer is a war plan that was adapted for domestic use procedures used by the U.S. Army in Vietnam. Although many facts still remain behind Pentagon smoke screens, Cable Splicer [documents] reveals the shape of the monster that the Ervin committee was tracking down."

During the time of Cable Splicer, several full-scale war games were conducted with local officials and police working side by side with military officers in civilian clothing. Many policemen were taught military urban pacification techniques. They returned to their departments and helped create the early SWAT (Special Weapons and Tactics) teams.

Rep. Clair Burgener of California, a staunch Reagan Republican who had attended the Cable Splicer II kickoff conference, was flabbergasted when shown Cable Splicer documents, stating, "I've read *Seven Days in May* and all those scary books … and they're scary! … This is what I call subversive." Subcommittee Chief Counsel Doug Lee read through the documents and blurted, "Unbelievable. These guys are crazy! We're the enemy! This is civil war they're talking about here. Half the country has been designated as the enemy." Snider agreed, stating, "If there ever was a model for a takeover, this is it."

The attacks of 9/11 and the War on Terrorism had provided the pretext for the activation of plans such as Cable Splicer, a clear violation of the Posse Comitatus Act. In June 2002, despite promises by the Bush Administration that it would not initiate any new intelligence reforms until after the joint congressional committees had completed their inquiry into the 9/11 attacks, the Pentagon quietly requested permission to create a powerful new position—Under Secretary of Defense for Intelligence. This request for yet another layer of authority was inserted into a Senate defense bill slated for congressional approval.

Stephen A. Cambone was confirmed by the U.S. Senate as the under secretary of defense for intelligence on March 7, 2003, and sworn in four days later. Cambone left this position following the resignation of Defense Secretary Donald Rumsfeld and was succeeded by retired Lt. Gen. James R. Clapper.

"The Pentagon's gambit has been such a brilliant stealth attack that many members of Congress aren't even aware it is happening, let alone what it means," noted reporter Linda Robinson in *U.S. News & World Report*. "No hearings have been held, and Pentagon officials portray it as merely an internal managerial matter with few broader implications. But intelligence officials and experts say that could not be further from the truth. The new under secretary position is a bureaucratic coup that accomplishes many Pentagon goals in one fell swoop."

Fears of secretive, overreaching agencies with military connections that might violate the Posse Comitatus Act appeared to find substantiation in January 2005, when news outlets reported that since 2002, the Pentagon's Defense Intelligence Agency (DIA) had operated an intelligence-gathering and support unit called the Strategic Support Branch (SSB) with authority to operate clandestinely anywhere in the world where it is ordered to go in support of anti-terrorism and counter-terrorism missions. The SSB previously had been operating under an undisclosed name.

Road signage becomes critical in military-type maneuvers. The Tacmar road signs help identify detention centers and work camps already in place across the United States, such as those at or near Grayling, MI; Fort Smith, AK; Palmdale, CA; Fort Devens, MS; Fort Dix, NJ; Fort Leonard Wood, MO; Nashville, TN; and Mineral Wells, TX. Such sites, rumored to number more than 600, are usually closed military bases surrounded by high chain-linked fences with the barbed wire on top pointing inward rather than outward, obviously to keep someone in rather than to keep people out.

If one is comforted by the thought of federal protection from terrorist threats, consider this scenario: A pimple-faced 18-year-old dressed in camouflage and armed with a fully loaded M-16 arrives at your door and informs you that you must leave your home and come with him because the authorities fear a biological attack in your city. If you protest and say you'll stay and take your chances, you are in violation of the law and subject to arrest, fine and imprisonment. After seeing his armed companions, you decide to join your neighbors in a military truck destined for a "relocation camp" situated many miles from your home. At the camp, you are instructed to stand in line for a vaccination against smallpox, anthrax or whatever the latest threat might be. If you refuse the inoculation, recalling that in past years many such vaccines were proven to be tainted, you are again subject to fine and jail.

If this sounds like an Orwellian nightmare, laws authorizing just such action had already been passed in several states and the District of Columbia by the end of 2002. Maine, New Hampshire, Maryland, Virginia, South Carolina, Georgia, Tennessee, Florida, Missouri, Oklahoma, Minnesota, South Dakota, Utah, Arizona, and New Mexico passed all or parts of the Model State Emergency Health Powers Act, which was drawn up as a model law at the behest of the federal Centers for Disease Control and Prevention following the anthrax attacks that occurred in the Capitol on the heels of 9/11. Other states have either rejected or stalled the legislation. But don't take comfort if your state is not among those passing this act as most of this overreaching law was incorporated into the Homeland Security legislation.

Under this legislation, authorities would be able to federalize all medical personnel, from EMTs to physicians, and enforce quarantines. They would have the right to vaccinate the public, with or without their consent, seize and destroy private property without compensation and ration medical supplies, food, fuel, and water in a declared emergency.

"[This act] goes far beyond bioterrorism," said Andrew Schlafly of the As-

sociation of American Physicians and Surgeons. "Unelected state officials can force treatment or vaccination of citizens against the advice of their doctors."

FEMA, designated as the lead agency under the Department of Homeland Security, also has plans in its files for the evacuation of cities and the use of sprawling temporary camps to house their residents. Under the pretext of planning for the War on Terrorism, FEMA has dusted off and augmented contingency plans to counter the effects of nuclear, biological and chemical attacks.

> //[Walmart Garden Centers] are fitted with iron bars and chain link fencing, locking roll-down overhead doors, and locking exit with a register, scanner, and key-pad swipe/card console. Might not [such garden centers] be a detention area where local dissidents can be detained for further processing and then relocation. And then they will be relocated to somewhere (with each truck driver using the Tacmar system, driving trucks on the wrong sides of the entire road system). So I guess they will just back the busses up to the loading dock of Wal-Mart, threaten us with rakes and shovels—they [will be] getting medieval on our asses—and conveniently relocate us to bases inside the United States ... Thanks Wal-Mart, and thanks to the Tacmar folks—for a really good laugh ... I happen to believe strongly in the theories surrounding the Illuminati—quite a stretch for many to consider! But this Tacmar thing ... their conclusions just don't seem very sound. //

One of the most ominous indications of government plans for something terrible in our future was the revelation that FEMA was storing hundreds of thousands, perhaps millions, of cheap plastic coffins measuring approximately seven feet long and three feet deep (more than one person per coffin?)

At least 500,000 such containers were photographed near Madison, GA, and posted on the Internet in late 2007. Researchers claimed the plastic coffins, which can be sealed to prevent leakage of contaminants, were ordered from a firm named Polyguard & Company LLC by the Veterans Administration and stored on land leased by FEMA. Polyguard was founded by Lee Schwab, a fourth-generation funeral director and licensed embalmer.

It was noted that Georgia is the home of the Centers for Disease Control.

By mid-2002, FEMA was notifying its vendors, contractors, and consultants to envision the logistics of millions of displaced Americans forced to leave cities that come under attack. The firms were given a deadline of January 2003 to be ready to establish such displaced person camps. FEMA made it known that it already had ordered significant numbers of tents and trailers to be used for housing.

Such plans were briefly brought to the public's attention in the summer of 2002 when then Attorney General John Ashcroft publicly proposed the establishment of internment camps for American citizens he deemed "enemy combatants."

And who would provide the muscle for such activity? After all, U.S. troops are spread thin all across the globe.

// Why are we all in denial over the possibilities? Didn't we hear about prison camps in Germany and even in the United States during World War II? Japanese individuals were rounded up and placed in internment camps for the duration of the war. Where was their freedom? You don't think it could happen to you? //

According to plans that stretch all the way back to the U.S. Program for General and Complete Disarmament in a Peaceful World, introduced before the United Nations in 1961 by President John F. Kennedy, American sovereignty will eventually be replaced with policing by UN Peacekeepers. This program called for "the disbanding of all national armed forces and the prohibition of their reestablishment in any form whatsoever other than those required to preserve internal order and for contributions to a United Nations Peace Force."

In mid-2007, President George W. Bush codified the consolidation of U.S. political power with his ominously worded National Security Presidential Directive/ NSPD 51 and Homeland Security Presidential Directive/HSPD-20, innocently entitled

"National Continuity Policy." In the interest of "continuity of government," this directive stated: "The president shall lead the activities of the federal government for ensuring constitutional government." The implication was that he would lead the entire government, not just the executive branch.

This takeover of the federal government was contingent on a "catastrophic emergency," broadly defined as "any incident, regardless of location, that results in extraordinary levels of mass casualties, damage, or disruption severely affecting the U.S. population, infrastructure, environment, economy, or government functions."

So, in the event of an emergency—which can be defined solely by the president—foreign troops, many already training within the U.S., will conduct relief operations, evacuations, relocations, house-to-house searches for weapons and the seizure of all resources.

> **// The only useful purpose that I can imagine breaking such a 'code' might serve is if we were to use those abandoned facilities ourselves—to organize a resistance. //**
>
> ATS MEMBER COMMENT

Sound unbelievable? It's already happened. In early September 2005, several convoys of Mexican Army troops drove into Texas ostensibly to aid in the Hurricane Katrina rescue efforts. Although the mainstream media reported these troops were unarmed, several accounts, citing witnesses, claimed some of the convoyed troops were armed with Heckler & Koch German assault rifles. In addition to the Army troops, the Mexican Navy sent two ships, eight all-terrain vehicles, seven amphibious vehicles, two tankers, two helicopters, radio communication equipment, and medical personnel to assist relief workers in Houston's Astrodome.

The announced entry of foreign troops to provide aid was contradicted by major media accounts of massive supplies gathered in major cities as well as reports that much of the aid was blocked from distribution. The *Los Angeles Times* reported: "Scores of police and volunteer firefighters from around the nation, as well as trucks loaded with donated water, were even now being prevented from entering New Orleans while troops conduct house-to-house searches."

At that time the FEMA director was Michael D. Brown, the first person hired by his long-time friend and former FEMA director Joe Allbaugh, who ran George W. Bush's presidential campaign in 2000. Brown subsequently resigned due to his mishandling of the Katrina rescue. Many observers felt that FEMA intentionally created a climate to justify foreign troops entering the U.S. The Associated Press reported that a U.S. military press office employee said he did not know the precise location of the Mexican convoys but thought they had been rerouted from Houston to Dallas. "If the army does not know the location of the convoys or why they are heading for Dallas, beside the fact that they are armed, isn't that an issue of national security?" questioned one researcher.

The last time Mexican troops were in Texas was in 1846, when soldiers from Mexico, which had refused to acknowledge the Rio Grande River as a border, were driven back. This incursion resulted in the Mexican-American War of 1848 in which Mexico lost about one half of its former territory. Texas Congressman Ron Paul was irate, stating, "Any Mexican troops here, period, is illegal and unconstitutional."

Such troops need to find their way around with speed and efficiency. Is this the true purpose of the Tacmar road signs?

Others have stated the belief that these signs and reflective markers found on the reverse side are coded to target vital sites, facilities, and resources to be confiscated and used by foreign troops. Some of these concerned persons include military personnel.

"While I was stationed in Beirut, Lebanon after the bombing in the '80s, I saw those markers [Tacmars] put on the back of their road signs to bridge language barriers among multinational peacekeepers doing military operations in the city," stated U.S. Navy Chief Petty Officer A. Phillips.

It's not all just about gun confiscation and maintaining order. According to FOX News, soldiers—either foreign or domestic—will enforce relocation and quarantines:

"Among the specific proposals are plans to allow soldiers to enforce quarantines in the event of a chemical or biological weapons attack ..."

Some researchers claim Tacmar road signs located just outside cities and towns mark land-fills, pits, cemeteries, and quarries already designated for mass graves in the event of a biological pandemic.

Naturally, the idea that someone is planning to incarcerate most of the population of the United States has been met with disbelief and derision.

"When first coming across this information I was in a state of total denial," noted one commentator. "How could this be? I believed our country was free, and always felt a sense of comfort in knowing that as long as we didn't hurt others in observing our freedom we were left to ourselves. Ideally we treated everyone with respect and honored their uniqueness and hoped that others did likewise. It took an intensive year of searching into the hidden politics to discover that we are not as free as we believe we are. If we are in denial, we don't see the signs that are staring at us, but keep our minds turned off and busy with all the mundane affairs of daily life."

So for now, the nation's road signs, like fluffy clouds, can be interpreted in any manner you would like. Only time will tell if the conspiracy-minded are onto something.

▶ **IS FREE/ALTERNATIVE ENERGY BEING KEPT FROM THE PUBLIC?**

▽ WHO

▶ The U.S. government and the oil industry

▽ WHAT

▶ Is there an active operation designed to suppress free and alternative energies?

▽ WHEN

▶ From the early twentieth century to the present day

▽ WHERE

▶ Such claims proliferate on the Internet and have been the subject of several books.

▽ WHY

▶ To ensure that the owners of the oil industry continue to maintain their monopoly on the Earth's energy, and to prevent the citizens of the world from having access to cheap—or even free—energies.

additional evidence and commentary:
www.abovetopsecret.com/book/energy

In early 1945 Nazi Germany was on its knees with the Russians pouring in from the East and the British and Americans pushing from the West. Yet, Nazi war production was at levels higher than in 1940 when the Reich was at its height.

The reason for this surprising production success was the Nazis use of synthetic oil. Basically landlocked (the North Sea was blockaded by Allied ships and submarines), Germany was forced to develop non-petroleum oils and grease. The most prevalent of the various methods used was hydrogenation processes, mostly developed within the I. G. Farben chemical combine, which produced synthetic oil from coal.

Since World War II, knowledge of synthetic oil and alternative energy sources has almost dropped from public view. Many researchers have concluded that a "free energy/alternative energy conspiracy" exists to keep such technology from the public. They contend that the use of various renewable and ground-breaking technologies that could provide energy at reduced cost—perhaps at no cost at all—are being deliberately suppressed and discouraged by both major governments and the oil industry.

The reasoning behind such suppression is simple: to preserve the economic status quo and ensure a large profit from ever increasing oil prices. Similarly, it is alleged that free energy cannot be allowed to gain a foothold in a capitalist system because that system would then utterly collapse if such energies and technologies were introduced on a widespread scale across the world.

Most adherents of this theory suggest that the conspiracy had its beginnings in the 1930s, and with the work of one Thomas Henry Moray, who claimed that he and his family had been threatened and shot at on several occasions, and that his laboratory had been ransacked by sinister sources as part of an organized effort to stop his free energy research.

Moray, who received a Ph.D. in electrical engineering from the University of Uppsala, reportedly succeeded in developing a continuous energy source that, to-day, is known as Zero Point Energy, an energy that can be freely extracted from the quantum-physical active vacuum space that surrounds us.

In the 1920s, Moray demonstrated his "radiant energy device" that seemed to operate without any discernible means whatsoever. He would call his device a "solid state detector," or "Moray Valve," and which consisted of a large antenna connected to a complex series of high voltage capacitors, transformers, and semicon-ductors. By reportedly stimulating the existing oscillations of radiant energy from space, the Moray Valve is said to have run for several days producing 50 kilowatts of power.

The demonstrations attracted mainstream newspaper attention, as well as scientists from Bell Laboratories and from the Department of Agriculture. None could determine how the device actually operated, and no evidence of fakery was ever found. To his credit, Moray refused to sell his technology to the corporate world, fearing that it would be misused, and he largely vanished into obscurity.

Others suggest that the research—and the subsequent cover-up—of free energy began much earlier with the scientific genius of Nikola Tesla, inventor of the Magnifying Transmitter, a device that was essentially a high-powered harmonic oscillator designed to allow for the unlimited transmission of electrical energy via wireless transmission.

Born at the stroke of midnight on July 9, 1856 in the Croatian province of Lika, Tesla was without doubt a scientific genius who, arguably, ushered in the age of electrical power single-handedly. Tesla completed his elementary education in Croatia, continuing his schooling in the Polytechnic School in Graz, and finishing at the University of Prague. He worked as an electrical engineer in Germany, Hungary, and France before emigrating to the United States in 1884.

Arriving in New York City with, quite literally, four cents in his pocket, Tesla soon found employment with Thomas Edison in New Jersey. However, personal dif-ferences between the two men soon led to their separation. Tesla then established a laboratory in New York City in 1887, where experiments ranging from the exploration of electrical resonance to studies of lighting systems were undertaken. Four years later, Tesla was at his creative peak. He developed, in quick succession, the induction motor, new types of generators and transformers, a system of alternating current power transmission, fluorescent lights, and a new form of steam turbine.

Tesla died of heart failure at the New Yorker Hotel, some time between the evening of January 5 and the morning of January 8, 1943. He was 86 years old. Interestingly, in the immediate aftermath of Tesla's death, the FBI ordered the government's Alien Property Custodian office to size all of Tesla's papers and property, despite the fact that he had U.S. citizenship. The FBI, the federal government, and the corporate world that supplied weapons to the military, had many reasons to be concerned by Tesla's activities.

Right up to the time of his death, Tesla had been working on what became known as his "Teleforce Weapon," a charged particle beam projector that was based upon a large Van de Graaff generator of unique design and a special type of open-ended vacuum tube. Tesla's invention also became known as the "Peace Weapon"—chiefly due to the fact that Tesla envisaged it having the ability to end all wars and discourage future ones.

In a letter to J. P. Morgan, Jr., on November 29, 1934, Tesla wrote: "I have made recent discoveries of inestimable value. The flying machine has completely demoralized the world; so much that in some cities, as London and Paris, people are in mortal fear from aerial bombing. The new means I have perfected afford absolute protection against this and other forms of attack."

He added, "These new discoveries, which I have carried out experimentally on a limited scale, have created a profound impression. One of the most pressing problems seems to be the protection of London and I am writing to some influential friends in England hoping that my plan will be adopted without delay. The Russians are very anxious to render their borders safe against Japanese invasion and I have made them a proposal which is being seriously considered."

Taking into consideration the fact that there is good evidence to demonstrate that both the First and Second World Wars were secretly orchestrated by powerful men with a long-reaching agenda, it seems likely that anyone, especially Tesla, whose "Peace Weapon" might have discouraged open warfare as well as the production of alternative energy sources that could have wrecked the all-powerful oil industry, had to be stopped at all costs.

Then there is the case of Wilhelm Reich. Born in 1897, Reich was an Austrian-American psychiatrist and psychoanalyst, who created a storm of controversy when he began researching what he believed were links between human sexuality and neuroses. Reich placed great emphasis on something he termed "orgastic potency," a previously unknown form of energy that Reich believed could revolutionize human health. The energy would ultimately become known as "Orgone." Indeed, according to Reich's theory, all forms of illness could be traced back to a depletion of Orgone energy within the body.

According to Reich, Orgone was the "primordial cosmic energy," blue in color, and which he further asserted, was both "omnipresent" and responsible for the Earth's weather, the color of the sky, gravity, the formation of galaxies, and the biological expressions of both emotion and sexuality.

Beginning in 1940, he conducted clinical tests on people who would sit in a box-like device constructed by Reich, known as the Orgone Accumulator, to soak in concentrated amounts of Orgone energy. As his research continued and became more ambitious, Reich began to develop smaller, portable devices that could specifically focus on enriching certain areas of the body, such as the immune system, as well as destroying localized tumors.

Having also tested his device on cancerous mice, Reich became convinced that he had indeed tapped into a previously unknown form of energy that had the potential to cure both physical and mental health conditions.

Needless to say, this did not please the U.S. psychiatric and medical communities, who wished to continue their hold—and ensure their profits—on issues pertaining to national healthcare, treatment and medicinal drugs. No one in the official world wanted to see the entire U.S. population cured of all its ills by an energy that was freely available to one and all.

Reich also claimed to have uncovered a life-threatening opposite of Orgone, which he termed Deadly Orgone, or DOR. Reich further maintained that DOR had been responsible for turning large parts of the Earth into desert. As a result, he began working on a device known as a "Cloud-Buster." It was Reich's belief that he could manipulate streams of Orgone energy in the atmosphere, something that could result in the production of clouds and rainfall. Realizing the potential spin-offs that this technology offered humankind, it was Reich's ambitious plan to see his "weather control" technology used all across the planet in areas decimated by drought, and as a means by which some of the huge deserts of the Earth could ultimately be turned into grassland, forest, and jungle.

Interestingly, Reich reportedly observed countless UFOs over Maine and also in the Arizona skies during the course of his Cloud-Busting experiments in the two states. He speculated that perhaps these UFOs were propelled by Orgone and released DOR as a form of waste. Reich even asserted that his Cloud-Buster could adversely affect potentially hostile UFOs in the event that an interplanetary war broke out.

Perhaps inevitably, faced with the knowledge that here was a man who was offering the people of Earth perfect health, free energy, and the ability to cure the planet's ills, the official world moved quickly to quash both Reich and his work. On February 10, 1954, the U.S. Attorney for Maine, acting on behalf of the FDA, filed a complaint seeking a permanent injunction under Sections 301 and 302 of the Federal Food, Drug, and Cosmetic Act, to prevent interstate shipment of Orgone-therapy equipment and literature.

Not surprisingly, Reich refused to appear in court, believing, with some justification, that no one in the legal world would be able to fully appreciate the importance of his discoveries or their potential to radically change the world and its people for the better.

In a letter to the court, Reich wrote: "My factual position in the case as well as in the world of science of today does not permit me to enter the case against the Food and Drug Administration, since such action would, in my mind, imply admission of the authority of this special branch of the government to pass judgment on primordial, pre-atomic cosmic Orgone energy. I, therefore, rest the case in full confidence in your hands."

The outcome was sadly predictable. As a direct result of his failure to appear in court, an injunction was granted on March 19, 1954 and a judgment was passed that ordered the destruction of all of Reich's written materials that in any way, shape or form referred to Orgone energy—including all copies of his ten published books.

And the bad news did not end there. In May 1956, Reich was arrested on a flimsy violation of the injunction when a colleague of his transported a small amount of Orgone-therapy equipment across a state line. Reich was charged with contempt of court. Reich refused to arrange a legal defense and, as a result, was brought in chains to the courthouse in Portland, Maine. Representing himself, he admitted to having violated the injunction and was sentenced to a two-year jail term.

A fellow psychiatrist and friend of Reich's, Dr. Morton Herskowitz wrote of the trial: "Because [Reich] viewed himself as a historical figure, he was making a historical point, and to make that point he had conducted the trial that way. If I had been in his shoes, I would have wanted to escape jail; I would have wanted to be free. I would have conducted the trial on a strictly legal basis because the lawyers had said, 'We can win this case for you. Their case is so weak, so when you let us do our thing we can get you off.' But he wouldn't do it."

And things only got worse for Reich. On June 5, 1956, officials of the FDA raided Reich's estate at Rangeley, Maine, and summarily destroyed all of his Orgone Accumulators and associated materials. Then, on August 25, 1956 and again on March 17, 1960, the remaining six tons of his books, journals and papers were burned in the former Gansevoort Incinerator to the west of New York's Meatpacking District. In March 1957, Reich was sent to Danbury Federal Prison, where he was examined by a psychiatrist who concluded that Reich was suffering from "paranoia manifested by delusions of grandiosity and persecution and ideas of reference."

Eight months later, on November 3, 1957, Reich died in his sleep—reportedly from heart failure—at the federal penitentiary at Lewisburg, Pennsylvania. At the time of his death, Reich was planning to apply for parole, upon which he envisioned returning to his research and work on Orgone, Cloud-Busters, alternative energies, and medical cures. Interestingly enough, in 2007 the 287-page file on Tesla was quietly removed from the FBI's website as was the 789-page collection on Reich. The disappearance of these and other files on inventors lends credence to those who claim the government, in league with corporate monopolies, is attempting to suppress alternative technologies.

Another energy innovator hounded by the U.S. government was Dr. Royal

Raymond Rife, who in the 1930s demonstrated the ability of precise electrical frequencies to disrupt viral and bacteria cells. An analogy to this effect is glass shattering when a singer's high note is sounded.

A Special Research Committee of the University of Southern California confirmed that Rife frequencies were reversing many ailments including cancer. By 1934, Rife had isolated a virus that bred cancer and stopped it by bombarding it with electromagnetic frequencies. He was successful in killing both carcinoma and sarcoma cancers in more than 400 tests on animals. According to several reports, Rife, along with other doctors, succeeded in using his frequencies to cure 16 cancer patients diagnosed as terminal by conventional medicine.

It did not take long for the medical establishment to realize that such a device not only would wreck the pharmaceutical industry but damage medicine in general since cures meant less visits to the doctor. Opposition immediately came from Dr. Thomas Rivers of the Rockefeller Institute, who had not even seen Rife's equipment in operation.

Overworked and underfunded, Rife and his associates were easy targets for attack. False claims were made against him, test procedures were altered causing his demonstrations to fail and impossible and diverting demands were made on Rife's research.

// The FDA's attack against Reich constituted a fraud upon the courts and the American people, and the Reich legal case continues to overshadow the better-known Scopes Monkey Trial in constitutional significance, in that an American court authorized the burning of scholarly books and the jailing of scientists for making unorthodox viewpoints. //

After declining an offer to partner with Morris Fishbein, then head of the American Medical Association, Rife's troubles turned more serious with lawsuits and health authorities attacking him from all sides. The university's Special Research Committee was disbanded, Rife was marginalized and his device today is available only as a costly research instrument employed by a few doctors and private citizens. Rife died a broken man in 1971.

For sci-fi fans, "Beam me up, Scotty" is perhaps the most widely, and instantly, recognized quote of all. Although attributed to *Star Trek*'s Captain Kirk, it is ironic that those four specific words were never actually uttered in even a single episode of what is probably the world's most-watched sci-fi television series of all time. This phrase was intended to convey the ability to travel from one location to another via what today we routinely refer to as teleportation.

The term, teleportation, was coined in the early 1900s by the American journalist and chronicler of all-things weird, Charles Fort. He used the word to describe something that he had a particular fascination with—the unexplained disappearances and appearances of people, animals, and objects.

Having combined the Greek prefix "tele" (meaning "distant") with the latter part of the word "transportation," teleportation was born, and was first used by Fort in his 1931 book *Lo!* Fort noted: "Mostly in this book I shall specialize upon indications that there exists a transportory force that I shall call Teleportation."

Literature from IBM described this phenomenon thusly:

> Teleportation is the name given by science fiction writers to the feat
> of making an object or person disintegrate in one place while a perfect
> replica appears somewhere else. How this is accomplished is usually not
> explained in detail, but the general idea seems to be that the original
> object is scanned in such a way as to extract all the information from it,
> then this information is transmitted to the receiving location and used
> to construct the replica, not necessarily from the actual material of the
> original, but perhaps from atoms of the same kinds, arranged in exactly
> the same pattern as the original. A teleportation machine would be like a
> fax machine, except that it would work on 3-dimensional objects as well
> as documents, it would produce an exact copy rather than an approximate
> facsimile, and it would destroy the original in the process of scanning it. A
> few science fiction writers consider teleporters that preserve the original,
> and the plot gets complicated when the original and teleported versions of
> the same person meet; but the more common kind of teleporter destroys
> the original, functioning as a super transportation device, not as a perfect
> replicator of souls and bodies.

Indeed, just such hazards were demonstrated in the sci-fi film *The Fly*.

If, one day, humankind develops the ability to instantly transport people, possessions and just about anything and everything to anywhere on the planet in an instant, not only would it revolutionize our world, it would also offer a technology that once again would take control away from the oil industries, and, arguably, usher in a new era of potentially unlimited energies. Little wonder, therefore, that its value, worth and feasibility has been denied at the official level.

The majority of people today consider teleportation to be a notion forever to be limited only to sci-fi novels and films. However, the U.S. Air Force for years has secretly taken an interest in this strange—and potentially world changing—subject. For example, consider an Air Force report entitled the *Teleportation Physics Study*.

The Air Force Research Laboratory, Air Force Materiel Command, quietly contracted the Study to Eric W. Davis of a Las Vegas-based outfit called Warp Drive Metrics. In August 2004 military officials made Davis's report available to the public.

Davis stated: "This study was tasked with the purpose of collecting information describing the teleportation of material objects, providing a description of teleportation as it occurs in physics, its theoretical and experimental status, and a projection of potential applications. The study also consisted of a search for teleportation phenomena occurring naturally or under laboratory conditions that can be assembled into a model describing the conditions required to accomplish the transfer of objects."

Interestingly, the Davis report noted that there appeared to be keen interest in official circles with respect to teleportation and its potential applications by the Department of Defense. "The late Dr. Robert L. Forward stated that modern hard-core sci-fi literature, with the exception of the ongoing *Star Trek* franchise, has abandoned using the teleportation concept because writers believe that it has more to do with the realms of parapsychology/paranormal (a.k.a. psychic) and imaginative fantasy than with any realm of science. Beginning in the 1980s developments in quantum theory and general relativity physics have succeeded in pushing the envelope in exploring the reality of teleportation. As for the psychic aspect of teleportation, it became known to Dr. Forward and myself, along with several colleagues both inside and outside of government, that anomalous teleportation has been scientifically investigated and separately documented by the Department of Defense," Davis wrote.

Davis's report carefully noted that there were a number of definitions for what might constitute teleportation. An extract from the report describes these definitions:

Teleportation—sci-fi: the disembodied transport of persons or inanimate objects across space by advanced (futuristic) technological means. We will call this Sf-Teleportation, which will not be considered further in this study.

Teleportation—psychic: the conveyance of persons or inanimate objects by psychic means. We will call this p-Teleportation.

Teleportation—engineering the vacuum or spacetime metric: the conveyance of persons or inanimate objects across space by altering the properties of the spacetime vacuum, or by altering the spacetime metric (geometry). We will call this vm-Teleportation.

Teleportation—quantum entanglement: the disembodied transport of the quantum state of a system and its correlations across space to another system, where system refers to any single or collective particles of matter or energy such as baryons (protons, neutrons, etc.), leptons (electrons, etc.), photons, atoms, ions, etc. We will call this q-Teleportation.

Teleportation—exotic: the conveyance of persons or inanimate objects by transport through extra space dimensions or parallel universes. We will call this e-Teleportation.

The *Teleportation Physics Study* is highly technical in nature, but it is worth noting Davis's conclusions with respect to the five areas of teleportation described above. He concludes that, based on present day capabilities, "p-Teleportation" would seem to offer the greatest potential. Davis noted: "p-Teleportation, if verified, would represent a phenomenon that could offer potential high-payoff military, intelligence and commercial applications. This phenomenon could generate a dramatic revolution in technology, which would result from a dramatic paradigm shift in science. Anomalies are the key to all paradigm shifts!"

In a section of the *Study* titled "Recommendations," Davis added: "A research program ... should be conducted in order to generate p-Teleportation phenomenon in the lab. An experimental program ... should be funded at $900,000–$1,000,000 per year in parallel with a theoretical program funded at $500,000 per year for an initial five-year duration."

When the Air Force declassified the *Study*, Lawrence Krauss of Case Western Reserve University and the author of *The Physics of Star Trek*, stated: "It is in large part crackpot physics," and added that it contained "some things adapted from reasonable theoretical studies, and other things from nonsensical ones."

Perhaps the Air Force, after reading Davis's document, agreed: "The views expressed in the report are those of the author and do not necessarily reflect the official policy of the Air Force, the Department of Defense or the U.S. government," was the statement made by the Air Force's Research Laboratory (AFRL) when questioned by *USA Today*.

Asked why the Laboratory had secretly sponsored the study, AFRL spokesman Ranney Adams said: "If we don't turn over stones, we don't know if we have missed something." Significantly, the AFRL added that: "There are no plans by the AFRL Propulsion Directorate for additional funding on this contract."

Unless circumstances change drastically, it would seem that despite the secret studies of the Air Force, teleportation—in the way that it is portrayed on *Star Trek*, at least—is destined to remain purely within the domain of sci-fi. Or is it?

The declassified documentation may not tell the whole story, if the following words of an *Above Top Secret* contributor prove to be valid. This member wrote:

> I am in the military, and am a computer programmer. I had a supervisor whom I became good friends with who got out of the military about a year and a half ago. He used to be stationed at Wright-Patterson AFB ... he ended up getting a contractor job working for the Air Force Research Laboratory located at Wright-Patterson.
>
> Pretty much everything they do at the Air Force Research Laboratory is classified, so I knew before I asked him what he was working on that he wasn't going to tell me, but I asked ...

IS FREE/ALTERNATIVE ENERGY BEING KEPT FROM THE PUBLIC?

One particular night I got a phone call from him … we got on the subject of work and he told me what he was working on. Apparently he was working on an actual teleportation device. His actual words were "like beam me up, Scotty." He wouldn't go into details but I definitely believed him. I've asked him about it since then and he acts like he doesn't know what I am talking about.

We might ask: was the Air Force's teleportation study really considered unfeasible in terms of offering real, tangible results? Or, is it possible that powerful men in shadowy positions did not wish to see the introduction of a technology that would render the oil and transportation industries as extinct as the dinosaur?

▸ IS THE FEDERAL RESERVE
A SCAM?

▽ WHO

▶ The Federal Reserve

▽ WHAT

▶ Is the Federal Reserve a Scam on the American Public?

▽ WHEN

▶ 1913 to the Present Day

▽ WHERE

▶ Such claims proliferate on the Internet and have been the subject of several books.

▽ WHY

▶ If there is no control over the Federal Reserve System by the American public, then there is no control over the nation's money supply, which makes all notions of freedom and democracy a cruel joke.

additional evidence and commentary:
www.abovetopsecret.com/book/federalreserve

When the republic of the United States was originally founded in the late 1700s, the largest bone of contention concerned the desirability of a central bank. There was no central bank until 1781.

The early American colonists printed small quantities of paper money and were prospering. Benjamin Franklin explained, "In the colonies we issue our own money. It is called Colonial Script. We issue it in proper proportion to the demands of trade and industry to make the products pass easily from the producers to the consumers ... In this manner, creating for ourselves our own paper money, we control its purchasing power, and we have no interest to pay to no one."

The English Parliament, at the urging of the Bank of England, stopped this practice. The Currency Act of 1764 prohibited the printing of currency. The colonists were forced to accept interest-bearing notes from the Bank of England. Franklin and others claimed it was this outlawing of debt-free money that caused economic depression and widespread unemployment precipitating the American Revolution.

The arguments for and against a central bank can be seen in the debates of Founding Fathers Thomas Jefferson and Alexander Hamilton. Hamilton believed in strong central government and a central bank overseen by a wealthy elite. Supporters of Hamilton's elitist ideals formed America's first political party, the Federalists. Hamilton, once described as a "tool of the international bankers," argued, "a national debt, if it is not excessive, will be to us a national blessing."

Jefferson knew from European history that a central bank could quickly become the master of a nation. "I sincerely believe ... that banking establishments are more dangerous than standing armies; and that the principle of spending money to be paid by posterity, under the name of funding, is but swindling futurity on a large scale," he wrote to John Taylor in 1816, adding, "Already they have raised up a money aristocracy … The issuing power should be taken from the banks and restored to the people to whom it properly belongs."

Jefferson further believed a central bank to be unconstitutional. "I consider the foundation of the Constitution as laid on this ground: That 'all powers not delegated to the United States, by the Constitution, nor prohibited by it to the States, are reserved to the States or to the People.' To take a single step beyond the boundaries thus specially drawn around the powers of Congress, is to take possession of a boundless field of power, no longer susceptible of any definition. The incorporation of a bank, and the powers assumed by this bill, have not, in my opinion, been delegated to the United States, by the Constitution."

But Hamilton and his wealthy friends won out. Even before the drafting of the Constitution, the Bank of North America was created by Continental Congressman Robert Morris in 1781. Morris tried to craft it into a central bank copying the Bank of England. It lasted just three years before being discontinued due to rampant fraud and the inflation caused by the creation of baseless "fiat" currency (money declared the only official unit of exchange).

Hamilton didn't give up and in 1791 headed the next attempt to form a central bank by establishing the First Bank of the United States, a move strongly opposed by Jefferson and his followers.

The First Bank of the United States also was closely modeled after the Bank of England and created a partnership between the government and banking interests. Twenty percent of the bank's capital was obtained through the federal government with the remaining 80 percent pledged by private investors, including foreigners such as the European Rothschild banking family. This bank also caused inflation by the creation of fractional-reserve notes. Money merchants prospered but the average citizen suffered. In 1811, when the bank's 20-year charter came up for renewal, it was defeated by one vote in both the Senate and the House.

But the costs of the War of 1812, along with chaotic financial conditions, prompted Congress to issue a 20-year charter to the Second Bank of the United States in 1816. This central bank ended in 1836, after President Andrew Jackson in

1832 vetoed a congressional bill to extend its charter, precipitating what became known as the "Bank War." Jackson, the first president from west of the Appalachian Mountains, denounced the central bank as unconstitutional as well as "a curse to a republic; inasmuch as it is calculated to raise around the administration a moneyed aristocracy dangerous to the liberties of the country." It may have been no coincidence that America's first assassination attempt was made on Jackson in 1835 by a man named Richard Lawrence, whose pistols misfired. Lawrence claimed to be "in touch with the powers in Europe."

There were other attempts to resurrect a central bank but none succeeded until the creation of the Federal Reserve System in 1913, in essence the third central banking system that has existed in the United States. It is well documented that the creation of the Fed was quite literally a conspiracy. Until well into the 1980s, the Fed was never referred to as a central bank. But today, newscasters routinely call it this.

This latest bankers' scheme came after a series of retractions of loans and the refusal to renew old ones created what became known as "bank panics" in 1873, 1893, and 1907. It was these contrived panics that led to calls for the establishment of a centralized banking system. Needless to say, the idea of a central bank was highly unpopular at the time with a public rightly fearful of giving a single, central authority power over the entire monetary system.

In the wake of the bank Panic of 1907, Congress created the National Monetary Commission, whose mandate was to initiate a program that would allow for a complete reformation of the United States banking system. Senate Republican leader and financial expert Nelson Aldrich oversaw the commission. Aldrich also set up two other commissions—one was designed to study the American monetary system in-depth, while the focus of the other was to investigate the European central-banking systems and provide reports on their activities.

After reviewing Germany's banking system, he came away greatly impressed. He now believed that a central bank was more preferable than the government-issued bond system that had existed in the United States, which he had previously championed.

Unsurprisingly, centralized banking was met with a great deal of opposition from American politicians of the day, many of whom were deeply suspicious of even the idea of a central bank, and some of who openly accused Aldrich of being biased as a result of his deep connections to wealthy bankers such as J. P. Morgan, as well as his daughter's marriage to none other than John D. Rockefeller, Jr.

In 1910, Aldrich and a variety of executives that represented the banks of J. P. Morgan, Rockefeller, and Kuhn, Loeb, & Co., secluded themselves for ten days on Jekyll Island, Georgia. The executives included Frank Vanderlip, president of the National City Bank of New York; Henry Davison, who was a senior partner of J. P. Morgan & Company; Charles D. Norton, the president of the First National Bank of New York; and Colonel Edward House, who later became President Woodrow Wilson's closest adviser and the founder of the controversial Council on Foreign Relations.

At the Jekyll Island meeting, the German banker Paul Warburg of Kuhn, Loeb, & Company directed the proceedings and was almost single-handedly responsible for the creation of what would become the Federal Reserve Act.

In his 1935 autobiography, titled *From Farmboy to Financier*, Frank Vanderlip recalled his memories of Jekyll Island: "I was as furtive as any conspirator. Discovery, we knew, simply must not happen, or else all our time and effort would have been wasted. If it were to be exposed that our particular group had got together and written a banking bill, that bill would have no chance whatever of passage by Congress. I do not feel it is any exaggeration to speak of our secret expedition to Jekyll Island as the occasion of the actual conception of what eventually became the Federal Reserve System."

Despite the undoubted historical and economic significance of the Jekyll Island meeting, the whole affair remained completely unknown to the public, and even the government, until a journalist named Bertie Charles Forbes wrote an article about it in 1916, a full three years after the Federal Reserve Act was passed.

Aldrich fought vigorously for the establishment of a private bank that would be largely free of government oversight and influence. Sensing strong opposition, he then presented an idea that became known as the "Aldrich Plan." This was a plan calling for the establishment of a National Reserve Association to succeed the National Monetary Commission. While the majority of Republicans and Wall Street bankers favored the Aldrich Plan, it lacked enough support to be passed by Congress. Aldrich was almost unanimously viewed as the absolute epitome of the "Eastern establishment" and his plan was overwhelmingly criticized and derided by both southerners and westerners alike, who perceptively noted that it was predominantly wealthy families and the large corporations that ran the country who would control the proposed National Reserve Association.

Conservative Democrats fought fiercely for a privately owned and decentralized reserve system that would be free of Wall Street's vice-like grip. The Nebraskan Democratic presidential candidate William Jennings Bryan said of the plan: "Big financiers are back of the Aldrich currency scheme." Bryan noted astutely that if it passed, big bankers would "then be in complete control of everything through the control of our national finances."

Even certain Republicans opposed the Aldrich Plan. Republican Senator Robert M. LaFollette and Representative Charles Lindbergh, Sr. both spoke out against the favoritism that they contended the bill granted to Wall Street. "The Aldrich Plan is the Wall Street Plan. I have alleged that there is a 'Money Trust,'" said Lindbergh, adding, "The Aldrich Plan is a scheme plainly in the interest of the Trust." In response, the Senate Banking Committee held what were known as the "Pujo Hearings," which firmly convinced the majority of the U.S. population that America's money was already in the hands of a select few on Wall Street.

It issued a report that stated in part: "If by a 'money trust' is meant an established and well-defined identity and community of interest between a few leaders of finance ... which has resulted in a vast and growing concentration of control of money and credit in the hands of a comparatively few men ... the condition thus described exists in this country today."

To counter such perceptions, the National Board of Trade appointed Paul Warburg to head a committee to convince Americans to support the Aldrich plan. The committee set up offices in the then forty-five U.S. states and began distributing printed materials about the central bank, its work, polices, ideas and ideals.

The political influence of newly-elected Democratic President Woodrow Wilson, along with a Democratic majority in both houses of Congress, led to the Aldrich Plan being renamed the Federal Reserve Act, proposed by Congressman Carter Glass, chairman of the House Banking and Currency Committee.

Shrewdly, Aldrich and other Jekyll planners loudly voiced opposition to this bill, although whole sections were identical to the Aldrich Plan.

Another problem for supporters of the bill was that early polling indicated that Democrat Wilson could not defeat Republican Howard Taft, who had already pledged to oppose any banking bill. In a maneuver which has been used successfully several times since, former President Theodore "Teddy" Roosevelt, also a Republican, was encouraged to run as a third-party candidate with large sums of money provided to his Progressive Party by two major contributors closely connected to J. P. Morgan. The scheme worked well. Roosevelt pulled votes from Taft so that Wilson, who already had pledged to sign the Federal Reserve Act, was elected by a narrow margin.

> **//**My fear is that when the [next] collapse comes, the ensuing riots will provide a wonderful justification for martial law. Gold confiscation, just like in the 1930s, will be the norm. While it is easy enough to hide gold, you won't be able to spend it without risking the criminal penalties resulting from not handing it over to the government's 'strategic reserves.' It is not often that I say this, but my view of the future is very bleak. Spreading credit crisis, runs on major banks, government ineptitude, voter apathy, the list goes on and on. Unfortunately I see no good outcome to our current situation and I believe it has been engineered as such. **//**

Charles Lindbergh, Sr. told Congress twenty-four hours before the bill was passed: "This is the Aldrich bill in disguise. The worst legislative crime of the ages is perpetrated by this banking bill. The banks have been granted the special privilege of distributing the money, and they charge as much as they wish. This is the strangest, most dangerous advantage ever placed in the hands of a special privilege class by any government that ever existed. The system is private. There should be no legal tender other than that issued by the government. The people are the government. Therefore the government should, as the Constitution provides, regulate the value of money."

After Wilson presented the bill to Congress, a group of Democratic congressmen, led by Representative Robert Henry of Texas, revolted and demanded that the "Money Trust" be destroyed before it could undertake major currency reforms. Henry's supporters were strongly opposed to the idea of regional banks having to operate without the government protections from which large banks would inevitably benefit. The group almost succeeded in killing the bill, but was mollified by Wilson's promises to propose antitrust legislation after the bill had passed.

Wilson signed the Federal Reserve Act on December 23, 1913; just two days before Christmas with some Congressmen already home for the holidays and with the average citizen's attention clearly elsewhere. "Congress was outflanked, outfoxed, and outclassed by a deceptive, but brilliant, psycho-political attack," commented G. Edward Griffin, author *The Creature from Jekyll Island*.

Frank Vanderlip, one of the Jekyll Island attendees and the president of National City Bank said, "Although the Aldrich Federal Reserve Plan was defeated when it bore the name Aldrich, nevertheless its essential points were all contained in the plan that was finally adopted."

Even the agrarian William Jennings Bryan, who had been appointed secretary of state after being instrumental in gaining the Democratic nomination for Wilson, quickly became disillusioned with the new act. In the pages of the November 1923 issue of *Hearst's Magazine* Bryan wrote: "The Federal Reserve Bank that should have been the farmer's greatest protection has become his greatest foe."

The Federal Reserve System today is composed of twelve Federal Reserve banks, each serving a section of the country, but dominated by the New York Federal Reserve Bank, the "first among equals." These banks are administered by a Board of Governors appointed by the president and confirmed by the Senate, usually a rubber-stamp procedure.

Today, the Board of Governors of the Federal Reserve System is an independent agency of the federal government. This board does not receive funding from Congress, and the terms of its seven-person membership of the Board span both multiple presidential and congressional terms. The Board is required to make an annual report of operations to the Speaker of the House of Representatives and is responsible for the formulation of monetary policy. It also supervises and regulates the operations of the Federal Reserve Banks, and the entire U.S. banking system in general.

Criticism of the Federal Reserve System is not new and some historical criticisms are reflective of current concerns. Indeed, there are those who believe the Federal Reserve System is shrouded in excessive secrecy. Meetings of some components of the Federal Reserve are held behind closed doors, critics note, and the transcripts of those same meetings are rarely released before a five-year time-passage.

William Greider, a former assistant managing editor of the *Washington Post* in his 1987 book *Secrets of the Temple: How the Federal Reserve Runs the Country* noted: "To modern minds, it seemed bizarre to think of the Federal Reserve as a religious institution. Yet the conspiracy theorists, in their own demented way, were on to something real and significant … [The Fed] did also function in the realm of religion. Its mysterious powers of money creation, inherited from priestly forebears, shielded a complex bundle of social and psychological meanings. With its own form of secret incantation, the Federal Reserve presided over awesome social ritual, transactions so powerful and frightening they seemed to lie beyond common understanding … Above all, money was a function of faith. It required implicit and universal social consent that was indeed mysterious. To create money and use it, each one must believe and everyone must believe. Only then did worthless pieces of paper take on value."

Some have sought to penetrate the secrecy and understand the true nature of the Federal Reserve, its history and real intent, however. And for their findings and conclusions we should turn our attention to Gary Allen and Larry Abraham who, in their seminal work, *None Dare Call It Conspiracy*, wrote:

> In order to show the hinterlands that they were going to need a central banking system, the international bankers created a series of panics as a demonstration of their power, a warning of what would happen unless the rest of the bankers got into line. The man in charge of conducting these lessons was J. Pierpont Morgan, American-born but educated in England and Germany. Morgan is referred to by many, including Congressman Louis McFadden, (a banker who for ten years headed the House Banking and Currency Committee), as the top American agent of the English Rothschilds.

By the turn of the century J. P. Morgan was already an old hand at creating artificial panics. Such affairs were well coordinated. Senator Robert Owen, a co-author of the Federal Reserve Act, (who later deeply regretted his role), testified before a congressional committee that the bank he owned received from the National Bankers' Association what came to be known as the "Panic Circular of 1893." It stated: "You will at once retire one-third of your circulation and call in one-half of your loans."

Historian Frederick Lewis Allen tells in *Life* magazine of April 25, 1949, of Morgan's role in spreading rumors about the insolvency of the Knickerbocker Bank and The Trust Company of America, which rumors triggered the 1907 panic.

Did Morgan precipitate the panic? Oakleigh Thorne, the president of that particular trust company, testified later before a congressional committee that his bank had been subjected to only moderate withdrawals, that he had not applied for help, and that it was the [Morgan's] sore point statement alone that had caused the run on his bank. From this testimony, plus the disciplinary measures taken by the Clearing House against the Heinze, Morse, and Thomas banks, plus other fragments of supposedly pertinent evidence, certain chroniclers have arrived at the ingenious conclusion that the Morgan interests took advantage of the unsettled conditions during the autumn of 1907 to precipitate the panic, guiding it shrewdly as it progressed so that it would kill off rival banks and consolidate the preeminence of the banks within the Morgan orbit.

Allen and Abraham recorded that: "The 'panic' which Morgan had created, he proceeded to end almost single-handedly. He had made his point. Frederick Allen explains: 'The lesson of the Panic of 1907 was clear, though not for some six years was it destined to be embodied in legislation: the United States gravely needed a central banking system.' When the Federal Reserve System was foisted on an unsuspecting American public, there were absolute guarantees that there would be no more boom and bust economic cycles. The men who, behind the scenes, were pushing the central bank concept for the international bankers faithfully promised that from then on there would be only steady growth and perpetual prosperity. However, Congressman Charles A. Lindberg, Sr. accurately proclaimed: 'From now on depressions will be scientifically created.'"

According to Allen and Abraham, "Using a central bank to create alternate periods of inflation and deflation, and thus whipsawing the public for vast profits, had been worked out by the international bankers to an exact science. Having built the Federal Reserve as a tool to consolidate and control wealth, the international bankers were now ready to make a major killing. Between 1923 and 1929, the Federal Reserve expanded (inflated) the money supply by sixty-two percent. Much of this new money was used to bid the stock market up to dizzying heights."

Allen and Abraham noted that the House Hearings on Stabilization of the Purchasing Power of the Dollar in 1928 disclosed that the Federal Reserve Board was working closely with the heads of European central banks. The Committee warned that a major crash had been planned in 1927. At a secret luncheon of the Federal Reserve Board and heads of the European central banks, the committee warned, the international bankers were tightening the noose.

"Montagu Norman, governor of the Bank of England, came to Washington on February 6, 1929, to confer with Andrew Mellon, secretary of the treasury. On November 11, 1927, the *Wall Street Journal* described Mr. Norman as 'the currency dictator of Europe.' Professor Carroll Quigley notes that Norman, a close confidant of J. P. Morgan, admitted: 'I hold the hegemony of the world.' Immediately after this mysterious visit, the Federal Reserve Board reversed its easy-money policy and began raising the discount rate. The balloon, which had been inflated constantly for nearly seven years, was about to be exploded. On October 24, the feathers hit the fan," explained Allen and Abraham.

Writing in *The United States' Unresolved Monetary and Political Problems*, William Bryan described what happened next: "When everything was ready, the New York financiers started calling 24-hour broker call loans. This meant that the stockbrokers and the customers had to dump their stock on the market in order to pay the loans. This naturally collapsed the stock market and brought a banking collapse all over the country because the banks not owned by the oligarchy were heavily involved in broker call claims at this time, and bank runs soon exhausted their coin and currency and they had to close. The Federal Reserve System would not come to their aid, although they were instructed under the law to maintain an elastic currency."

Commenting on all this, Allen and Abraham said:

The investing public, including most stock brokers and bankers, took a horrendous blow in the crash, but not the insiders. They were either out of the market or had sold 'short' so that they made enormous profits as the Dow Jones plummeted. For those who knew the score, a comment by Paul Warburg had provided the warning to sell. That signal came on March 9, 1929, when the *Financial Chronicle* quoted Warburg as giving this sound advice: "If orgies of unrestricted speculation are permitted to spread too far, the ultimate collapse is certain to bring about a general depression involving the whole country." Sharpies were later able to buy back these stocks at a ninety percent discount from their former highs.

To think that the scientifically engineered Crash of '29 was an accident or the result of stupidity defies all logic. The international bankers who promoted the inflationary policies and pushed the propaganda which pumped up the stock market represented too many generations of accumulated expertise to have blundered into "the great depression."

Prior to the 1930s, paper bills could be redeemed for gold, since Section 10 of the Constitution specifies gold and silver as the only lawful tender. Older Federal Reserve notes bore the inscription, "... redeemable in lawful money at the United States Treasury, or any Federal Reserve bank." The original purpose of money—to represent tangible goods and services—has been forgotten, as has the term "usury," which is charging interest on any loan. Usury was once considered a sin by the Christian churches and, until recently, usury—defined as excessively high interest—was a crime punishable by fine or jail.

Money today is increasingly mere electronic blips in a computer accessed by plastic cards at ATMs. There is nothing to back it up. Yet this illusory money is loaned at interest by great institutions. As the total amount of money grows, its worth decreases. This is called inflation, in effect a built-in tax on the use of money. And inflation can be manipulated, upwards or downwards, by those who control the flow of paper money, or these electronic blips.

Only two U.S. presidents have attempted to issue interest-free money: Abraham Lincoln who printed "Greenbacks" to finance his war against the Southern Rebellion; and John F. Kennedy, who in 1963 issued "United States Notes" through the

U.S. Treasury rather than "Federal Reserve Notes." It may not be sheer coincidence that both of these men were shot in the head in a public place. It has proven hazardous to one's health to thwart the international bankers.

It is highly pertinent to note the following statement of Congressman Louis McFadden, Chairman of the House Banking and Currency Committee, who stated firmly: "It [the Great Depression] was not accidental. It was a carefully contrived occurrence. The international bankers sought to bring about a condition of despair here so that they might emerge as the rulers of us all."

Those are wise words to remember decades later, in a fearful time with debt—both governmental and personal—ballooning ever upward in a faltering U.S. economy.

Indeed, members of the *Above Top Secret* forum are acutely aware of the potential for something similar happening today as evidenced by several comments on the site.

If the purpose of the Federal Reserve is to balance the budget and to manage the national money supply to the benefit of the public, then the answer to the question "Is the Federal Reserve System a scam?" must be "Yes."

▶ ARE CHEMTRAILS FOR REAL?

▽ WHO

▶ No one in authority will admit to the existence of chemtrails.

▽ WHAT

▶ High-flying aircraft that lay down long trails of non-dissipating cloudy trails.

▽ WHEN

▶ These trails have been observed on any given day at any given time, both day and night.

▽ WHERE

▶ These trails have been observed in almost all NATO countries.

▽ WHY

▶ This is the real question since no one will admit this is happening.

additional evidence and commentary:
www.abovetopsecret.com/book/chemtrails

In about 2002, a retired Army Intelligence officer was visiting a friend who was still in the military, stationed at White Sands Proving Ground in New Mexico.

During their chat, the serviceman boasted about the security at White Sands, stating that no aircraft were allowed to fly over its restricted airspace.

The former intelligence officer, well aware of the issue of chemtrails, pointed to a high-flying jet leaving a white trail clear across the sky directly above them. "What about that airplane?" he asked.

After looking directly at the jet above them, his companion replied with a smirk, "What plane?"

This then is the crux of the problem concerning what has come to be known as "chemtrails." No one in a position of authority will admit that they exist, much less who is responsible, and what purpose they may serve. Unlike many mysteries, this one is visible to anyone who cares to look up on the days that large jets weave narrow and continuous vapor/chemical trails through the sky.

Beginning in about 1997, observant persons in the United States, Canada, the United Kingdom, and Europe starting noticing the long trails in the sky that failed to evaporate like the common condensation trails from normal aircraft.

Condensation trails, or contrails, have been a fixture in the skies since World War II when high altitude bombers would leave a trail of condensation behind their engines.

Any aircraft engine, jet or piston, produces warm, moist air which, when injected into the cold, dry air of the upper atmosphere, results in a trail of water vapor or ice crystals that stream out behind the craft. Once these particles return to a cooler state, they evaporate back into the air. This vaporization can take place within 10 seconds or stretch to more than an hour depending on the temperature and humidity in the atmosphere. Since contrails primarily contain water, they present no real hazard to the population. Contrails do not normally occur under about 30,000 feet.

Chemtrails present another story. These trails do not evaporate but spread out and eventually form a cloudy haze over the entire sky. As World War II veteran David Oglesby noted after observing chemtrails in the sky above his California home: "The trails formed a grid pattern. Some stretched from horizon to horizon. Some began abruptly, and others ended abruptly. They hung in the air for an extended period of time and gradually widened into wispy clouds resembling spider webs. I counted at least 11 different trails."

The official debunking line that all observed trails in the sky are simply condensation trails falls apart when, as described by numerous observers, a short contrail and a lengthy chemtrail are seen simultaneously in the same portion of sky and at approximately the same altitude.

In 2001, there may have been a brief admission to the reality of chemtrails. Ohio Rep. Dennis Kucinich, who served as chairman of a subcommittee of the House Committee on Oversight and Government Reform, introduced his unsuccessful Space Preservation Act of 2001, designed to ban the deployment of weapons in space. But also included in this legislation was chemical, biological, environmental, climate changing, or tectonic weapons and, notably, chemtrails. The latter was later stricken from the failed bill. In 2004, while campaigning as a presidential candidate, Kucinich responded to a question about chemtrails by stating, "Chemtrails are real."

In a 2000–2001 study in Houston, Texas, Mark Steadham, using Flight Explorer software, found that over the course of 63 days of observation military aircraft were laying down white plumes which lasted for eight hours or more while commercial airliners flying at the same altitude left contrails that persisted for no more than 25 seconds. Stranger still were observations of aircraft not filing flight plans and hence, not recorded by the FAA and shown in the flight software. "It was discovered that the jets that were responsible for leaving highly persistent trails that last for hours did not ever appear on Flight Explorer and were documented for 8 separate instances, including one instance with two jets in formation," reported Steadham. For his full study, visit www.chemtrailcentral.com/report.shtml.

Chemtrails often occur at altitudes and in conditions where it would be impossible for a contrail to form. Whereas contrails are composed of water vapor, they are whitish in color and produce no "halo" effect in sunlight; chemtrails, on the other hand, appear oily and produce rainbow effects, especially in the late afternoon sun. Contrails cannot be stopped without shutting off the engines but chemtrails have been observed ending even as the aircraft producing it flies onward.

In the late 1990s and early 2000s, people—and even some local TV stations—were reporting strange white sticky substances being found on homes, yards, and vehicles. It was lace-like and would hang from trees and shrubbery as if it had fallen from the sky. Chemical analysis found this substance contained aluminum oxide, barium, polymers, and even traces of pathogens. People in the vicinity of this substance reported ill effects such as asthma, fatigue, headaches, dizziness, joint pain, and flu-like symptoms.

Apparently, whatever was being concocted was improved, as there have been no such reports in recent years. A Harvard School of Public Health team determined that aerial particulates as small as 10 microns in diameter can constitute a serious health menace. Consider that a human hair is about 100 microns wide. Referring specifically to second-hand smoke, research associate Vaughan Rees reported, "Toxic particles from secondhand smoke can settle on furniture or on floors, and we are assuming that will also occur in cars on child-restraint seats. Children tend to touch things with their hands, and put their hands in their mouths. So children can also be exposed to contaminants in that way." Obviously, adults are as susceptible as children to tiny particles in the air.

The Harvard study determined that respirable suspended particles can be inhaled and can transport carcinogens and other toxic substances deep into the lungs resulting in respiratory illnesses like bronchitis, emphysema, and asthma.

It is known that many pathogens may be found in the upper atmosphere, which is an indication that illnesses brought on by chemtrails may not be an intentional part of the program. They may be inadvertently brought to earth by the chemtrail haze. This undoubtedly is a small consolation to those who suffer from such contamination.

Germ warfare experts and medical authorities agree that a high-altitude spraying program is a most inefficient method for distributing bacteria and viruses. There seems to be little evidence that the chemtrails are designed to cull the human population, as was believed by many in the early days of the spraying.

One Canadian research foundation concluded that the much-discussed but little-publicized chemtrails might be an attempt to hide a sickening military secret. Professor Donald Scott, president of the Common Cause Medical Research Foundation, claimed that chemtrails are a belated attempt by U.S. military and intelligence chieftains to stop the spread of a debilitating disease first concocted in the early 1980s.

According to Scott's account, the military began developing diseases in the 1970s that were infectious but not contagious. In other words, they developed an ailment, which could be spread to enemy troops but would not pass into other populations. One such disease was based on a zoonosis, a disease that can be transmitted to humans by animals, in this case brucellosis. Brucellosis is a bacterial disease usually found in cattle that can cause undulant fever in humans.

> **//** Keep looking up and you'll eventually see contrails and chemtrails side by side in the air and once you see two planes of similar size laying trails at the same altitude and they don't match, then you know something is amiss. **//**

ATS MEMBER COMMENT

By manipulating this disease, researchers were able to design a disabling bacterium that disappeared following infection. Troops could be infected yet exhibit no signs of the bacteria when examined by a doctor.

According to Scott's report, such a bacteria was tested during the summer of 1984 at Tahoe-Truckee High School in California, where individual rooms were fitted with an independent recycling air supply. A teacher's lounge was designated as the infection target. Seven of eight teachers assigned to this room became very ill within months.

The high school was only one of several locations where the specially designed pathogens were tested, some distributed by aerosol sprays and others by the use of contaminated mosquitoes.

Scott reported that one hundred million mosquitoes a month were bred at the Dominion Parasite Laboratory in Belleville, Ontario, during the 1980s, then tested by both Canadian and U.S. military authorities after being infected with brucellosis. Some observers believe the viral epidemic reported around New York City in recent years may have been the result of these infected mosquitoes.

The testing of unsuspecting victims was conducted by both the military and CIA, according to Scott, and monitored by the National Institutes of Health as well as the U.S. Centers for Disease Control.

Encouraged by what they felt was a successful test, military leaders reportedly passed the brucellosis bioagent to none other than Saddam Hussein, who in the mid-1980s was fighting a protracted war against Iran at the behest of the CIA.

In 1986, with the approval of Vice President George H. W. Bush, Saddam received shipments of both *brucella abortus*, biotypes 3 and 9, and *brucella melitensis*, biotypes 1 and 3.

After Saddam had obtained a stockpile of the brucellosis, a terrible discovery was made—this designer bacteria had mutated and become contagious.

According to Scott's report, Saddam used this pathogen on American troops during the Persian Gulf War in 1991, resulting in the illness referred to as Gulf War Syndrome. More than 100,000 Gulf War vets now suffer from this syndrome, which causes chronic fatigue, loss of appetite, profuse sweating even at rest, joint and muscle pain, insomnia, nausea, and damage to major organs.

Much of this information may be found in a 1994 report by Senator Donald W. Riegle, Jr., entitled, "U.S. Chemical and Biological Warfare-related Dual Use Exports to Iraq and Their Possible Impact on the Health Consequences of the Persian Gulf War."

Troops initially were told that no such infection existed and that the problem was mostly in their minds. Slowly, over the years, authorities were forced to admit that something had triggered severe illness in many Gulf War veterans.

By then a variant of the brucellosis had spread to the civilian population.

Many people began suffering from general debilitation and tiredness.

When it became know that the contagion was spreading into the general population, top officials with the National Institutes of Health and the Centers for Disease Control as well as the Defense Department and the Department of Health and Human Services began a program of misrepresentation of the disease to mask their role in its origin. The illness was claimed to be connected to the Epstein-Barr virus and was labeled "Chronic Mononucleosis." This has now become known as Chronic Fatigue Syndrome. Like the veterans before them, victims of this ailment were told it was merely a psychological condition.

One victim, Dr. Martin Lerner of William Beaumont Hospital in Royal Oak, MI, told his peers in the American Society of Microbiology that his bout with this mysterious disease left his heart damaged. Dr. Lerner and others suspected that Chronic Fatigue Syndrome is caused by viral infection.

Top-level officials, concerned both with the spread of the contagion and with the risk that their role in its origin would become publicly known, moved to counteract the pathogen. This program may be another explanation for chemtrails.

As explained by Scott, "We have learned ... that a patent was issued in 1996 for an aerosol vaccination process which would permit the vaccination of wild life and domestic herds by spraying them or their disease vectors (birds) from the air ... We have noted that many of the sightings of chemtrails are over migratory bird flight paths ... The chemtrails program may well be a belated effort by the U.S. and Canadian governments to get the brucellosis genie back in its bottle."

Only occasionally have members of the corporate media seen fit to mention chemtrails and then it disappears from the airwaves quickly. In 2000, a weatherman, who was not the primary weather specialist at a Dallas-Forth Worth TV station, on an early news broadcast mentioned that in response to many calls concerning the long trails in the sky, he was told that it was a military experiment but that there was no call for alarm. The story never aired on later news broadcast. Other news outlets reported similar explanations over the years but the U.S. military has consistently denied any such experiments and the mass media for the most part has parroted such denials.

One notable exception to this apparent news blackout was the Discovery

Channel, which in February 2007 aired a program devoted to the issue of chemtrails. It was a classic case of misdirection. The program, *Best Evidence*, was entitled "Chemical Contrails" and focused on whether jet-aircraft vapor trails may be toxic. The first third of the program fairly presented the concerns of several citizens and researchers concerning the aerial trails, which appeared much different from the usual vapor trails. The following third was a boring description of various scientific equipment, including a jet engine, which was to be used to test burn particulates from the jet's exhaust. The final third was an exhaustingly detailed analysis of the burnt fuel that showed no pathogens or any other harmful chemical or metal in the fuel waste.

From this presentation, it was made plain that nothing unusual was to be found in jet vapor trails. But for those who viewed this program closely, the fatal flaw became easily apparent. First, the show's narrator stated that the U.S. military had refused to allow its jet fuel to be tested, which left out the prime suspect of the chemtrails. For their test, the show's producers had used commercial jet fuel purchased from a local airport. No wonder the burned fuel showed no unusual properties. No one has ever accused normal jet fuel of being contaminated with chemicals or pathogens.

// How come one day there are numerous trails crisscrossing each other in the sky but on the next day, with no change in the climate, there are no trails in the sky. Did all aircraft suddenly stop flying? //

Last, but not least, it has been established, both by observation and photographs, that chemtrails emanate from lines along aircraft wings, not from the engines. This alone demonstrates that chemtrails constitute an aerial spraying program. It also nullifies any meaningful test on spent jet fuel.

One Louisiana TV station in late 2007 took upon itself the task of testing water captured under a crosshatch of aerial trails. KSLA-TV News in Shreveport found exceptionally high levels of barium, an alkaline earth metal rarely found in nature as it quickly oxidizes in air. An excessive amount of barium is toxic, affecting the nervous system and the heart. State health officials confirmed to the TV station the danger of barium to the human nervous and immunization systems but hesitated to link this danger to chemtrails.

Barium, along with aluminum oxide, already had been identified among the contents of chemtrails by other tests. During a three-month period in 2002, three separate rainwater and snow samples from Chapel Hill, North Carolina were collected and submitted for formal double-blind laboratory analysis. Therese Aigner, an accredited environmental engineer, found significant amounts of barium, aluminum, calcium, magnesium, and titanium in the samples, all of which had a verified chain of custody. Ms. Aigner concluded that that the consistency of the findings indicated "a very controlled delivery (dispersion) of chemtrails by aircraft in your area." She added that whoever was responsible for the chemtrails was violating more than a half dozen federal laws and regulations.

Apparently, yet another ingredient of chemtrails is tiny synthetic filaments called polymers. Polymer chemist Dr. R. Michael Castle reported that some of polymers he studied in connection with chemtrails can cause "serious skin lesions and diseases when absorbed into the skin."

// There is no way to explain the media's refusal to investigate or give coverage to this story except that they are fully aware of it and are under bogus 'national security' orders to spike the story. //

ATS MEMBER COMMENT

Yet the government, with help from a compliant corporate mass media, still refused to even consider the issue. Politicians appeared to have been given the runaround when it comes to chemtrails. In response to a 2001 inquiry by California Senator Dianne Feinstein, Air Force Col. Walter M. Washabaugh, chief of the Congressional Inquiry Division, after a lengthy explanation of condensation vapor trails and explaining that recent sightings are a result of ever increasing air traffic, wrote: "The Air Force's policy is to observe and forecast the weather to support military operations. The Air Force is not conducting any weather modification experiments or programs and has no plans to do so in the future. In short, there is no such thing as a 'chemtrail'—the actual contrails are safe and are a natural phenomenon. They pose no health hazard of any kind."

Since no one in authority will admit to what is happening right in front of the public's eyes, researchers have been forced to speculate on what chemtrails are all about.

Once the idea of population control is put aside, the next best explanation appeared to be some form of weather modification or control. Experiments in this area date back to the 1950s, so it seems reasonable to assume that some advancement has been made. Concerns over weather modification were not eased by the 1996 publication of an Air Force research paper entitled "Weather as a Force Multiplier: Owning the Weather in 2025." The paper concludes that although "offensive weather-modification efforts would certainly be undertaken by U.S. forces with great caution and trepidation, it is clear that we cannot afford to allow an adversary to obtain an exclusive weather-modification capability." To this end, the paper states, "Efforts are already under way to create more comprehensive weather models primarily to improve forecasts, but researchers are also trying to influence the results of these models by adding small amounts of energy at just the right time and space."

Anyone familiar with past government secret projects, such as the B-1 "Stealth" bomber, knows that if the military publicly speaks of a technology, even as a future possibility, it has already been developed.

Many researchers of chemtrails believe that heavy metal particles are being sprayed into the upper atmosphere in an attempt to form a barrier, a heat shield, against solar radiation. Just such a proposal was made years ago by Dr. Edward Teller, known as the father of the hydrogen bomb and the "Star Wars" missile defense system. Teller, in a paper entitled "Global Warming and the Ice Ages: Prospects for Physics-Based Modulation of Global Change," proposed the introduction of reflective metal particles into the atmosphere to reflect ultraviolet rays and thus decrease the effects of global warming. He also took note of the difficulty in persuading the public to allow such a program that would pollute their air with metal particles, many known to be harmful to humans.

An old journalistic credo states, "Follow the money." Losses to the agriculture and insurance industries could be catastrophic if the world continues to suffer the effects of global warming, a phenomenon disparaged by many hired experts until its effects became undeniable. If flooding in the Mississippi Valley, drought and fires on the West Coast and unusually strong hurricanes, tornadoes, and storms continue, the United States insurance industry could face bankruptcy, bringing down the entire national economy. Since so many foreign currencies are based on the U.S. dollar, this would precipitate a worldwide economic crisis. Apparently, someone feels the deaths of chemtrail-susceptible people, whether the very young or old, is acceptable to prevent this.

It also has been suggested that the injection of heavy metal particles into the atmosphere will aid in various military activities, such as enhancing radar and communications and even boosting the effects of the High Frequency Active Auroral Research Program (HAARP), a vast array of powerful transmitting dishes located near Gakona, Alaska. Officially, HAARP is designed to study the uppermost portion of the Earth's atmosphere, the ionosphere. However, critics of the program claim this powerful array can be used as a weapon, to deliver energy blasts equal to an atomic bomb, destroy communications across the planet and even influence human behavior by broadcasting human brainwave frequencies.

Another scary purpose behind the chemtrails was voiced by a retired military intelligence officer who became particularly interested in chemtrails after being doused with chemicals from the air that seriously affected his health. This man participated in the Army's "remote viewing" program, where he took a mental look for the purpose behind the chemtrail program. What he got was summed up in one word—"terraforming," an attempt to alter the environment of the planet.

The case for the reality of chemtrails is strong but until there is some official recognition of this activity, the tax-paying public will be left only to speculate on its originators and purpose.

▶ IS THERE A NAZI BASE
IN ANTARCTICA?

▽ WHO

▸ The German Nazis of World War II

▽ WHAT

▸ Speculation has abounded since the War that the Nazis built a hidden base in Antarctica.

▽ WHEN

▸ Construction in the Antarctic began even before the war.

▽ WHERE

▸ South of Africa is an area of Antarctica called Queen Maud Land which the Germans renamed *Neuschwabenland*.

▽ WHY

▸ Officially built as a scientific base, rumors have persisted that this base was used as a refuge for escaping Nazis after the war.

additional evidence and commentary:

www.abovetopsecret.com/book/nazibase

Rumors have persisted for years that Nazis escaping from Europe at the end of World War II—perhaps including Hitler himself, his ashes, or his Secretary and Deputy Fuehrer Martin Bormann—went to a secret base in Antarctica.

It has been further claimed that at such a base flying disks were constructed that were so sophisticated that a secret Nazi empire has exerted significant control over world events and governments to this day.

However, evidence for the existence of an Antarctic Nazi base containing UFOs is scant, consisting primarily of the known exploration of Antarctica's Queen Maud Land, named by Norwegian whalers after Queen Maud of Norway, a granddaughter of England's Queen Victoria, and some scattered, unproven reports.

The historical facts are well documented. German exploration of Antarctica reaches back into the 1800s. But the most noted expedition was the 1938 expedition lead by *Kapitan* Alfred Ritschér to Queen Maud Land, situated east of the Weddell Sea, named for the English seal hunter James Weddell.

Prior to the start of the expedition, the German Society of Polar Research invited the famous explorer Richard E. Byrd to Hamburg where he showed expedition members a documentary of his Antarctic exploration and told them what conditions to expect.

Ironically, less than 10 years later, then U.S. Navy Admiral Byrd would lead a military expedition—some claim an assault force—to Antarctica.

Kapitan Ritschér, an arrogant but competent man, renamed the area *Neuschwabenland* in honor of his flagship the *Schwabenland*, a floating laboratory that belonged to the Lufthansa airline company. It carried two amphibian

aircraft weighing 10 tons each as well as a complement of scientists and techni-
cians. Ritschér's expedition had been under the direct orders of *Reichsmarschall*
Hermann Goering, Rudolf Hess and other influential members of the secretive
Thule Society.

Officially on a mission to study the feasibility of whaling in those waters, Ritschér proceeded to drop small swastika flags along separate flight paths to the South
Pole, eventually staking out more than 600,000 square kilometers for the Reich.

Ritschér was fascinated by reports from Weddell who wrote of finding ice-
free areas in Antarctica. In one 1823 report, Weddell wrote, "The ice in this region
had completely disappeared, the temperature is mild, birds were observed flying
around the ship, and groups of whales frolicked in the wake of the craft." Unfortunately, bad weather forced Weddell to return home. Despite several subsequent expeditions, including those of the famous Commander Richard Byrd in the early 1930s,
no one has reported finding this sanctuary of warm water and thriving plant life.

It has been suggested that the Ritschér expedition found just such a place,
one that contained huge ice caverns filled with warm water and living plants. It is
speculated that the soil of Antarctica is remarkably rich and can grow nearly any
plant, once ice-free.

> **//**It is true that Admiral Robert Byrd led an expeditionary/inva-
> sion force into Antarctica in 1947 and the force sustained losses;
> whether those losses were due to adverse weather conditions or
> hostilities the fact remains that a combat ready force was indeed
> taken down there. **//**

ATS MEMBER COMMENT

Reportedly, the Germans discovered areas containing caves, one of which
was reported to have led to a large underground lake warmed from geothermal heat.
Reportedly, knowledgeable persons in both Norway, who tried to claim possession of
Queen Maud Land before the Germans, and Britain were aware of these ice-free areas
but chose to suppress this information as well as leave them off maps to prevent
other nations from trying to lay claim.

While the idea of ice-free sanctuaries in Antarctica has been brushed off by many as absurd, the recent mysterious happenings concerning Lake Vostok, with its 60–70 degree temperature water along with reported magnetic anomalies, give tantalizing evidence that there may be some truth to this.

Antarctica theoretically is the perfect secluded hideaway, as it is approximately 5,600 miles from Africa, 4,760 miles from Australia and 1,870 miles from the southernmost tip of South America.

Ritschér and the *Schwabenland* returned to Hamburg on April 12, 1939, amid much fanfare. However, with war fears rising that year and Hitler's attack on Poland in September, the German expedition was quickly forgotten by all but the Nazi High Command.

By mid-1940, submarine bases had been built in *Neuschwabenland* that became the sites of a great buildup of supplies and materials in addition to servicing U-boats operating in the South Atlantic. This site served as the southernmost point in a Nazi triangle of influence including South Africa and Argentina. Construction of this far-flung Nazi base continued throughout the war and its major base became known as New Berlin or "Base-211."

German Navy Grand Admiral Karl Dönitz stated in 1943, "The German submarine fleet is proud of having built for the Fuehrer in another part of the world a Shangri-La on land, an impregnable fortress."

Was this "Shangri-La" in Antarctica? The Norwegian Nazi, Vidkun Quisling, made another intriguing statement during his trial at Nuremberg in 1945. He said, "I believe I fought for a just cause and I refused to run away from my responsibilities when the Nazis, shortly after their final collapse, offered to convoy me aboard a submarine to safe refuge."

Addressing the question of how the Nazis could have kept such a large base secret, author W. A. Harbinson explained, "Regarding the possibility of the Germans building self-sufficient underground research factories in the Antarctic, it has only to be pointed out that the underground research centers of Nazi Germany were gigantic feats of construction, containing wind tunnels, machine shops, assembly plants, launching pads, supply dumps, and accommodation for all who worked there, including adjoining camps for slaves—and yet very few people knew that they existed."

Compounding the mystery of what the Nazis were up to in Antarctica was the strange appearance and disappearance of some German U-boats at the end of the war. By March 1945, the total number of Nazi submarines had reached 463, according to British historian Basil Liddell Hart. He then noted that 159 U-boats surrendered to the Allies while another 203 were scuttled by their crews. Simple math indicates that more than 100 Nazi subs were unaccounted for after the war ended.

An unmarked German U-boat surrendered to the Argentine Navy on June 10, 1945, but no further details were released. Exactly one month later, the U-530 surrendered at Mar del Plata, Argentina, and just over a month later, on August 17, 1945, the U-977 also surrendered at Mar del Plata. That same month, another sub— the U-465—was scuttled off the coast of Patagonia.

These were large subs, designed for transporting quantities of supplies and material. U-530's Chief Torpedo Officer Wilhelm Bernhart revealed that his sub had landed at Antarctica and offloaded several crates that Bernhart believed to contain documents as well as Nazi relics.

In the aftermath of World War II, there were several military missions to Antarctica, the most documented of which was the 1947 expedition by Admiral Richard E. Byrd. But there are reports of British expeditions even before Byrd.

James Robert, a civil servant with an agency of the British Ministry of Defence as well as a World War II historian and writer, claimed to have twice interviewed one of the last surviving members of a British force sent to Antarctica in late 1945.

"Unfortunately for Britain, though victorious in the War, it was bankrupted and humiliated by the two new superpowers. But Britain was in a position to regain some pride and surreptitiously upset its supposed allies with the final, decisive battle against the surviving Nazis: a battle that would never be recorded in the history books; a battle that would make its claims on the continent more legitimate; but, most importantly, a battle that ended the war that it had been compelled to wage," Robert wrote in 2005. He explained, "Operation *Tabarin* [named for Paris nightclub] was activated as a measure of monitoring German activities on the Antarctic continent. The known British bases were mainly on the Antarctic Peninsula, in places such as Port Lockroy and Hope Bay, and on the islands surrounding the peninsula, such as the secret bases on Deception and Wiencke Islands—though some were set up on the continent. The most secret of all has not, and more than likely never will be, disclosed. The base at Maudheim, near the Mühlig-Hoffmann Mountain Range in Queen Maud Land, alternatively, was so secret that it was never given a name or even a grid reference on official maps."

Could the Nazis have established a base in Antarctica and kept it both secretive and operational for over 50 years? One would think not, but consider that the Nazis in Germany had underground research factories that were great feats of construction and engineering, containing winding tunnels, machine shops, assembly plants, launch pads, supply depots and accommodations for all men who worked there—and yet very few people knew that these facilities existed until the end of the war ... Also since the end of WW2 there has been wave after wave of UFO sightings—in all parts of the world but especially the U.S. and South America. Makes one wonder if there might be a connection.

It was from this secret base that Britain launched its attack on the Nazis, according to the unnamed survivor, a member of the British special forces. Robert presented this account of the man's story, which began when this trooper was taken to the Falkland Islands for special arctic training in the fall of 1945. Led by a veteran of the Norwegian resistance and accompanied by an unnamed scientist, this special unit of British soldiers traveled to Antarctica. The trooper said they "were to investigate 'anomalous' activities around the Mühlig-Hoffmann Mountains from the British base in Maudheim. Antarctica, so we were told, was 'Britain's secret war.'"

The trooper told Robert:

> The original scientists and commandos [at Maudheim] had found an "ancient tunnel." Under orders, the force went through the tunnel but only two returned before the Antarctic winter set in. During the winter months, the two survivors made absurd claims over the radio about 'Polar Men,

ancient tunnels and Nazis." Radio contact was finally lost in July 1945, and ominously for our mission, going into the unknown, the last broadcast brought us all further anxiety as we listened to the fear in the voice: "... the Polar Men have found us!" was screamed before contact was lost.

Warily approaching the Maudheim base, the soldiers were startled to discover a survivor of the earlier expedition. This man said another survivor had fled to another bunker and was followed by a Polar Man. One of the British soldiers opened the bunker and crept inside.

"Once inside, a silence descended across the base, followed moments later by two gunshots. The door was opened and the Polar Man dashed to freedom. None of us was expecting what we saw, and the Polar Man had fled into the surrounding terrain so quick that only a few token shots were fired. Out of fear and awe at what we had seen, we all decided to go into the bunker. Go in we did, and two bodies were found.

> *It may be worth remembering that running secret underground bases requires more than mindless minions for James Bond types to sneak past and/or mow down when the situation gets out of hand ... Yup, electricity. Electricity from where? As far as I know, there were maybe two sources in wide use in WWII: hydroelectric and fossil fuels. Hydroelectric? In the snow? Even with conservation, the Nazis would run out of lights and freeze within a year. Also, where would they get their food, enough for say 5,000 technicians, soldiers and administrative staff? Go shoot penguins and harpoon orcas? Do orcas even visit the Antarctic? I'm not a zoologist ... Soooooo ... They must be getting their juice, spare parts and ReichBurgers from somewhere. How? Deliver with submarines. Or even regular cargo ships (avoid icebergs!) Or airdrops (expensive, you need an airstrip). How far from the coast is it? So, who in the past might POSSIBLY be friendly to a bunch of defeated Aryan goose-steppers? (And don't say the U.S.!! We all know about Project Paperclip) Who would get along just FINE with them? Gee, I wonder which country THAT could be? *

The soldier who had pulled the short straw was found with his throat ripped out, and, more heinous, the survivor had been stripped to the bones," Robert was told.

Regrouping, the soldiers made their way to the tunnel described by the survivor and entered. On the way, the survivor described how members of his expedition had discovered the tunnel and followed it to a vast underground cavern apparently warmed by geothermal heat.

"The Nazis had constructed a huge base into the caverns and had even built docks for U-boats, and one was identified supposedly. Still, the deeper they traveled, the more strange visions they were greeted with. The survivor reported that 'hangars for strange planes and excavations galore' had been documented," Robert reported.

The first British expedition had been discovered and made a fighting withdrawal being chased by Nazis and Polar Men. Six members of the expedition party were caught and executed.

Arriving back at the Maudheim base, the survivors decided to split up. One man lured a Polar Man into his bunker where he was locked in. The other, the man relating this tale, locked himself in another bunker. Unfortunately, his radio was damaged in the fighting and he had to wait to be rescued with no communication with the outside world.

After hearing the survivor's story, the Brits investigated the tunnel and were amazed to find it in a valley devoid of ice, which reminded them of the Sahara Desert.

According to the story told to Robert, the Polar Man returned to their camp and was killed. He apparently was a product of Nazi genetic manipulation. The soldier told Robert, "The scientist decided that the Polar Man was 'human' but, it seemed, had been able to produce more hair and withstand the cold far more effectively. The corpse, after a brief post-mortem, was stored in a body bag, and with the cold could be preserved until a more meticulous dissection could occur."

The expedition, with all the explosives they could carry, entered the tunnel, which seemed to stretch for miles. Finally, they came to a vast and artificially lit cavern filled with men working with large amounts of equipment. Stealthily, they began to plant explosives.

The soldier's story continued:

Throughout the day, mines were laid and more photos were taken; and with the odds of not being detected looking good, a hostage was taken, as well as proof of the Nazi base, the "Polar Man," and photographs of new, and quite advanced, Nazi technology. When the mission to place the mines that would destroy the base had been accomplished, as well as substantial proof of the base gathered, we headed towards the tunnel—but, alas, we were spotted, and more of the Polar Men and a troop of Nazis gave chase. Upon reaching the tunnel, we needed to put an obstacle in the way to slow down our enemy long enough for the mines to detonate. Some mines were placed at the entrance to the tunnel, and when the explosions were heard we were hopeful that not just the base had been comprehensively destroyed but so, too, the enemy forces giving chase. We were wrong.

The mines did indeed close the tunnel, but, for those Nazis and Polar Men behind, the chase was still on. In a fighting retreat, only three of the 10 escaped the tunnel: the Norwegian, the scientist, and myself. The rest had fallen gallantly in making sure that some of the party survived. Upon reaching the safety of the dry valley, enough mines were laid to close the tunnel permanently. After the mines were detonated, there was no evidence of any tunnel ever existing ... We returned to the Maudheim base where we were evacuated and flown back to the safety of the Falkland Islands Dependencies. Upon reaching South Georgia, we were issued with a directive that we were forbidden to reveal what we had seen, heard, or even encountered. The tunnel was explained away as nothing more than a freak of nature; "glacial erosion" was the scientist's specific term. The "Polar Men" were nothing more than "unkempt soldiers that had gone crazy"; the fact that they were German was never submitted into the report, and any notion of the mission going public was firmly rebutted. The mission would never be made official, though certain elements of the mission were to be leaked to the Russians and the Americans. So my last Christmas of World War II was spent on the Antarctic continent in 1945, fighting the same Nazis that I had fought against every Christmas since 1940. What was worse was the fact that the expedition was never given any recognition, nor the survivors any credit. Instead, the British survivors were de-mobbed from the forces, whilst the scientist and his report would soon disappear, the mission never to be known about except by the select few.

This account of an anonymous source by Robert would be easy to dismiss except that the details closely match a separate account given by U-boat 530's Captain Bernhart as published in his 1988 book *Adolf Hitler and the Secrets of the Holy Lance*, co-authored by Col. Howard Buechner, a respected New Orleans physician and former medical officer with the U.S. Army's 45th Infantry Division during World War II.

According to Bernhart's story, on May 1, 1945, a Col. Maximilian Hartmann delivered the ashes of Adolf Hitler and his still-living wife, Eva Braun, to the commander of the U-977 to be sent to the Nazi base in Antarctica. At their destination, a shore party of 16 men set out for a hidden Nazi base. Bernhart claimed to be one of these men, which explained why he was chosen years later to retrieve treasures in Antarctica.

//At the end of the day, when it comes to secret Nazi bases, if one existed in those icy wastes we'd know about it by now. After all, we live in an age where a spy satellite can peer down through the atmosphere and read a newspaper over your shoulder, and your telephone, radio and Internet communications can be tracked, traced and monitored at the touch of a button. Even if such a base were underground, there'd be surface activity at some stage, even if it were just some stir-crazy Ober-lieutenant sneaking outside for a quick cigarette! //

Bernhart's strange tale to Col. Buechner included an account concerning the recovery of the fabled *Heilige Lance* or Holy Lance also known as the "Spear of Destiny." This relic is reportedly the spear of a Roman soldier named Gaius Cassius who became known as Longinus. By legend, Longinus used the spear to pierce the side of Jesus on the cross, not as punishment, but to mercifully shorten his agony. This spear is still exhibited in the Hofburg Museum in Vienna. It is said to be a relic of great power for whoever possesses it and can be used for good or for evil.

Bernhart claimed the spear on display in Vienna is a fake. He claimed the real spear, along with other Nazi treasures, was sent by Hitler to Antarctica in the keeping of Col. Hartmann in 1945 but was recovered in 1979.

Buechner said Bernhart showed him the logbook from the 1979 expedition, which used helicopters to reach the deserted Nazi base. Bernhart recounted:

> Our lights penetrate the steel tunnel, which extends for approximately ten meters. When we arrive at the end of the tunnel, we find ourselves in a huge cavernous area. It seems warm. As we search the cavern with our lights, we notice frozen pillars of ice in strange and grotesque shapes. We penetrate into the cavern the distance of about 300 meters. It is at this point that we came to a smaller cavern, which turned towards the right and ended in a room approximately 80 meters in width and ten meters in height. It is here that the Reich treasures are hidden!!!
>
> At this point stands a small obelisk about a meter in height, which marks the spot. There is an inscription which reads as follows: "There are truly more things in heaven and 'in' earth than man has dreamt. (Beyond this point is AGHARTA.) [Signed by Nazi occultist Karl] Haushofer, 1943."
>
> Our lights immediately fall upon the treasure, which consists of eight large bronze chests. This makes two for each man and will require two trips. Can we do it? This remains to be seen. Each one of us grasps a bronze box in his hands. Oddly enough, they do not seem as heavy as we had imagined.

"[A] base in Antarctica wouldn't be able to control anything ... but it would be a good place to hide if you were the last remnant of an ideologically fanatic regime. Also ... it would be a good place to develop weapons you could blackmail the world with. I'm not saying that I believe all the legends that have popped up over this ... I just think it's extremely unusual to see such a heavy military escort for a scientific expedition in an undefended region of the Earth. It's overkill ... and overkill matters in government because it equals waste and the possibility that the taxpayers will get mad at you. **"**

ATS MEMBER COMMENT

Hartman was soon disappointed to realize that the weight of the boxes, in total, is too heavy for his team to carry back to their waiting helicopter. Four of the boxes had to be left behind.

Bernhart concluded, "The trek back is energy consuming and difficult. We stop to rest several times along the return route. The chests are growing heavier and heavier as we go along. We have to stop and rest more frequently. Finally we reach the [helicopter] just as complete exhaustion is setting in … Shortly before we are ready to leave, the chest containing the Holy Lance is opened. We all watch with profound fascination as Klauss knocks the bronze pin from the clasp. Inside the chest is a faded leather case along with a variety of other items. We carefully open the case. It is there! The Holy Lance! The Lance that pierced the side of our Lord Jesus Christ!"

Bernhart claimed that the other chests were taken unopened and that he only knew the identity of four items recovered in Antarctica—the Holy Lance, a bronze plaque prized by Hitler, a 1934 watercolor painting by Hitler entitled "Germania and the Appointment of the Gods at the Beginning of the World" and the infamous "Blood Flag," a sacred Nazi relic from the 1923 "Beer Hall" Putsch.

The Spear, along with the other Nazi treasures, was returned to Europe by Hartmann where he claimed today they remain hidden by a Nazi secret society calling themselves the Knights of the Holy Spear.

Following his own research, Col. Buechner came to believe Bernhart's story.

While all of this could be chalked up as utter fantasy, it fails to explain the well-documented 1946–47 military expedition to Antarctica code named "Operation Highjump" led by Admiral Richard E. Byrd. The task force was under the command of Admiral Richard H. Cruzen and continues to be the largest Antarctic expedition ever organized. It remains a mystery what convinced the Navy to fund this massive task force to Antarctica or why it was rushed into operation so soon after the war ended.

Reportedly, President Harry Truman tried to stop the expedition at the last moment but was compelled to relent upon the advice of his military advisors. Obviously, there was some overriding urgency and importance to this mission.

Officially named the United States Navy Antarctic Developments Program, this U.S. Navy operation reached their destination on January 15, 1947, and lasted only into February 1947. This force consisted of 4,700 men and 13 ships—including an aircraft carrier with six twin-engine transport planes and helicopters. Byrd made it plain that the operation's objectives were not diplomatic, scientific or economic—but military. According to the military, the expedition was hastily mounted to take advantage of the first Antarctic summer after the war.

Near the end of January 1947, during a two-prong reconnaissance sweep of Antarctica, an ice-free area was discovered by one of the force's flying boats. Byrd described it as a "land of blue and green lakes and brown hills in an otherwise limitless expanse of ice." Newsmen echoed the words of the Nazi Navy Commander Dönitz by calling this area "Shangri-La."

Rumors have circulated for many years regarding the true objectives of Highjump. One idea was that the United States was attempting to gain as much new territory in Antarctica as possible in light of the turmoil following the end of World War II. Another was that the U.S. was determined to lay claim on any uranium found there as well as the possibility of using the subcontinent as an atomic test site. But the most enduring rumor has been that, in light of the British failures during the Tabarin operations, the U.S. military was sent to wipe out a secret Nazi base.

Publicly described as crew training, a test for "new material under extreme Antarctic conditions" and determining the feasibility of maintaining permanent American bases in Antarctica, Highjump was declared a success. However, it was never stated why such a massive task force was needed to test materials nor why the force, equipped for a six to eight month operation, returned after only eight weeks. It has also never been explained why Byrd personally flew a mission that flew over the German territory of *Neuschwabenland*. And the deaths of several task force members were never fully explained. Official reports stated they died in a plane crash—one report stated it "blew up"—and other accidents.

Another fact that undermined the argument that the expedition was merely for exploration was that while members took more than 70,000 photographs of the Antarctic coastline, none were made with the reference markers necessary to match the photos together for a comprehensive view. This "technical error" was corrected the following year by a much smaller expedition.

It has been long reported that Byrd, upon his return from Antarctica, warned of the possibility of attack from the polar regions by aircraft of incredible speed. These remarks were reported in the March 5, 1947 edition of *El Mercurio* in Santiago, Chile. Reporter Lee Van Atta, who had accompanied Byrd, wrote, "Admiral Richard E. Byrd announced today that it is necessary for the United States to put into effect defensive measures against enemy airmen who come from the polar regions. The admiral said, 'I have no intention of scaring anyone but the bitter reality is that in case of a new war, the United States would be in a position of being attacked by aircraft that could fly with fantastic speed from one pole to the other.'"

*//*In 1958 which was the IGY (International Geophysical Year) many nations decided to combine resources and explore and research many areas of the earth, but mainly in the Antarctic. This was also the time when the Antarctic treaty was being drawn up between all the various nations that had claimed sovereignty down there. Now the U.S. had never had a single Antarctic expedition up to that date, and would have been excluded from being part of the Antarctic treaty. So as part of the IGY scientific program, the U.S. offered to use its vast military resources to fly over the whole continent and photograph it and produce accurate maps and other scientific data. The name says it all "Operation Highjump" and that is exactly what it was. There are no alien bases, no Nazi submarine pens, no secret underground cities. Only the conspiracy nuts believe this stuff. I have never before heard that 1,000 Americans died down there, that is a lot of people and is just not believable. Anything like that would have become famous and extremely well known and be a part of general knowledge. I have spent two winters and nearly three years of my life in the Antarctic and have had a long thirty year interest in the Antarctic and all the bases down there. It never happened, sorry ... *//*

Adding to the confusion over what actually happened in 1947 in Antarctica was a manuscript made public in the 1970s that purported to be a secret diary written by Byrd. It was released by someone or some group called the International Society for a Complete Earth and purported to be an account of a flight to the *North Pole* by Byrd on February 19, 1947.

After recording some routine flight data that mimicked entries from a 1926 account of Byrd's Arctic flight, Byrd reported sighting a small mountain range with what appeared to be a valley lined with green trees with a river or stream flowing through it. This diary also reported spotting a large animal that resembled a wooly mammoth. The diary continued:

> Ahead we spot what seems to be a city!! This is impossible! Aircraft seems light and oddly buoyant. The controls refuse to respond!! My God!
>
> Off our port and starboard wings are a strange type of aircraft. They are closing rapidly alongside! They are disc-shaped and have radiant quality to them. They are close enough to see the markings on them. It is a strange symbol I shall not reveal ... I tug at the controls again. They will not respond!! We are caught in an invisible vice grip of some type!
>
> Our radio crackles and a voice comes through in English with what perhaps is a slight Nordic or Germanic accent! The message is, 'Welcome, Admiral, to our domain. We shall land you in exactly seven minutes. Relax, Admiral, you are in good hands.' I note the engines of our plane have stopped running! The aircraft is under some strange control ...

This narrative states that after a floating landing, Byrd and his radioman were taken on a conveyance with no wheels to the city, which "seems to be made of a crystal material." There, with his radioman detained, some sort of elevator took Byrd deep down into the Earth to a room glowing with rose-colored light seeming to come from the walls. A man with "delicate features and with the etching of years upon his face" entered and spoke, saying:

> I bid you welcome to our domain, Admiral. We have let you enter here because you are of noble character and well-known on the Surface World ... You are in the domain of Arianni, the Inner World of the Earth ... I shall tell you why you have been summoned here. Our interest rightly begins just after your race exploded the first atomic bombs over Hiroshima and

Nagasaki, Japan. It was at that alarming time we sent our flying machines, the "*Flugelrads*," to your surface world to investigate what your race had done ... You see, we have never interfered before in your race's wars and barbarity, but now we must, for you have learned to tamper with a certain power that is not for man, namely, that of atomic energy. Our emissaries have already delivered messages to the powers of your world, and yet they do not heed. Now you have been chosen to be witness here that our world does exist. You see, our culture and science is many thousands of years beyond your race, Admiral ... Your race has now reached the point of no return, for there are those among you who would destroy your very world rather than relinquish their power as they know it ... So, now, I say to you, my son, there is a great storm gathering in your world, a black fury that will not spend itself for many years.

After rejoining his radioman, the pair was escorted to their plane, which was somehow lifted into the air with the engines returning to full power. As they regained control and set a course for the American base, a voice came over the radio saying, "We are leaving you now, Admiral. Your controls are free. *Auf Wiedersehen!*"

According to this diary publication, Byrd was taken to the Pentagon where he was held for nearly seven hours. Then he was reminded that he was a military officer and was ordered to remain silent about his North Pole experience.

Obviously, Byrd could not have had such an encounter at the North Pole while leading Operation Highjump at the South Pole. There is also the problem of him sighting mountains, trees and a mammoth at the North Pole in February, which is a time of total darkness. Such inept hoaxing only further clouds a subject filled with enough mystery already.

While all these unconventional accounts of Antarctic exploits sound more like a something developed for the Sci-Fi Channel than real-life exploits, there remains a tantalizing quality to them. With the recent announcement of the pre-historic Lake Vostok; the 1999 discovery of a virus in Antarctica to which there seemed no immunity by human or animal as well as the strange deaths of both humans and penguins dating back to at least 1913, there are definitely aspects of that polar region which have defied conventional explanation.

Germany did lay claim to vast areas of Antarctica on the eve of World War II. There was substantial activity by both German surface ships and submarines in the

South Polar region both during and after the war when numerous U-Boats were missing. Add to this the fact that the hastily-mounted Highjump military expedition returned home shortly after it arrived in Antarctica and Byrd warned of craft that could fly from pole to pole at fantastic speed and you have the makings for a real conspiracy theory.

As for the tales of secret Nazi bases or hidden civilizations, perhaps they are only made-up tales, Antarctic legends, which coincidentally surface from separate sources. Or perhaps they represent bits and pieces of a gigantic secret that has been kept from the public for more than 60 years.

▶ **WHO KILLED JFK?**

▽ WHO

▸ John Fitzgerald Kennedy, thirty-fifth president of the United States

▽ WHAT

▸ Kennedy was assassinated by gunfire, struck by at least two bullets.

▽ WHEN

▸ He was shot at about 12:30 p.m. on Friday, November 22, 1963 and pronounced dead about a half hour later at a local hospital.

▽ WHERE

▸ The assassination took place while JFK was riding in a motorcade through Dealey Plaza on the west end of downtown Dallas, Texas.

▽ WHY

▸ According to official pronouncements, the accused assassin, Lee Harvey Oswald, wanted to make a name for himself. But as will be seen, there was much more involved.

additional evidence and commentary:
www.abovetopsecret.com/book/jfk

///

In 1901, a lone-nut anarchist named Leon Czolgosz assassinated President William McKinley. Vice President Teddy Roosevelt became president. Less than two months after McKinley's death, Czolgosz had been convicted and executed in the electric chair.

By the 1960s, no one remembered Czolgosz, even though at the time anarchists suspected Czolgosz of being a government agent.

But nearly 50 years after the assassination of President John F. Kennedy, the entire world still recognizes the name of Lee Harvey Oswald.

Czolgosz was not forgotten because he had a name difficult to pronounce but because it was determined that he was the sole cause of McKinley's death and the whole affair was styled a tragic occurrence and forgotten, unlike Kennedy's death which is still mired in obfuscation and controversy.

And, unlike the McKinley assassination where the shooting of the president occurred in plain sight and the assassin captured immediately, no one saw who fired the shots in Dallas. Oswald was captured about an hour later in another part of the city. As late as the 1970s, former Dallas Police Chief Jesse Curry said, "We could never place him [Oswald] in that window with the rifle."

Less than an hour after the shooting, Oswald was taken into custody in a south Dallas theater after an employee reported he had sneaked in without buying a ticket. Oswald maintained his innocence during his two days in police custody, proclaiming to newsmen, "I didn't shoot anybody. I'm just a patsy!" On Sunday morning while being taken from Dallas city jail during a publicly announced transfer, Oswald was fatally shot by Dallas nightclub owner Jack Ruby, a man with close connections to both Dallas authorities and the Mafia.

Today, it is clear that the Dallas Police were tipped off as to the identity of their suspect by U.S. Naval Intelligence. Dallas Police Lt. Jack Revill has stated publicly that he rode back to police headquarters from the Texas School Book Depository (TSBD) with a Naval Intelligence agent. Once back at police headquarters, Revill made out a list of Texas School Book Depository employees. Heading this list was the name Harvey Lee Oswald with an address of 605 Elsbeth in Dallas. Of course, his name was Lee Harvey Oswald and the Elsbeth address was never given nor recorded on his TSBD employment records. During the time of the House Select Committee on Assassinations, a Lt. Col. Robert E. Jones of the 112th Military Intelligence Group at Fort Sam Houston in San Antonio testified that on the day of the assassination, he got a call from one of his agents in Dallas who told him that a suspect by the name of A. J. Hidell had been arrested in connection with the assassination. Jones said he checked military intelligence files and found that the name Hidell cross-referenced to a Harvey Lee Oswald. The file carried the address of 605 Elsbeth. Revill got this same misinformation from the Naval Intelligence agent. If military intelligence tipped off the Dallas Police to Oswald, it is strong substantiation for Oswald's claim that he was set up.

> **"I think the magic bullet theory is one of the most ridiculous things ever put upon the American people."**

ATS MEMBER COMMENT

Controversy and uncertainty began the very day Kennedy was killed. Initial news stories stated that Secret Service agents first thought that the president was hit by a burst of gunfire from an automatic weapon from the area of the infamous Grassy Knoll, located on the northwest corner of Dealey Plaza. A rifle discovered by lawmen in the Book Depository was initially described as a 7.95-mm German Mauser but later that day this was changed to a 7.65-mm Italian Mannlicher Carcano, a World War II gun termed the "humane weapon" by the Italians because of its inaccuracy. Government investigators said Oswald had ordered the rifle from a magazine that advertised a 36-inch long Carcano. Yet the rifle still displayed in the National Archives is 40-inches long.

A paper bag was found in the Texas School Book Depository, which authorities claimed was used by Oswald to smuggle a rifle into the building where he worked. However, the bag showed no sign of containing a rifle and FBI documents were conflicting, one stating the paper matched wrapping paper available in the depository while another stated it did not. No explanation for these discrepancies was ever given.

One explanation may have been the fact that the FBI unlawfully seized all the evidence. Against existing procedures, as well as law, all of the assassination evidence was taken from the hands of the Dallas Police by the FBI on the evening of the assassination. Yet, the FBI was not officially called into the case until Tuesday, November 26, following a meeting between the FBI and Dallas authorities. In other words, top officials of the FBI had all the assassination evidence to themselves with no chain of evidence or oversight for two full days before this mass of material became the official evidence in the case. From that point onward, controversy and questionable evidence plagued all investigations into JFK's death.

For example, the day after the assassination, an official FBI document signed by Director J. Edgar Hoover stated, "No latent [finger]prints of value were developed on Oswald's revolver, the cartridge cases, the unfired cartridge, the clip in the rifle, or the inner parts of the rifle." On Sunday, the rifle was returned to Dallas and on Monday morning was transported to Miller Funeral Home in Fort Worth where Oswald's body was being prepared for funeral. Mortician Paul Groody said he was present when FBI agents placed Oswald's dead hand on the rifle and that he had a hard time cleaning ink off Oswald's hand in time for his burial. That evening, Dallas District Attorney Henry Wade blurted out to reporters "Oh, have I mentioned, we found his fingerprints on the rifle."

Less than a week following the assassination, President Johnson closed off all congressional and state investigations of the murder by appointing a special commission headed by Chief Justice Earl Warren. Warren had initially turned down this appointment saying it was improper for one branch of government to investigate another but was coerced into service by President Johnson who told him that if he didn't determine that Oswald was a lone assassin, it might lead to World War III.

One key member of what came to be called the Warren Commission was

Allen Dulles, long-time director of the CIA who had been fired by Kennedy for the Agency's part in the ill-fated 1961 Bay of Pigs Invasion. Dulles's mentor, Chase Bank President John J. McCloy, was another influential member of the commission. Both were prominent members of the Eastern establishment centered within the Council on Foreign Relations.

By selectively choosing evidence and ignoring contradicting testimony, the Warren Commission in 1964 concluded that Oswald was the lone assassin and that they could find no evidence of conspiracy. Contrary to the notion that suspicions over the Kennedy assassination is a recent development, polls conducted in late 1964 indicated that a substantial number of Americans (more than a third) declined to accept this official conclusion but remained largely quiet in the wake of media support for the commission's work.

In later years, three commission members—Rep. Hale Boggs and Senators John Cooper and Richard Russell—all voiced their own skepticism regarding the commission's conclusions. The most vocal of the three, Boggs, took a plane flight in Alaska and was never seen again.

Many crucial pieces of evidence, including the fact that Oswald had neither the weapon nor the marksmanship to commit the assassination, were never reported to the public. The Warren Commission Report did admit that three metal shims had to be placed under the rifle's telescopic sight to make it accurate enough to test and that Oswald's Marine records showed in his last shooting examination he qualified as "Marksman" by only two points. Marksman is the lowest of the three military shooting categories—marksman, sharpshooter, and expert. Fellow Marines stated Oswald on the firing range often could not even hit his target, much less the bull's-eye.

Although the law demanded an inquest be conducted in Dallas before Kennedy's body could be removed, federal agents forcibly whisked his corpse from Parkland Hospital at gunpoint. The body was returned to Air Force One at Love Field where takeoff was delayed while Lyndon B. Johnson was sworn in as the thirty-sixth president, an unnecessary action as the U.S. Constitution makes clear the line of succession. Johnson later claimed that Kennedy's brother, Attorney General Robert Kennedy told him to conduct the swearing-in ceremony. However, Robert Kennedy denied this.

Only two days after the assassination, the FBI issued a report stating that Kennedy was first struck in the back, a separate shot struck Connally and a third shot entered the right side of Kennedy's head killing him. This was a plausible scenario assuming only three shots were fired. But it did not take into account the wounding of bystander James Teague. In late spring 1964, although the Warren Commission had tried to ignore the account of Teague's wounding, an assistant U.S. attorney in Dallas sent a letter and photograph of a bullet strike on the Main Street curb and the commission was finally forced to deal with this evidence of a fourth shot.

Since an admission that Kennedy and Connally were struck by separate bullets or that a fourth shot had been fired made the idea of one lone assassin impossible within the six-second time frame of the assassination, an alternative theory was required. This was advanced by a young assistant attorney on the commission's staff—Arlen Specter, now a senior senator from Pennsylvania. Specter proposed that the first shot passed through both Kennedy and Connally, the second shot missed striking a curb and slightly wounding Teague and the third bullet was the fatal shot to JFK's head.

Specter's proposal became known as the "single bullet theory" or more aptly, the "magic bullet theory." It is the foundation of the lone-assassin theory.

A thorough examination of the president's body should have resolved any questions over the number of shots and from which direction they came. But this was not to be.

Kennedy's body was given an autopsy late on Nov. 22 at Bethesda Naval Hospital in Washington. It was so flawed—the three Navy doctors were not even allowed to examine his clothing for bullet holes—that controversy has raged over its conclusions ever since. The body had already been sent off for burial when the autopsy doctors learned that a three-inch gaping gash in Kennedy's throat masked a bullet wound. Original autopsy notes were burned and then rewritten.

// Anyone watch X Files? The episode about the history of Cancer Man, where they allege he was the one to assassinate both Kennedy and Martin Luther King Jr.? While I seriously doubt that there is a chain smoker in charge of a shadow government who pulled the trigger on both historic figures, there are some very interesting similarities in both assassinations—Both were shot sniper fashion from long to intermediate range with a high powered rifle. Both of the TRUE snipers fled and were never captured, although a 'fall guy' was pre-selected in both cases, complete with a 'drop gun' (in both cases, not the same model, or even the same caliber that actually killed either person). In both cases, both the 'drop guns' and the crime scene were prepped with planted fingerprints and other evidence pointing to the fall guys. I am not going to go on into possible reasons, motives, or make guesses at who did it, what they gained from it, etc. I will say, knowing what I know about military tactical marksmanship, both assassinations were likely performed by military grade snipers, likely pulled originally from their duties by the CIA, or someone posing convincingly as the CIA. //

ATS MEMBER COMMENT

To add to this confusion, Jerrol F. Custer, who took the autopsy X-rays of Kennedy's body, and Floyd Riebe, who took the autopsy photographs, in 1992 stated publicly that the X-rays and photos then being presented by the government were not the ones they took during the autopsy.

Suppression of evidence, destruction of evidence, alteration of evidence, fabrication of evidence, and intimidation of witnesses—all criminal acts under the

U.S. legal system—are demonstrable in the aftermath of JFK's death. But the lone-assassin theory held, being continually supported by a compliant and uncritical news media.

However, in early 1967, New Orleans District Attorney Jim Garrison, a former FBI agent, after making a study of the Warren Commission's 26-volumes of evidence, concluded that JFK was indeed killed as the result of a conspiracy and had identified two local men as suspects—David Ferrie, a man with both U.S. intelligence and mafia connections, and Clay Shaw, the influential and respected director of the city's International Trade Mart.

Shaw had a shadowy background with connections to an international firm named Permindex, whose board of directors was composed of former Nazis, intelligence operatives and European royalty. Furthermore, Shaw had dealt with the CIA for years and was promised help by then CIA Director Richard Helms.

Ferrie, a defrocked Jesuit priest and airline pilot fired after being arrested for homosexuality, was the center of a matrix of oddball characters which included Shaw, former FBI Special Agent Guy Banister, anti-Castro Cubans, mafia chief Carlos Marcello, prominent cancer doctor Alton Ochsner, and Lee Harvey Oswald.

Before Ferrie could be brought to trial, he was found dead from a blow to the neck. His death was ruled an accident.

Shaw, on the other hand, was tried and in 1969 was quickly found not guilty by a New Orleans jury, although a poll of the jury taken after the trial indicated they believed Garrison's contention that a conspiracy existed to kill Kennedy. They simply did not believe enough evidence was presented to convict Shaw. Several persons testified they knew of a "Clay Bertrand," who was overheard plotting against Kennedy. Garrison failed to convince the jury that Shaw and Bertrand were the same man.

It was later determined that Shaw had indeed lied about his relationship to both Ferrie and Oswald, and was, in fact, aided in his defense by the CIA. Shaw's jail admittance card on which he gave the alias "Clay Bertrand" was not allowed into evidence.

In the late 1960s and early 1970s, while the public remained skeptical of the lone-assassin theory, it was not considered a suitable topic for polite discussion and the mass media offered precious little contradictory material.

The official story held—Oswald did it all alone, he did not know Jack Ruby, Ruby was not connected to organized crime, Oswald was not connected to David Ferrie, Oswald was an expert shot, and Oswald had no connection to the U.S. government as his mother claimed.

In the years following the Garrison prosecution, a large number of books and magazine articles were published calling the Warren Commission's conclusions into question. One by one, the official facts concerning Oswald and the assassination fell away. According to more than a dozen witnesses, Oswald did know Jack Ruby, he was pictured in a Civil Air Patrol photograph with David Ferrie, he only made the minimum shooting rating by two points, and a wealth of information indicated Oswald's intelligence work for the government, including a 201 (employment) file with the CIA.

By the late 1970s, a Gallup Poll showed 80 percent of the American public believed Kennedy died at the hands of a conspiracy.

So much evidence was made public that a congressional committee was established to reinvestigate the assassination. Based on two separate sets of acoustical studies of a Dallas Police dictabelt recording of the assassination and "other scientific evidence," the House Select Committee on Assassinations in 1979 "established a high probability that two gunmen fired at President John F. Kennedy."

This conclusion of conspiracy was downplayed by the corporate media as typified by the statement of *New York Times* Associate Editor Tom Wicker, who wrote in a foreword to the Select Committee's report, "The most avid public attention, however, will inevitably be centered on the House committee's startling contention that a second gunman was in Dealey Plaza, indicating a conspiracy to kill President Kennedy. In the absence of any explanation whatever of his or her supposed presence and actions, or of what the committee majority believes happened in Dallas ... I decline to accept this latest of so many conspiracy theories."

Once again, the truth of the Kennedy assassination became simply a matter of trust—did one trust the government and media or the witnesses and evidence?

In 1991, the mass of new evidence was presented to the American public in the Oliver Stone film *JFK*, which was assailed by the corporate mass media as "fantasy" even before it opened in theaters. Stone led a demand for a new inquiry citing the fact that so many JFK assassination files were still locked away by the government.

The film and the public demand for openness resulted in Congress naming a new panel to again look at the evidence. The Assassinations Records Review Board accumulated an immense amount of material from government agencies and archives but failed to make any conclusions on their findings and the whole matter again was swept under the rug.

// [I] think it was Sam Giancana and the Chicago mob, of which Jack Ruby was connected, endorsed by Lyndon Johnson and wealthy Texas oilmen who supported him, and with at least some small amount of CIA backing so it would go off without a hitch. Giancana was mad and wanted Bobby, the attorney general at the time, off his outfit's tail, and he grew to hate John Kennedy as well. LBJ wanted power and JFK was about to shut down the CIA, so they were more than happy to help. //

One item discovered by the board was a memo written by Warren Commission member and future un-elected President, Rep. Gerald R. Ford, in which Ford ordered the authors of the Warren Report to change their wording from "a bullet had entered [Kennedy's] back at a point slightly below the shoulder to the right of the spine" to "a bullet entered the back of the neck slightly to the right of the spine."

This change of location of the back wound by a politician with no known medical experience subsequently allowed Specter's argument that one bullet had passed through Kennedy's neck and gone on to cause five wounds to Texas Governor John Connally. This single-bullet theory was disputed early on by both Connally's physician, Dr. Robert Shaw, and by Connally himself, although Connally went on to voice support for the conclusions of the Warren Commission.

Despite the near-overwhelming evidence of multiple assassins and obvious cover-up at the level of the federal government, the corporate mass media continued to cling to the theory of Oswald as a lone assassin and viciously attacked those who would say otherwise. Sycophants set up websites and went on talk shows, diverting the public's attention to irrelevant and distracting details while disparaging any conspiracy talk.

In recent years, major books were published in an effort to counter the growing public acceptance of conspiracy in JFK's death. Gerald Posner, in his 1993 book *Case Closed* even published a computer simulation claiming to prove Oswald's sole guilt. Posner failed to inform his readers that aside from the obvious fact that computers can only present conclusions based on the information with which they are programmed, the computer analysis was done by Failure Analysis Associates for use in a mock trial of Oswald for the American Bar Association and that a parallel analysis for the defense provided computer support for Oswald's innocence. Only the prosecution analysis was presented in Posner's book.

> **//**I heard that it was the driver who shot JFK. Everyone who was [close] enough to see what happened was killed or had an 'accident.' **//** [Editor's note: see the chapter on Hoaxes.]

ATS MEMBER COMMENT

Posner, in an effort to reconcile the evidence against the single-bullet theory, argued that the Warren Commission had the lone-assassin theory right but the sequence of the shots wrong. He speculated that the first of three shots struck a tree branch and was deflected, striking the Main Street curb and bystander Teague, and it was the second shot that passed through both Kennedy and Connally. He offered no explanation for how he could have possibly known that a bullet hit a tree branch.

Likewise, in 2007, Charles Manson prosecutor Vincent Bugliosi presented the public with a 1,600-page prosecution (not so) brief against Oswald entitled *Reclaiming History*. It should have been entitled *Reclaiming the Warren Commission*. Bugliosi's book even included two pages of a made-up conversation between a fictitious mobster he named "Vito" and Jack Ruby and no mention of the fact that right after the assassination, Bill Newman, one of closest witnesses to the fatal head shot, told a Dallas TV station that the shot came from behind him on the "knoll." Throughout his book, which was given huge corporate mass media attention, Bugliosi continually castigated conspiracy researchers with such names as "silly buffs," "zanies," "cuckoo birds" and "crackpots."

Both Bugliosi and Posner enjoyed widespread acclaim from the corporate mass media, yet both followed in the footsteps of Johnson's handpicked Warren Commission—cherry-picking the evidence, filling pages with irrelevant data, mocking anyone who would speak of conspiracy, and avoiding any information that might tend to exonerate Oswald. It appeared that these books were not designed to convince a thoughtful reader, but instead to provide national headlines and sound bites that continue to cloud the issue.

By 2007, whole new generations were being subjected to mass media presentations—films, TV documentaries, books and articles—again proclaiming Oswald's sole guilt while presenting no evidence of his innocence, such as JFK's official autopsy report, the Dallas Police paraffin test showing no gunpowder on Oswald's hands or face, voice stress analysis indicating Oswald's truthfulness in proclaiming his innocence, or the documented cover-up of vital evidence by federal authorities.

The Kennedy assassination, like the Roswell and 9/11 controversies, devolves down to simply a question of trust. With the evidence in disarray and mired in controversy, one can either trust the federal government's pronouncements of Oswald's sole guilt or trust the mountain of evidence that tears giant holes in those pronouncements.

In 1963, Kennedy's death was legally just another Texas homicide, as there were no laws concerning presidential assassinations. It is the demonstrable cover-up on the part of federal authorities that transformed that homicide into a national coup d'etat.

▶ DID JOHN TITOR COME
FROM THE FUTURE?

▽ **WHO**

> ▸ A person, or persons, calling themselves John Titor.

▽ **WHAT**

> ▸ John Titor came to be the name used by someone claiming to be a time traveler from the year 2036.

▽ **WHEN**

> ▸ Titor's messages were posted on the Internet beginning on November 2, 2000 and ending on March 24, 2001.

▽ **WHERE**

> ▸ His postings appeared initially on several Internet bulletin boards, primarily on sites concerned with time travel. They were later reproduced and expanded on other sites.

▽ **WHY**

> ▸ This mystery is an example of "either/or" in that Titor was either a fraud or a time traveler. Many people continue to argue over which description is correct.

additional evidence and commentary:
www.abovetopsecret.com/book/titor

While the mystery and controversy over the John Titor issue has never resolved his claims to being a time traveler, it has served to demonstrate the power and reach of the Internet.

What began as a series of anonymous postings to some bulletin boards soon became an Internet phenomenon.

Although most were quick to brand his story a total hoax, his detailed descriptions of a grim and desolate future fascinated many Net surfers. Perhaps he articulated many of our own hidden fears. In any case, the John Titor story quickly spread. By mid-2004, almost 50 websites were devoted to his story.

The messages initially were signed simply "Timetravel_0" but after January 2001, when the postings began to appear on some Art Bell forums which required a name, the name John Titor came into use. During one exchange, Titor was asked point blank if John Titor was his real name. His reply, "John Titor is a real name," did not provide a definitive answer.

In short, Titor claimed to be a soldier living in 2036 Florida who was sent by the military via a time machine back to our time to obtain an IBM 5100 computer. He said this older model was needed to correct software problems in his time as the 5100 had the ability to use old IBM code to reconcile incompatible programming languages of the future.

His most astounding claim was that the United States, having fallen into a civil war beginning in 2004, will be devastated by a nuclear war in 2015. Most major cities will be destroyed and the nation will be split into five separate divisions, each with its own president.

Titor stated he made a stop in the year 2000 to visit family members and collect photographs lost in the civil war. He said he also felt compelled to warn people about the coming wars as well as their diet.

He said many lives will be lost in his future through Creutzfeldt-Jakob Disease (CJD), today a rare but incurable degenerative brain disorder which leads to loss of brain function and death. Some researchers have compared Creutzfeldt-Jakob to the current growth of Alzheimer's patients. It is a disease from infectious particles of protein (prions) comparable to bovine spongiform encephalopathy (BSE) commonly known as Mad Cow Disease. According to Titor, this disease is contracted through the ingestion of infected meat and will grow to epidemic proportions in his future.

Titor described his time machine as containing "two magnetic housing units for the dual micro singularities [and] an electron injection manifold to alter mass and gravity micro singularities." Singularities are defined as distinctive and unique or in quantum physics as a point in spacetime when matter is infinitely dense. He also said it contained three separate computers along with a cooling and X-ray venting system, gravity sensors, or a variable gravity lock, and four primary clocks containing caesium, a silver-gold alkali metal used in today's extremely accurate atomic clocks.

> **//** [I]t was accepted by scientific circles in 1904 that rocket propulsion in space was impossible because the rocket's gases had nothing to push against. This logic was one of the reasons why [rocket pioneer Robert] Goddard had to (later on) receive funding from people like Henry Ford ... he was considered a 'quack' and many scientific circles shunned him. **//**

This description of the time machine, which he said was mounted in the rear of a 1967 Chevrolet Corvette convertible, has been described as "a pastiche of pop-science terminology." The somewhat fuzzy photos of his time machine that he posted depicted what appeared to be parts from a military surplus store. However, Titor must have had some insight into advanced quantum physics since black holes, vortex singularities, and zero point energy are currently on the cutting edge of recent research.

Never forget that more than half of the Manhattan Project scientists, creators of the first atom bomb, sincerely believed that a nuclear chain reaction could not be stopped but would set the atmosphere on fire and incinerate the entire Earth. Luckily for us, they were wrong. All new science is initially considered nonsense or magic.

Not too long ago, great scientists like Sir Isaac Newton believed that time was akin to a fired arrow, shooting out straight and true in only one direction. Einstein altered this perception with his theory that time wound around through the universe much like a river. Today, some speculative physicists believe that, again like a river, time sometimes forms eddies or whirlpools, vortexes providing shortcuts through both time and space.

// His timeline is a different timeline to ours, ours is just very similar. (Within 1–2% if I recall according to his story). //

The Casimir Effect has demonstrated that two electrically conducting metal plates brought close together in a vacuum can create a space that negates gravity. Since gravity and time seem to be interrelated, canceling one may cancel the other. This relationship can be seen within the UFO literature in which witnesses often describe loss of time as well as the cessation of all electromagnetic devices when a UFO is nearby.

Once past Titor's eyebrow-raising statements about nuclear war and contaminated meat deaths, he also shows a keen knowledge of recent time travel theories by asserting that everything that can happen does happen in a multi-dimensional universe. In other words, rather than living in a linear time-space dimension, we actually occupy one timeline in an infinite number of timelines, somewhat like being the needle on an old phonograph record. We only perceive the groove in which the needle rests while all about us are many, many other grooves.

In addressing objections to time travel on the basis of time paradoxes—you know, if you went back in time and killed your grandfather, would you still exist?—Titor wrote, "It has always surprised me why that concept [of multiple timelines] is so hard for people to imagine and accept. Nothing would happen. The universe would not end and there are no paradox problems that threaten existence ... Temporal spacetime is made up of every possible quantum state. The Everett-Wheeler model is correct. [This is the universal relative state theory postulated by Princeton physicist Hugh Everett and his thesis advisor John Archibald Wheeler] I have met and/or seen myself twice on different world lines. The first was a training mission and the second is now. I was born in 1998 so the other 'me' is the second on this world line. There is a saying where I come from, 'Every possible thing that can happen or will happen has already happened somewhere.'"

// Hell, why not warn us that there would be a massive terrorist attack on U.S. soil in a little over a year?" [referring to Titor's 2000 postings] //

ATS MEMBER COMMENT

British science writer Jenny Randles, in her 2005 book, *Breaking the Time Barrier* presented compelling examples of recent discoveries in physics indicating the very real possibility of time travel. She noted that "a race to build a time machine has been going on since at least the Second World War." So the notion of time travel—especially one working within a series of parallel timelines—is not as far fetched as it may seem to those who have not kept up with recent research.

Titor's predictions of future history become less acceptable.

It appeared that Titor was making predictions from the standpoint of our present knowledge. For example, he failed to specifically mention the attacks of Sept. 11, 2001, accepted by now as a turning point in U.S. history. He did, however, mention huge arsenals of weapons of mass destruction in Iraq, a concept believed by most Americans prior to the 2003 invasion.

It is understandable that someone could have missed the underreported news stories in 2003 of massive anti-war demonstrations in every American city in the weeks leading up to the U.S. invasion of Iraq. Some of these demonstrations were larger than the largest anti-war demonstrations during the Vietnam War. Simply because the corporate-controlled mass media does not headline a story does not mean it didn't happen. Others might point out that a man from a future that had experienced global nuclear war and the death of millions might not have been that concerned about 3,000 dead in 2001, when, according to Titor, he was three years old.

But it is understandable that all but the most credulous would suspect the Titor postings as a fake, a "quite well researched and executed hoax," as noted on the ATS forum. "But a hoax nonetheless …"

It is easy to dismiss Titor because of his contention that the United States would begin to slide into civil war beginning in 2004. Obviously, the nation is not yet in any kind of shooting war. However, for those astute observers of the national scene who are not caught up in the matrix of the corporate mass media, there are discernible and frightening signs of a degeneration of the national spirit since the controversial election of 2004.

Everyone recalls the contentious (s)election of 2000. Most citizens expected honest investigations and that the system would correct itself. The 2004 election ended any thought that the political system could be salvaged by traditional means. Despite the fact that "computer glitches" were blamed for votes wrongly going to President Bush, his cousin and opponent, John Kerry, declined to pursue the matter. The law of averages, of course, would dictate that computer glitches should have been meted out roughly equally in each candidate's favor. Instead, all mistakes meant votes for Bush.

*//*Now [2004], we haven't seen any Waco type events so far. Nor any Civil Unrest leading up to this coming election. *//*

In the near future, 2004 may well be marked as the beginning of real and deep-seated distrust of the federal government which might degenerate into local confrontations with authorities such as the 1992 shooting of Randy Weaver's wife and dog by federal agents at Ruby Ridge, the 1993 Waco debacle, and the 2007 New Hampshire standoff between federal agents and Ed and Elaine Brown who barricaded themselves in their solar and wind-powered home after being convicted of not paying income taxes.

Already there is a great disparity of outlook between individualistic and freedom-loving Americans living in small towns and rural areas and denizens of the inner-city urban areas who have been conditioned to think of government as the provider of food and the panacea for all their ills.

If whoever is elected president in 2008 continues to push for the North American Union and other New World Order policies against the desires of the majority of Americans, the stage could indeed be set for outbreaks of violence, which most likely would divide along urban-rural lines.

Another point to consider is how quickly the world can change. In August 1939, the world was at peace. One year later, it was embroiled in a world war.

> **//**He was guessing about the civil war. At the time there was a big fuss about the 2000 U.S. elections, (he hinted that Florida's votes would be discounted at one stage). He timed the 'civil war' to start around the next U.S. elections. [A] fairly safe guess at the time because it was still four years down the track. He didn't mention the War on Terror because he didn't know. He, like the rest of us, didn't see it coming. **//**
>
> ATS MEMBER COMMENT

As for nuclear war in 2015, this will remain to be seen but the stage is being set. Russia is rearming and beginning to launch bomber practice missions again in response to President Bush's plans to place offensive missiles in Eastern Europe. Chinese military officials have stated publicly that war with the United States is "inevitable." More than two dozen small "suitcase" atomic weapons are missing from the defunct Soviet Union, and many smaller nations, such as Pakistan, India, Israel, North Korea and Iran, now have, or are rumored to be developing, nuclear capability.

In the midst of the squabbling over the science and politics in this story, many seemed to miss the message that Titor said he wanted to bring from the future.

// [Titor] specifically stated that the civil unrest began around/because of the [2004] election. He also stated that there was no general date on which the war 'began,' rather, people felt that it began around 2004 in retrospect. Also, when did WW2 start? If I asked a British member of ATS they'd say 1939 ... an American member would say 1941 ... a Chinese member would say 1933. When he gives the date of 2004 he is not giving an exact date like December 7, 1941 ... because the war was amorphous for a few years. It was only around 2008 that most people acknowledged that a civil war was occurring ... a real person from the future wouldn't categorize information the way we do. For him, everything that's going on [2004] in the [Middle East] is just a series of minor skirmishes that form a prelude to a much larger and more dramatic war. It's unreasonable to expect someone from 32 years in the future to have the same focus that we do. If you or I went back to as little ago as 1990, we might fail to mention the first WTC bombing, the Khobar towers bombing, or the war in Rwanda. Someone going back to the 1930s might not mention the sinking of the *Reuben James* [the first U.S. Navy ship sunk in World War II]. *//*

On November 21, 2000, Titor posted this message, "How can you possibly criticize me for any conflict that comes to you? I watch every day what you are doing as a society. While you sit by and watch your Constitution being torn away from you, you willfully eat poisoned food, buy manufactured products no one needs and turn an uncaring eye away from millions of people suffering and dying all around you. Is this the 'Universal Law' you subscribe to? Perhaps I should let you all in on a little secret. No one likes you in the future. This time period is looked at as being full of lazy, self-centered, civically ignorant sheep. Perhaps you should be less concerned about me and more concerned about that."

From the future or not, this message from Titor seems to be right on the mark.

▸ WHO BUILT THE SPIDERY
DRONES?

▽ WHO

▶ The U.S. government and military

▽ WHAT

▶ The creation of futuristic, man-made aircraft that are based on captured, or crashed, alien technology.

▽ WHEN

▶ From at least the 1980s to the present day.

▽ WHERE

▶ Such claims proliferate in books and on the Internet.

▽ WHY

▶ To utilize alien technology as a weapon of war and surveillance.

additional evidence and commentary:
www.abovetopsecret.com/book/drones

One Monday in June 2007, a security guard patrolling a wooded area near Maxwell Air Force Base in Montgomery, Alabama, thought he saw a hubcap hung up in a tree.

"**A**s I looked around, I could see this thing. It was not attached *to* the tree. It was not *in* the tree. It was to the *side* of the tree! And it had these elongated wires that stuck out of the top and just sort of curved and went up and sort of disappeared. They looked like they just sort of faded out. They didn't stop, they just faded out."

This witness described the hovering object as looking like a ceiling fan or even a mechanical dragonfly with appendages or antennae sticking out from it. Before the object moved off slowly, he got the impression it was watching him. "When I saw this thing, it was like, 'Oh, my God!' It was staring at me!! It just gave me the heebie jeebies ... Doing that type of work myself, I know what it feels like to be under surveillance. I have night vision equipment and all this other stuff. That's what I do. And I felt like this thing was watching me. I had this gut feeling that this thing is either taking pictures of me or it's looking at me, scanning, and that was the feeling that I had. I just had this feeling that this thing knew I was there and it was watching me."

This was only one of the more recent sightings of very unorthodox, alien-like, metallic devices that soar and hover in the air. Apparently unmanned, they have come to be known as the "drones."

As human technology continues to develop at an ever-increasing pace, our ability to differentiate between what may be a genuine UFO and what may simply be the latest, futuristic-looking, unmanned aerial vehicle (UAV) designed for, and utilized by, the government and the military, has become severely blurred.

This was amply demonstrated throughout 2007, when numerous people across the United States reported seeing aerial devices of a distinctly strange nature that some perceived as being alien in origin while others concluded they were simply prime examples of next-generation military hardware.

The controversy may have begun on May 10, 2007, when a person signing with the name "Chad" posted the following story to the Coast to Coast website:

"Last month (April 2007), my wife and I were on a walk when we noticed a very large, very strange 'craft' in the sky. My wife took a picture with her cell-phone camera. A few days later a friend (and neighbor) lent me his camera and came with me to take photos of this 'craft.' We found it and took a number of very clear photos … the craft is almost completely silent and moves very smoothly. It usually moves slowly until it decides to take off. Then it moves very quickly and is out of sight in the blink of an eye. More than anything, I simply want to understand what this is and why it is here?"

Chad later followed up this post with this report:

… I see this thing very often. Since it first appeared, I have probably seen this thing maybe eight different times since the first appearance. My friend and I went out the next day after I first saw it to get the photos, but it was not there. Then we tried again the next day, and we found it within like 30 minutes and followed it for a while. Most of the time I see it out of windows in my house, I have seen it very close. It is very easy to photograph and many neighbors aside from my friend have also seen it.

It is almost totally silent but not quite. It makes kind of "crackling" noises. It's hard to describe them but they are only intermittent and not very loud, but you can notice them. Sometimes there is a very slight hum that sounds kind of mechanical, almost like when you are near very large power lines. But it is nothing like a jet engine; it is very quiet for the most part.

It moves like an insect. If you have ever seen a bug on a pond, it is kind of like that. It is very smooth and slow most of the time, but then every now and then it will rotate very quickly and go very fast in another direction, then stop, and repeat the process all over again. There is just something very unnatural about the way it moves.

Chad ended by stating, "Also, I have had maybe four headaches in the last week, and I am normally not the kind of person who really ever gets them. Also my wife has been tired and fatigued lately. She is about a month pregnant, and the doctor said fatigue is normal around this time, but I worry that it is a lot. Basically what I'm worried [about] is that this 'craft' has got some kind of radiation or something. Like I said, it sounds like power lines if you get close enough to it. Obviously I am worried for our health, especially with a baby on the way. I don't know if they are related, but again, this is why I really hope someone can answer these questions!"

In addition to submitting his report, Chad also supplied Coast to Coast with a number of the photographs that he took of the unknown object. They clearly show some sort of aerial device, and one which looks like a large wheel with five randomly spaced and sized spokes, atop which is sat a curved, funnel-like structure.

And the controversy was far from over.

On May 12, an anonymous woman filed a report with the Mutual UFO Network describing her own encounter with a near-identical craft seven days earlier in Nevada. She wrote:

> My husband and I were in Lake Tahoe over the weekend. We left on Friday afternoon and came back Monday morning. On Saturday at about 7 p.m., I was walking out to my car to get a sweater when I saw this thing in the sky. It was pretty close I think, but still above the trees. It was moving and spinning slowly, heading towards my right. I was startled and confused at first and wanted to take a picture, but our camera was still inside so I took two pictures with my camera phone before it passed behind the roof of the house. I ran around to the other side and was yelling to my husband to come out. We came around the other side and saw it just as it was going down behind some trees. He didn't get a good look at it, but he saw enough to convince him that it was something really strange.
>
> We decided to take a drive around the area to see if we could see it again, but we never did. We didn't see it the next day either. Since we were renting the cabin for the weekend we didn't know any nearby residents but I would bet at least a few other people saw it. It was very visible and very strange looking. I was definitely a little freaked out but my husband didn't seem very bothered by it. He was more interested in it than scared.

He wanted to drive around a lot longer trying to find it than I did! It didn't make any noise except for a very, very faint sound that is hard to describe but sounded like something vibrating. We both heard the sound although just barely. It moved in a very straight line when it went over the house but when we saw it on the other side of the house, when it was going down behind the trees, it made a very sharp turn. It didn't move like a helicopter or airplane, it was very "exact."

The woman concluded: "We did see one person on our drive who was a few blocks away taking a walk and asked him if he saw it, and he said no. Then we asked him if he heard any weird noise and tried to describe it as best we could, and he said he might have but he wasn't sure. By this time it was at least 20 minutes since we first saw the thing so who knows."

> **//**It's almost glaringly obvious to nearly all casual observers and commentators now that that the whole drone/Isaac/CARET drama is a yarn... **//**

ATS MEMBER COMMENT

Interestingly, aside from the fact that the object photographed at Lake Tahoe possessed four, rather than five, spoke-like appendages, it was virtually identical to the drone seen and photographed by Chad in Bakersfield, California.

On May 20, there was a new development. A source identifying himself as Rajinder Satyanarayana of Capitola, California, posted the following to the Internet that described an encounter with a practically identical craft:

This week I was visiting my fianceé's parents in Capitola (we were actually there to tell them about our engagement, in fact). We were eating dinner on the back porch when we noticed this "object" sort of hovering in the sky. The camera was still out from earlier so I grabbed it and tried to get some clear shots of it. It took off over the roof shortly after, so I ran into the street in front of the house to follow, trying to get more shots without wobbling around too much (which was harder than it sounds). It then came in lower over a telephone pole, where I was able to get a few more pictures, before it finally took off into the distance pretty fast. I thought it was gone but noticed it was still visible, so I grabbed a few more pictures.

At one point a car stopped to look as well. No one had any idea what this thing was but everyone in the car was visibly freaked out by it. Once it was gone they told me to call the news and drove off. I'm not sure who else saw it in the neighborhood since I don't live down there, but I'm sure at least a few others must have noticed it. It was way too weird and way too close to go unnoticed. Once it was gone and I caught my breath, I could barely stop my hands from shaking for the next hour or so. Needless to say, this is all we talked about for the rest of the night. None of us can figure out what it was (and that's saying something, because my fiancé's dad is a mechanical engineer). We sent a copy of the photos to their newspaper but haven't heard back yet. I dunno how long that kind of thing takes. There's also some writing on this thing, which I didn't recognize (and I read both English and Hindi). You can see it in a few of the pictures. I have no clue what this thing is so I'm putting it out there to see if anyone else saw it.

The next development came in early June, when a source describing herself as "Jenna L" posted a story at *UFO Casebook* on behalf of a witness identified only as Stephen.

Jenna L wrote: "Hi! My name is Jenna and I participate in a listserv for photographers in Saratoga, CA. Today a member named Stephen posted some pictures he took yesterday [June 5] for a class assignment in the area around Big Basin. The pictures very clearly depict some kind of large object in the sky, and he was able to get two clear shots and one out-of-focus shot before it apparently disappeared. I recognized certain details on this object immediately because a friend had sent me your About.com article on different UFOs that have appeared recently with a similar appearance."

Jenna posted Stephen's story:

Hey Guys. Okay, where to begin. Yesterday, I was up around Big Basin for my assignment like I've been mentioning for the last couple weeks—the theme for those that don't remember was photographing something at a small scale against a large scale backdrop to contrast scales and to play with depth of field etc—I chose to photograph a couple of flower/weed things growing right on the edge of a drop off with the valley in the background—I'm still using the Rebel XT I bought off Mark which is a SLR, so I'm looking at everything through a viewfinder when I notice something appear in the distance, like just pop out of nowhere.

I look up and there is this huge who-knows-what-the-xxxx floating in the distance and rotating very slowly and jerkily. Almost by reflex I take another shot which is focused in on it this time and go to stand up but practically fall over because I can't even think straight.

I was able to get one more shot which came out kind of blurred and then the thing vanished—like as in now you see it, now you don't—I attached the pictures so you guys can check them out before I really decide to do something with them—are these going to make the 6 o'clock news or what—any feedback would be great before I make a major decision here. Also by the way, I attached three pictures. The first is when it first appeared right as I was taking a shot of the flowers but I wanted you guys to see everything I saw. Sorry I only got 3 pix, but this thing was seriously gone in like a matter of secs.

On June 11, a further development came from broadcast journalist Linda Moulton Howe. She had been contacted by a source known as "Ty" who claimed to have photographed one of the now-familiar drones near Saratoga, California.

Ty stated, "… it was really, really big and looked like it came from the same place as Chad's drone. It had the same weird 'upside down jellyfish' thing on the top, and similar looking ring structures. What was different here, though, was how much more stuff was on it. It had a ton of different rings, all connected to a big column in the center … I don't have to tell you that this thing is intense to behold!"

There is no doubt that the governments of both the United States and Britain are working on some decidedly unusual and novel aircraft designs that might be mistaken for UFOs and the work of extraterrestrials. For example, in the summer of 2007 a series of noteworthy events occurred. First, the British Police Force unveiled its latest spy in the sky: a circular shaped vehicle, barely three-feet in diameter and topped with four small, helicopter-style blades that can fly to a height of 1,500 feet and spy on people engaged in, as the police termed it, "public disorder" and "antisocial behavior"—in other words, Big Brother surveillance technology.

Shortly afterwards, the U.S. Army revealed that it had succeeded in developing its own futuristic, UFO-like craft—the MAV, or Micro Air Vehicle. This device, developed by Honeywell, features a lift-augmented, ducted-fan propulsion system offering complete vertical-take-off capabilities. The MAV is a small device, equipped with four sturdy legs and could quite easily be mistaken for what we might envision an alien spacecraft to look like.

The drone controversy reached surreal proportions on October 9, 2007, when the *Washington Post* published an article titled "Dragonfly or Insect Spy? Scientists at Work on Robobugs." This article addressed controversial claims that various U.S. agencies—such as the Department of Homeland Security, the Office of the Director of National Intelligence and the Secret Service—were possibly employing minute, insect-sized, and insect-shaped drone devices to secretly spy on U.S. citizens at home and enemy personnel on battlefields abroad.

While the idea that the military possesses the capability to build a robotic, flying spy that is ingeniously disguised as a dragonfly might make the skeptics scoff, it is a fact that more than three decades ago the CIA was working on such a device. Known as the "Insectothopter," it mirrored to an eerie degree the appearance and movements of an insect, and was only cancelled as a result of its inability to maneuver properly when faced with strong crosswinds.

Indeed, the sheer proliferation of such UFO-style devices today prompted the U.S. Army Command and General Staff College to issue a 2007 report which, in part, stated that the huge increase in UAV's could "render military airspace chaotic and potentially dangerous."

The stories of the British Police Force's drone, the U.S. Army's MAV—and even that of the Robobugs—pale in significance when compared to yet another drone-like device that also became public midway through 2007—the "CARET Drone." CARET reportedly was an abbreviation for a Commercial Applications Research for Extraterrestrial Technology program. According to one source, these drones are human-built craft based upon reverse-engineered alien technology.

It was in June 2007 that a source identifying himself only as "Isaac" came forward and claimed to know the startling truth behind the drone-like UFOs. Isaac asserted that his knowledge came from working on an official and classified Department of Defense (DoD) project in the mid-1980s—the Commercial Applications Research for Extraterrestrial Technology program. He said the purpose of the project was to create aerial vehicles very much like those shown in the drone photographs. He added that these devices incorporated both alien and man-made drone technology.

Isaac was very careful to protect his identity and stressed he was not interested in making himself "vulnerable to the consequences of betraying the trust of my superiors." His desire for anonymity obviously diminished Isaac's credibility but the depth and detail of his claims were intriguing.

Isaac admitted he had no personal experience of working with the specific drones in the various photographs that had appeared earlier in 2007. However, he did state that he had worked with and viewed "many of the parts visible in the craft ... in the Big Basin photos."

According to Isaac, the ability of the drones to largely evade detection was due to the fact that they utilized technologies that rendered them invisible to the naked eye. However, localized and inadvertent "radar-jamming" from nearby military bases, Isaac explained, could temporarily and accidentally disrupt the drones' cloaking systems. The result would be that anyone who happened to be in the vicinity at the time the drones were affected by the jamming would gain a perfect view of them until their invisibility was restored.

Isaac said he had always been interested in computer science, and following postgraduate work in electrical engineering he went to work for a series of high-tech industry jobs before being recruited by the DoD. In 1984, after some uneventful time with DoD, Isaac was brought into the top secret Commercial Applications Research for Extraterrestrial Technology (CARET) program. He said apparently he was selected because of his knowledge, intelligence, and loyalty.

By the early 1980s, Silicon Valley had become a veritable juggernaut of technology, a fact that did not go unnoticed by the U.S. government and the military. According to Isaac, the official world's interest in recruiting personnel from the area was due to the fact that the U.S. government had in its possession an unknown quantity of highly-advanced alien technology that it wished to understand and exploit for its own purposes.

"One of the best examples of the power of the tech sector was Xerox PARC, a research center in Palo Alto, California, [that] was responsible for some of the major milestones in the history of computing. XPARC served as one of the models for the CARET program's first incarnation," Isaac explained.

This "first incarnation," according to Isaac, involved people such as himself, civilian scientists who were contracted by the DoD, but who had no actual military training or background. These people had only limited involvement with official secrecy, yet they were "suddenly finding [them]selves in the same room as highly classified extra-terrestrial technology."

For two months, Isaac said he and his colleagues received regular briefings from military officials concerning the technology with which they would be working as well as stern and ominous warnings of what would happen to them if they dared breathe even a solitary word of the project outside of cleared and official channels.

On being exposed to the alien technology for the first time, Isaac recalled, "There are very few moments in life in which your entire world view is turned forever upside down, but this was one of them. I still remember that turning point during the briefing when I realized what he'd just told us, and that I hadn't heard him wrong, and that it wasn't some kind of joke."

// If [Isaac's story] is the continuation of a hoax, this guy definitely knows what he's doing and is very good at it... //

Interestingly, Isaac said that although the CARET project was one that operated under the auspices of the Department of Defense, the primary goal of the project leaders was to introduce the technology into the commercial world, rather than keep it solely in the hands of the military. Isaac explained this line of thinking: "One of CARET's most appealing promises was the revenue generated by these product-ready technologies, which could be funneled right back into black projects. Working with a commercial application in mind was also yet another way to keep us in a familiar mind state."

The project was not without its problems, according to Isaac. He said one of the biggest problems centered on trying to persuade the military to share its acquired alien technology on a large scale. Such dispersion was considered essential if the project to reverse-engineer the materials into the DoD's "drone-project" was going to succeed.

"We started the program with a small set of extraterrestrial artifacts along with fairly elaborate briefings on each as well as access to a modest amount of what research had already been completed. It wasn't long before we realized we needed more though, and getting them to provide even the smallest amount of new material was like pulling teeth," said Isaac.

There were some indications that despite the importance of the CARET work, there were other DoD projects that seemed to have greater access to even more exotic extraterrestrial technologies. Isaac stated, "One downside to CARET was that it wasn't as well connected as other operations undoubtedly were. I never got to see any actual extra-terrestrials, not even photos, and in fact, never even saw one of their complete vehicles. Aside from the word 'extraterrestrial' itself, we rarely heard any other terms like 'alien' or 'UFO' or 'outer space' or anything."

So-called anti-gravity power systems were the focus of much of the research, Isaac explained, adding that "the technology we were dealing with was so out of this world that it didn't really matter all that much what your background was because none of it applied. The physicists made the most headway initially because out of all of our skills, theirs overlapped the most with the concepts behind this technology."

Over time, however, Isaac began to suffer as a result of the extremes of security, bureaucracy, and the strange and surreal nature of what he was learning. The work began to take its toll and by 1987, Isaac said he was "utterly burned out."

Additionally, Isaac said he was far from happy with the approach that the

> **//** I am sold, hook, line and sinker. Call me naïve, stupid or whatever, but I really feel that this is the real deal. **//**
>
> ATS MEMBER COMMENT

military was taking to the whole issue of extraterrestrials visiting the Earth. "I always felt that at least some form of disclosure would be beneficial, but as a lowly CARET engineer I wasn't exactly in the position to call shots," he said.

About this time Isaac decided to take matters into his own hands. "I was sure that I would be able to sneak certain materials out with me. I wanted to do this because I knew the day would come when I would want to write something like this and I knew I'd regret it until the day I died if I didn't at least leave the possibility open to do so," he stated.

Isaac began to secretly photocopy classified CARET documents "by the dozen" and hide the papers under his shirt and "around my lower back, tucked enough into my belt to ensure they wouldn't fall out." He added, "I'd often take upwards of 10–20 pages at once. By the time I was done, I'd made out with hundreds of photocopies, as well as a few originals and a large collection of original photographs. However, I've taken the proper steps to ensure a reasonable level of anonymity."

Isaac claimed not to know if CARET still exists today. It may exist as it did in the 1980s or it may have been absorbed into some other project. He pointed out that "for what it's worth, during my time there I never heard anything about invasions, or abductions; it never came up. So at the very least I can say my intent is not to scare anyone. My view on the extraterrestrial situation is very much a positive, albeit still highly secretive one. One thing I can definitely say is that if they wanted us gone, we would have been gone a very, very long time ago and we wouldn't even have seen it coming."

Linda Moulton Howe, the one person with a journalist's background who continued to dog the drone story, both located and interviewed drone witnesses and published drone material on her website, Earthfiles.com.

More than one computer scientist offered some support for the CARET story. Arthur A. Reyes, a senior lecturer and assistant professor in the Computer Science & Engineering Department at the University of Texas at Arlington, wrote: "I find Isaac's writing style and the content of his narrative to be consistent with that of a knowledgeable and experienced engineer or engineering manager. Isaac's use of jargon such as 'big-O notation,' 'context-sensitive languages,' 'style manuals,' 'workflow,' the distinction between software and hardware, etc., is correct, concise and insightful. I find nothing in Isaac's narrative to indicate fiction." Joe Schumacher, a retired computer engineer, said that the CARET photos depicted devices that closely matched equipment he had worked on while employed by one of the "Big 3" computer companies.

And that's where matters rest. As it developed, the controversy created a storm of debate at *Above Top Secret*. For some, the whole affair was deemed nothing more than a gigantic hoax but others were not so sure.

Since the late summer of 2007, no further significant data and no further evidence—pro or con—has surfaced in the CARET controversy. There have been no new photographs, with the exception of some obvious hoaxes and a piece of film posted to YouTube. Apparently someone had taken one of the legitimate drone photos and animated it with computer software, allowing debunkers to dismiss the entire issue. Others claim the drones are still around; only their cloaking technology has been improved.

One thing is certain, whether the work of hoaxers, human scientists, alien engineers, or a curious and convoluted combination of all three, it seems that the UFO drone controversy is here to stay.

▸ **WHAT PASSED BY THE SPACE SHUTTLE *ATLANTIS*?**

▽ **WHO**

▸ The *Atlantis* STS-115 space shuttle's six-person crew

▽ **WHAT**

▸ Preparations for a landing back on Earth were delayed due to the discovery of an unidentified object sighted between the shuttle and the Earth. It was simply described as "small and dark."

▽ **WHEN**

▸ The *Atlantis* was launched on September 9, 2006, and arrived at the space station on September 11. The delay due to the unidentified object took place on September 19.

▽ **WHERE**

▸ In Earth orbit, the object was seen between the shuttle and the Earth.

▽ **WHY**

▸ This item made news because it delayed the landing of the *Atlantis* until September 21, 2006. The shuttle glided to a safe landing at the Kennedy Space Center in Florida at 6:21 a.m. (EDT) after a mission to resume construction of the International Space Station.

additional evidence and commentary:
www.abovetopsecret.com/book/shuttleufo

Following the safe return of *Atlantis*, Commander Brent Jett, a veteran shuttle astronaut, remarked, "It was critical that she perform well and she did. It was a pleasure to fly her and it's great to be home."

While in space, the crew conducted three successful spacewalks mainly devoted to preparing a truss segment and its solar arrays, which had been brought into orbit by the *Atlantis*. The 17.5-ton truss was to provide power and data services for the space station. The solar arrays, unfurled on Sept. 14, spanned 240 feet and were said to double the station's power generation capability once operational. STS-115 was the 116th shuttle flight and the 19th mission to visit the space station. *Atlantis* has now flown 27 times and made six trips to the station.

The *Atlantis* STS-115 mission was NASA's first operational attempt to resume construction on the International Space Station following the *Columbia* disaster of 2003. The loss of the *Columbia* had been ascribed to damage to the heat shield.

But the thing that prompted the most interest from ATS members was something that appeared in space as the shuttle prepared for its return to Earth.

The mystery object appeared during the shuttle's flight system checkout prior to its return to Earth—which included a firing of the ship's thrusters shaking the craft—prompting NASA officials to speculate the two events were related. "We shake the ship pretty good when we do this," said NASA space shuttle program manager Wayne Hale. Both flight controllers and shuttle astronauts noticed several bits of debris or "mystery objects," which appeared to float out from the ship's cargo bay following the checkout shaking.

A flight controller spotted the small object in *Atlantis*'s vicinity backlit by the Earth about 15 minutes after checkout. Officials suspected the object may have been something as simple as ice or ceramic gap-filler or perhaps a piece of plastic dangling from *Atlantis*'s heat shield.

There was even some controversy about whether this was one object or several. NASA officials tried to relegate the incident to one small object, yet the astronauts themselves reported as many as three in what appeared to be a triangular formation.

NASA early on eliminated the idea that the objects may have been pieces of the shuttle's heat shield tiles or carbon composite panels as these were checked both after launch and again after about nine days in orbit.

"It could be a little something up close or a bigger something a little farther away, it's a bit of a mystery," said Wayne Hale at the time of the object's discovery. "We're principally going about the task of making sure that the orbiter is safe for reentry and landing regardless of what that may have been."

"It was definitely moving away," Commander Jett reported. He added that he was able to get several photos of the small object but that it was too far away for any details. He said it was traveling away from the shuttle at what appeared to be a constant speed of about one or two feet per second

*//*What is ... significant is that NASA tried to claim that the objects from STS-75 were camera reflections, or the way the camera was seeing 'particles.' But now in STS-115 these are considered real objects, not dust particles or a type of lens flare or reflection. *//*

ATS MEMBER COMMENT

The mystery object, coupled with poor weather predicted for the Kennedy Space Center Landing Facility, caused a postponement of the shuttle's return.

Oddly, a series of accelerometers, which record stresses or potential impacts along *Atlantis*'s wing leading edges, recorded about eight events about the time of the shuttle's flight systems checkout. Hale said the accelerometers also reported phantom signals during *Atlantis*'s liftoff, although no impacts or damage were found.

In early October, NASA revealed that an unknown object had pierced a radiator mounted on one of the ship's two cargo doors but assured the public that the strike did not endanger either the ship or its crew.

"Although it's small, by comparison, it may be the second largest impact we've been able to detect on a payload bay door," stated NASA spokesperson Kyle Herring. "It did not do any other damage to the vehicle other than penetrate the radiator."

The unknown object was suspected to be either a micrometeoroid or some other piece of orbital debris. It caused a small, one-tenth of an inch puncture in the shuttle's aft starboard radiator and appeared to leave a 0.031-inch exit hole along with a nearby crack.

NASA concluded, "The nature of the object that hit the shuttle radiator isn't known."

ATS MEMBER COMMENT

//The theory by one of the guys that made the NASA video footage—smoking gun documentary makes an interesting hypothesis that the 'hole' is in fact an effect caused by a gravity based drive. The speculation is that gravity is so intense in the area of the hole that light can't penetrate it and bends around it. Thus the object is in fact disc shaped but the propulsion system makes it appear like a torus (donut). **//**

Due to its small size, proximity to the *Atlantis*, and the shaking of the pre-return checkout, the object was most likely something shaken loose from the shuttle, a micrometeorite or one of the more than 1,000 pieces of space debris orbiting the Earth which are a major hazard to space flights.

Some scientists have warned that the continued buildup of space debris—junk—may be creating an impenetrable shield around the planet which might end all Earth-launched space shots due to the danger of being struck by a piece. It would certainly be ironic if human attempts at space flight ended up placing the entire planet in quarantine.

▶ **WHAT HOVERED OVER O'HARE GATE C17?**

▽ WHO

▸ Various airline employees, air travelers and airport workers at Chicago's O'Hare International Airport.

▽ WHAT

▸ Many persons reported seeing a saucer-shaped object hovering over O'Hare's Gate C17 for several minutes before shooting upward with such intensity it left a hole in the cloud cover above the airport.

▽ WHEN

▸ The object was seen by both airline and airport workers about 4:30 p.m. on November 7, 2006.

▽ WHERE

▸ The first sighting was by a United Airlines ramp worker who was directing a United Airlines jet at Gate C17.

▽ WHY

▸ This is one of the most recent and well-documented UFO sightings. While there does not seem to be a final determination on what exactly hovered over Gate C17, the incident provides a springboard for the novice to journey into the enduring mystery of UFOs.

additional evidence and commentary:
www.abovetopsecret.com/book/ohare

One of the most recent—and publicized—UFO events occurred on November 7, 2006. A circular object was observed over O'Hare for several minutes before shooting upward and leaving a hole in the cloud cover.

Witnesses described a circular object between six and twenty-four feet in diameter that was noiseless, metallic, dark gray and with no visible lights. Some witnesses stated the object was spinning or rotating but others reported no motion. Initially, the object was stationary, hovering just below the 1,900-foot cloud cover in an overcast sky.

After hearing a report on the object over an internal United Airlines radio, one manager ran outside for a look. The unnamed manager told a newsman, "I stood outside in the gate area not knowing what to think, just trying to figure out what it was ... if somebody was bouncing a weather balloon or something else over O'Hare, we had to stop it because it was in very close proximity to our flight operations."

On November 14, 2006 The National UFO Reporting Center (NUFORC) noted the incident on its website and the next day, NUFORC Director Peter Davenport spoke of the incident on George Noory's *Coast to Coast* nationally-syndicated radio program. Davenport said, "In my opinion, because I know the quality of the witnesses, and because I know the nature of the documents that were generated, it is one of the most dramatic cases of the year 2006 that this center has handled."

By December 13, a senior aircraft mechanic, interviewed on the Jeff Rense radio program, told of sighting the disc-shaped object while in a Boeing 777 being taxied down a runway. According to Davenport, the NUFORC had tipped the *Chicago Tribune* to the O'Hare story but no story was forthcoming.

The O'Hare incident finally was reported in a front-page story in the *Chicago Tribune* written by reporter Jon Hilkevitch on January 1, 2007. Hilkevitch said he wrote that the paper had been alerted to the story in mid-December but that this notation was edited out of the final printed version. Hilkevitch said he interviewed six O'Hare workers, all of whom gave a similar description of the object but from different vantage points.

The next day, the O'Hare story was finally picked up; the Associated Press distributed a much-edited and shortened version of Hilkevitch's story. Such media outlets as *USA Today* and National Public Radio subsequently carried the story.

In an interview following the release of his news article, Hilkevitch said what impressed him about this story was the witnesses. "[They were] all aviation professionals, very credible sources and they are very serious. They are not saying what they saw was a, you know, a spaceship from another planet, but it was unidentified, it was in restricted airspace, and they were concerned from a safety standpoint."

Hilkevitch's journalistic hackles were raised when initially both United Airlines and the Federal Aviation Administration said there were no reports on the object. He knew better.

> **//** This is potentially a HUGE story. There has to be at least one picture. Of course, by the time it gets 'released' it will probably be grainy and resemble something that could have been made in 1960. **//**
>
> ATS MEMBER COMMENT

"What was interesting to me was that United Airlines, after receiving numerous reports, including from high-level management officials, decided to deny that they got any such reports! I don't know if they ... felt embarrassment, or [feared] maybe people would think United Airline employees are kooks, or something, by reporting this. But it's very odd. The FAA, at first, too, said they didn't know what I was talking about when I went to them. They had no reports of this. It wasn't until I put a Freedom of Information [Act] Request in and they got back to me saying well, we're going through the communication tapes from O'Hare tower and by golly, there is a lot of chatter here about this UFO."

Seeking quotes for his story, Hilkevitch found official statements dismissive. According to FAA spokeswoman Elizabeth Isham Cory, no [air traffic] controllers saw the object, and a preliminary check of radar found nothing out of the ordinary. She theorized the event was caused by a "weather phenomenon" and added that the FAA anticipated no further investigation.

O'Hare air traffic controller and union official Craig Burzych said, "The UFO report has sparked some chuckles among controllers in O'Hare tower. To fly 7 million light years to O'Hare and then have to turn around and go home because your gate was occupied is simply unacceptable."

Talk show host Jeff Rense observed, "Regrettably, the story in the *Tribune* contains the usual, nauseating put-downs, denials, and dismissals by FAA staff and controllers who, of course, 'didn't see a thing' ... which suggests either they are lying, were asleep on the job, or were grossly negligent. We'll choose number one. Another typical FAA cover-up at work.

"The U.S. media, and the U.S. government for that matter, have treated the massively important subject of countless unidentified flying craft—and the entire ET issue—with official derision, abuse, obfuscation, and outright silence for over 60 years. This cover-up is one of the blackest marks in the history of so-called professional journalism in America and the world," added Rense.

Some commentators concluded that the event might have been produced by an atmospheric vortex phenomenon, created by a vortex backwash produced by an airliner taking off. "You can conjecture all day long on that point if you wish to do so, but it's futile in this case," responded Davenport. "First of all, airplanes don't fly over [airport] gates, they fly over runways. So your surmise, I think, is not appropriate in this case ... This object was seen by many people to accelerate so fast and go straight up in the clouds that their eyes were unable to follow it."

After dismissing the O'Hare incident as a meteorological phenomenon based on the lack of necessary conditions such as the presence of ice crystals or rain, a detailed report (Case 18) issued in March 2007 by the National Aviation Reporting Center on Anomalous Phenomena (NARCAP) concluded the object would have to have been "something objectively and externally real to create the [Hole in Cloud] effect" which could not be explained "by either conventional weather phenomena or conventional aerospace craft, whether acknowledged or unacknowledged."

After noting the dismissive attitude of the FAA and other officials in post-9/11 America, the report stated, "It is interesting that an incursion over one of the busiest aviation facilities in the world would receive such superficial attention."

Although at least two photos, reportedly of the O'Hare object, were made public after the NARCAP report was published, neither has been substantiated, and the usual cries of fakery surfaced.

// I for one think the photos are hoaxes, but I will leave it up to the experts to figure that out. //

One ATS member was a witness. This account of the sighting was posted:

I first sighted it while at the intersection of Irving Park Rd. and Mannheim Blvd., and again for just a bit when I got to the parking lot of the international terminal. I was picking up a friend, an American Airlines cockpit officer who was flying in from Charles de Gaulle International Airport. His plane, scheduled for a 4:55 p.m. arrival time, was delayed because of the object.

The ostensible cell phone photo could have been the object, in that the UFO's perceptible coloration did alter somewhat depending on the viewer's angle. When I saw it from Mannheim, it appeared much paler, but as I moved closer to underneath it, it darkened … my impression is that it was highly reflective, with the upper part mirroring the lighter sky and the underneath mirroring the darker areas (as well as being naturally shaded). "Mirroring" is actually an awkward word, as the "texture" of the craft didn't seem highly polished, but it's the only word I can think of that somewhat applies. I do know that there are other photos, as I saw a fair number of people, even several on Mannheim, take photos with cell phones or digital cameras.

It was definitely an object, not a lenticular cloud or any other weather phenomenon. At its closest, it was no more than a quarter of a mile from me, and I saw it fly off. It was very clearly a controlled craft of some sort. There were no lights in use on it at that time ... the winds were light that day ... too light to require any directional TO or landing alterations.

//To the person that asked why UFOs would be at O'Hare Airport: If you were 'spying' on a civilization in a flying craft, would you not want to see if the civilization that you are 'spying' on has the same capabilities? I certainly would, and an airport seems like an excellent place to study human air-travel doesn't it? //

The one clear thing in the O'Hare incident is that something happened above Gate C17 that does not appear weather-related and both airport and FAA officials are not being forthcoming in their explanations.

▸ WHAT FLEW OVER PHOENIX?

▽ WHO

▶ The residents of Arizona

▽ WHAT

▶ A formation of lights said by many to be attached to a mile-long aerial object.

▽ WHEN

▶ Between 7:30 and 10 p.m. March 13, 1997

▽ WHERE

▶ The large V-shaped object moved silently southeast down through Arizona to along a 300-mile populated corridor from the Nevada state line through Prescott Valley and Phoenix to the northern edge of Tucson. Later in the night, a series of bright lights were sighted on Phoenix's southern horizon.

▽ WHY

▶ This is one of the more recent and certainly the most well documented UFO incidents to be reported in the mainstream media.

additional evidence and commentary:
www.abovetopsecret.com/book/phoenixlights

The public finally learned near mid-1997 that something strange had occurred over the city of Phoenix earlier that year. They also learned that military flares had been dropped, so the media dropped the entire issue.

Few have continued to follow the story but those who have now know that the incident cannot be brushed off with the excuse that those residents of the Phoenix area confused flares for a gigantic UFO. The former governor of Arizona admitted to CNN in 2007 that he saw the object and that it was "otherworldly."

Although referred to as the "Phoenix Lights," the sightings began much farther north of the city on the evening of March 13, 1997. Citizens of at least five other cities reported seeing a huge object shaped much like a boomerang moving slowly toward Phoenix. One report of an early sighting came from Henderson in the far northwest corner of the state at about 6:55 p.m.

Soon reports were coming in from Chino Valley, Prescott, Prescott Valley, Dewey, Cordes Junction, Wickenburg, Cavecreek, and many other communities to the north and west of Phoenix.

Cruising down through the most populated areas of the state, the object reached the Superstition Mountains east of Phoenix about 7:30 p.m. In the darkening skies, the object initially was seen as points of light. Depending on their vantage point, citizens reported first six lights, then eight and some even a ninth. The lights appeared to move in a coordinated fashion as though attached to a common structure.

Calls flooded local law enforcement and media offices but no one had an explanation for the object that was witnessed by thousands. Air traffic controllers at

Sky Harbor International Airport told reporters and UFO investigators that they saw nothing on their radar screens.

About 10 p.m. aerial lights again were seen south of Phoenix and the Gila River.

Initial photographs and tape recordings of the lights indicated an object very low to the ground as mountains can be seen in the background giving perspective to photo analysts. Studying scale based on elevation from the ground and distance from the camera, experts concluded the photographed object was more than a mile in length. A group of real estate agents gathered at a housing development in north Phoenix used known landmarks and surveying stakes to estimate the object was even larger—perhaps two miles in length. They also reported seeing bright lights along the object's leading edge described as "blue-white," to "yellow-white," to "amber." They even reported seeing a line of windows or portholes containing the "silhouettes of people."

> **//**Like many, I was fascinated with this case back in 1997 soon after it occurred and I first saw the story on CNN and *USA Today*. Here was a major UFO sighting on a massive scale, captured on video, and showed on major media outlets! Wow! ... But, soon my elation turned to disappointment after seeing the flares explanation marvelously illustrated on television documentaries, etc. So, like many others, I filed this case into the neat, but explained category. Little did I know how much, much more there was to the story. **//**

Many witnesses said the gigantic object was perceptible only by the fact that it blotted out the sky above it and reflected the city lights below it. No one reported any loud sound connected to the object although some stated there was a soft whispering like "rushing wind."

Peter B. Davenport, director of the National UFO Reporting Center (NUFORC), said discrepancies in the various descriptions of the object together with the large number of communities involved, "raised early suspicions that multiple objects were involved in the event, and that they perhaps were traveling at high speed. These suspicions would be borne out over subsequent months, following extensive investigation by many individuals. The investigations pointed to the fact that several objects, all markedly different in appearance, and most of them almost unbelievably large, passed over Arizona that night."

Davenport also noted that as the object moved slowly to the south over Phoenix, it appeared to "fire" a white beam of light at the ground. "At about the same time, the seven lights on the object's leading edge suddenly dimmed and disappeared from the witnesses' sight. The object moved off in the general direction of Sky Harbor International Airport, a few miles to the south, where it was witnessed by two air traffic controllers in the airport tower, and reportedly by several pilots, both on the ground and on final approach from the east," he reported, adding, "One of the witnesses in Scottsdale, a former airline pilot with 13,700 hours of flight time, reported seeing the object execute a distinct turn as it approached his position on the ground. He noted that he witnessed many lights on the object as it approached him, but that the number of lights appeared to diminish as it got closer to overhead."

One key witness was Lynne Kitei, a respected physician with the Arizona Heart Institute, who after spotting the hovering lights over the city, ran inside to fetch her video camera. Back on her patio, Kitei was able to videotape only three lights of the original six she had seen. Nevertheless, her tape became one of the best pieces of evidence shown by the media.

"Some people deny it even exists, that it all feeds into a logical explanation," Kitei says. "That's OK if it gives them comfort. Everyone [comes to knowledge] in their own time."

Typical of the numerous reports from ordinary Phoenix residents was that of Mike Fortson, a former member of the U.S. Navy's Ceremonial Guard, who carried security clearances and participated in events from state dinners in the White House to funerals at Arlington National Cemetery. Fortson recalled:

> I awoke from a brief nap in my recliner and leaned over to tell my wife
> that I was going to bed. I glanced to the clock on the television; it was
> 8:30 p.m. As I walked down the hallway to the master bedroom, I noticed
> the bedroom window was open. The weather was most pleasant this March

13 evening, temp. 75 degrees, clear and no wind ... typical Arizona spring evening. As I pulled the window closed, my eyes were attracted to the three huge, bright white lights angled down and very low to the ground. "Plane crash!" I thought. These lights were way too low and angled in a way nothing I know of could pull out of ... coming from the north and heading south was one, single structure that looked like a giant boomerang. (The description of boomerang, chevron (best), and V-shaped object all apply.) This object stuck out like a sore thumb in the evening sky due to the fact we were looking north towards the Phoenix metro area, and the city lights gave us a gray background in which to view this huge black V-shaped object. It was so low to the surface we could not believe it. I remember saying, "what the hell is that?"

The huge V-shaped craft was moving slowly to the south ... One thing that I remember the most is how this craft "floated" approximately 30–40 mph. There was no visual means of propulsion and absolutely no noise. The altitude and speed of the craft never changed.

... there was a bright bottom quarter moon setting in the western horizon. I said to the wife, "we're gonna get more detail, look, it's going right into the light of the moon." But instead of greater detail of this huge V-shaped craft, what we saw still amazes us. As the front of the V-shaped craft entered the light of the moon, this black chevron shaped object became translucent in bright light! We could still see the bottom quarter moon through the object, but instead of bright white, it [the moon] was a dingy yellow. As the V-shaped craft exited the bright moon, it became a solid black object again. We watched as the entire craft passed through this. Seeing a solid object going into and coming out of, was black. But as the craft passed between us and the bright, white moon, it was translucent.

There was no question in our minds that what we saw was not of this Earth. Our total sighting was approximately 1 minute and 45 seconds.

Fortson went on to describe the aftermath of the Phoenix sightings: "I was listening to talk radio most of the [next] day. I had not yet decided to call in. Mainly because of the debunking that was already going on. They [radio hosts] really made the callers feel ignorant and silly from the beginning. I was really getting upset. I have never experienced anything like this before. Without investigation ... conclusions were being drawn. This was very frustrating. And this is why I believe so many that had seen this massive craft refused to call in or report their sighting. One so called expert said, 'this is why people shouldn't look up!' Everyone laughed … The first day was terrible for the witnesses. Instead of trying to find out just how many witnesses there were statewide, they would just ridicule and insult the intelligence of those who called in. I was really starting to boil … after seeing those late night videos time and time again…it was getting to me … for that was not what we had seen Thursday evening at 8:30 p.m. from our home in Chandler. And after taking just so much … I finally made the call. I searched UFO on the Internet. After looking for a few seconds I found MUFON."

// [A]s usually seems to be the case in these types of unusual airborne events, conflicting information initially arrived from the local Air Force authorities. Witnesses who called the Luke Air Force Base with reports noted that the female operator stated that they were being flooded with calls. A day later, on March 14, 1997, the same Luke Air Force personnel were quoted as stating they had received no calls concerning the matter. Mr. Davenport of NUFORC produced phone records showing that he himself had called the base to report the lights on more than one occasion that night straightforwardly disproved these statements. //

Officialdom apparently moved to defuse the situation. In a masterstroke of disinformation, someone ordered the Maryland National Guard to overfly the Gila Bend Barry M. Goldwater Firing Range to the south of Phoenix and drop flares. This was done between 9:30 and 10 p.m. on the night of March 13. The cluster of lights from the flares were both seen and videotaped.

Curiously, although the Phoenix incident was covered in several small area newspapers, it was not mentioned in the *Arizona Republic*, Phoenix's major daily, the wire services, or the national media for three months. In its June 18, 1997 edition, *USA Today* carried a front-page article on the Phoenix incident and soon many national media outlets joined in the reporting.

With the incident now garnering news headlines, the Public Affairs Office at

Luke AFB announced that their investigation had determined that the lights seen in Phoenix were military flares launched from A-10 "Warthog" aircraft at approximately 10 p.m. Enterprising reporters who checked with the Maryland Guard were assured that their craft had indeed launched flares on March 13. Case closed.

The announcement of these maneuvers came despite the fact that back in March officials at Davis-Monthan Air Force Base in Tucson reported no military maneuvers were taking place that night at the Barry M. Goldwater Range. At the time of the June news interest, their story changed, stating that the person on duty that night had failed to look at the proper logbook.

Also months after the incident, Lt. Col. Ed Jones, of the Maryland Guard, suddenly came forward to support the flares story. He said he was one of the A-10 pilots over Arizona that night. Jones, who became assistant director of operations for the 104th Fighter Squadron of the Maryland National Guard, said his flight was cruising over southwestern Arizona on the last night of maneuvers called "Operation Snowbird" because they were winter visitors.

> **//** I was inspired by this thread and thought I would give this a try for myself. I tried it on the Phoenix Lights Wikipedia entry. I was surprised to see some interesting edits. I found 6 edits by Army National Guard Bureau (Manassas, Virginia). **//**

Returning east, Jones said he reminded the pilots to eject their leftover flares. He explained that as it was their last night on maneuvers, it was more cost-effective to eject the flares than to offload and store the munitions upon returning.

According to Jones, "One of our guys had about ten or so left, so he started to puke them out, one after another. So every few seconds or so, when the next flare was ready to go, he hit the button and launched it."

Despite this description of separately dropped flares, Jones said he looked back and saw an evenly spaced string of lights over the desert. He added the flares seemed to hover because heat from the flare rose into the parachute.

No one thought to question the discrepancy between the 8:30 p.m. sightings of a large object that blocked out the stars and the 10 p.m. lights from the flares. "The sad part [is] 99 percent of all the so-called investigations was on these lights videos ... nearly all witnesses to the March 13, 1997 UFO flyover were in the eight o'clock hour!" said witness Fortson, who added it was the "perfect diversion."

UFO researcher, author, and webmaster of *UFO Casebook* Billy Booth explained that the flares explanation "is totally unfounded for several reasons. First of all, flares do not move in unison, fall toward the ground, and then fly back up into the air, and move across many miles without changing their relative positions. Secondly, many witnesses had made reports of the giant lights hours before the reported time of the launch of the flares."

Booth's assessment was supported by Phoenix witness and retired Northwest Airlines Captain Trig Johnston, who stated, "the flare theory is just a cover story and I can prove it." He explained that the types of flares that the military claimed to have dropped are meant to be used at about 1,000 feet altitude to illuminate the ground so that troops on the ground can see the terrain." Yet, the flares dropped near Phoenix were estimated to have been between 10,000–15,000 feet high so as to be seen in Phoenix. "Why are they dropping ground illumination flares so high?" Johnston asked. "I was there, what I saw in Phoenix at 10:22 p.m. in Phoenix was not flares, it was a solid boomerang shaped object, nearly a mile wide."

Fortson said on March 16 he joined several other witnesses along with Mutual UFO Network Arizona representatives to view videos of the Phoenix lights. "That's when I first spoke up to them and said, 'that's not what we saw!' I described in front of all present and on film, for the very first time just what we saw at 8:30 p.m., not at 10 p.m., Nannette and I saw a solid V-shaped craft, not distant lights. We had no problem determining it was one object as it came through the gray background of the city lights, the enormous black craft stuck out like a sore thumb. It was low and slow and it did not make any noise. And as I exclaimed during the sighting, 'that son-of-a-bitch is a mile long!'

"Dr. Bruce Maccabee [a prominent investigator who studies UFOs scientifically] came to Phoenix and examined all the videos, I believe through a scientific method of triangulation he perceived them to be shot pretty close to the same time—approx. 10 p.m. Mountain Standard Time. I believe he calculated them to be a distance from Phoenix of about 30–36 miles and had to have been ignited around 16–17,000 feet. I would refer you to his conclusions he made that are on file at his website. Personally, I trust his conclusions because he was the only one who approached this from a scientific point of view. You see, the lights were just too far away."

Several persons near Luke Air Force Base reported not only seeing the lighted object but also witnessing interceptors being launched from the base. The Air Force, however, denied any such activity.

One reported incident might have revealed why more information on such events has not been forthcoming from the military. A young man who claimed to be an airman at Luke AFB telephoned the National UFO Reporting Center at 3:20 a.m. on March 14 to report that two USAF F-15C fighters had been "scrambled" from his base and had intercepted one of the objects. "Although the presence of F-15s could never be confirmed, the airman provided detailed information which proved to be highly accurate, based on what investigators would reconstruct from witnesses over subsequent weeks and months. Two days after his first telephone call, the airman called to report that his commander had just informed him that he was being transferred to an assignment in Greenland. He has never been heard from again since that telephone call," said NUFORC's Davenport.

On the morning of June 19, 1997, due to growing national interest in the Phoenix incident and many anxious calls from the city's residents, Republican Governor Fife Symington III announced he was instigating a full investigation of the case. "We're going to get to the bottom of this. We're going to find out if it was a UFO," he stated. He later said that officials with the Air Force were "perplexed" and could offer no explanation.

Later that same afternoon, Symington called together a hasty news conference and told reporters he had found the "guilty party" behind the Phoenix Lights. Symington's chief of staff, Jay Heiler, was then brought in handcuffed to state troopers dressed as a space alien, complete with rubber "alien" mask. Everyone got a big laugh, except the frustrated citizens of Phoenix.

"It was an insult to the intelligence of the witnesses," said Phoenix City Councilwoman and Vice Mayor Frances Emma Barwood. "The message to Arizona citizens was that reporting this was stupid."

Barwood, who did not personally see the lights over the city, nevertheless became the only elected official to question the government's flares story and to demand an objective and in-depth investigation. She said the mere mention of the incident at a council meeting prompted more than 700 calls from witnesses in the city. For her trouble, she was voted out of office. "The government never interviewed even one witness," she recalled.

// ...[L]ooks like the government is trying hard to skew/censor information. Lights reflected off commercial airliners, swamp gas, Venus etc... Got something to hide? **//**

"All I wanted them to do was investigate this," she later explained. "I never said anything about extraterrestrials ... How could they possibly not know about these huge craft flying low over major population centers? That's inconceivable, but it's also frightening."

In 1998, Barwood ran for the office of Arizona secretary of state. But the political powerhouses were all against her.

"In a state that has bounced two governors from office in 10 years, the race for secretary of state—next in line to the top—is worth following," editorialized the *Arizona Republic*. "Toss in a candidate whose pet political pursuits include UFOs and government cover-ups, and voters in this year's Republican primaries have one of the more intriguing contests for an otherwise unheralded office. The differences between Frances Emma Barwood and Betsey Bayless could not be more striking—dogmatic firebrand vs. calculated neutrality, grassroots outsider vs. political appointee, and advocate vs. administrator."

Her opponent, Betsey Bayless, a Maricopa County Board of Supervisors appointee well connected with the local power structure, garnered about $200,000 in campaign funds compared to Barwood's $22,000. Barwood lost.

Illustrating the standards of mainstream media reporting on the Phoenix incident were headlines such as "The Hack and the Quack." Name-calling and insinuations replaced objective reporting of the facts and witnesses.

But in 2007, the scales of this controversy tipped in favor of the unearthly when former Gov. Symington appeared on CNN to declare that he himself was a witness to the strange unidentified flying object over Phoenix. He said he saw a large triangular "craft of unknown origin" with lights, moving slowly. "It was dramatic. And it couldn't have been flares because it was too symmetrical. It had a geometric outline, a constant shape," said Symington. To journalist Leslie Kean, he stated, "It was enormous and inexplicable. Who knows where it came from? A lot of people saw it, and I saw it too."

Symington explained his antics at the June 1997 news conference were due to the fact that Arizona was "on the brink of hysteria." "I wanted them to lighten up and calm down, so I introduced a little levity. But I never felt that the overall situation was a matter of ridicule," he said. Adding that he wanted to make amends to his constituents and set the record straight, Symington reflected, "If I had to do it all over again I probably would have handled it differently."

> **//** [T]here's the issue of a very large object seen by many much earlier ... that's the one I'm interested in. As many have said, the flare drop might have been to muddy the earlier sightings. This might have been done incidentally without the knowledge of the MD Guard Unit, simply following their project guidelines. **//**

ATS MEMBER COMMENT

Now out of office, Symington gave this description of his sighting, "The lights were really bright and it was just fascinating, and it was enormous, it just felt otherworldly, you know in your gut you could just tell it was just otherworldly ... I suspect that unless the Defense Department proves us otherwise, I think it was an alien spacecraft."

In 2000, responding to a class action suit by Phoenix witnesses in the U.S. District Court in Phoenix, the Department of Defense claimed it could not find any information about the incident. This apparent loss of reports coupled with the flares story prompted former Gov. Symington, himself a veteran pilot, in 2007 to compare the Phoenix sighting with the November 2006 sighting at Chicago's O'Hare International Airport which the FAA explained away as a "weather phenomenon."

"I wish that government entities would stop trying to shut down these investigations by putting out some flakey story," he said.

Incredibly, on April 21, 2008—almost exactly eleven years and one month after the 1997 sightings—Phoenix residents again were treated to odd lights in the night sky. And again the explanation offered was flares.

Shortly after 8 p.m. on that Monday night, residents reported seeing bright red lights in the sky over the city. Although some observers reported seeing military jets near the objects, a spokesman at Luke Air Force Base denied any official air activity that night.

One man who managed to videotape the sighting was Brad Drenning, the sales manager for an electronics company. Drenning told reporter Linda Moulton Howe, "There were four lights pretty much in a straight line and they were hovering in just the same area. They weren't drifting with any kind of air currents. They were staying in one location."

But as Drenning began to videotape the objects, they began to move. "I got my camera out and started to videotape. The lights stayed in the same area and then they started moving in different formations. The first 2:49 [minutes] of my video-tape, there are two red objects in a pair to the left and two red objects in a pair to the right, kind of angled to each other. Then came other patterns like a square and a trapezoid and like a kite. The four red lights changed formation several times ... Our entire sighting was around 14 minutes. I would say there were approximately six to seven different formations, each lasting about 1.5 to 2 minutes each before the next pattern formed. Toward the end, the lights separated apart with two higher on the left and two lower on the right and they sat there for a minute or so. Then one-by-one, they took off, or went out, or whatever. Then the last one, the fourth and final one, sat there for another three or four minutes before it eventually looked as if it had gone farther away from us until we could not see it any longer."

One explanation was offered the next day when the *Arizona Republic* reported that a 44-year-old Phoenix resident named Lino Mailo "saw his neighbor launch several helium balloons with flares attached to them from the back porch of his north Phoenix home. Mailo said the balloons took off about 8 p.m., right before the mysterious lights were spotted."

"I feel bad for the people freaking out about this," Mailo told the newspaper. "I could've put this whole thing to rest."

While most everyone seemed to accept Mailo's explanation, it is worthwhile to note that while neither the North American Aerospace Defense Command, the FAA nor local air traffic controllers could offer any explanation for the lights, an FAA spokesman said that agency would not investigate the sightings.

Also, there was no explanation why the balloonist was never identified or questioned about his helium balloon launches.

Some observers of the lights questioned the helium balloon story. Drenning, for example, stated, "It was unlike anything I have ever witnessed. If it were a balloon or flare—I've been in the military—over time if there is any kind of air current, those will usually drift with the air current. They will drift in one direction or another. That is correct. These sat and hovered in one area. They didn't have any drifting. You'll see this in the video—in the other 10 minutes, they are very distinctive formations that were created. If it was some type of balloon, in my opinion, there is no way that anything else could have done that. What it was, I have no idea, but it does not make sense that it was a flare or balloon or something of that nature."

> **// I'm still undecided as to what actually happened that night. But what I do know, it was NOT the result of flares. //**
>
> ATS MEMBER COMMENT

At the time of this writing there was still no definitive answer as to what caused the red lights over Phoenix in 2008. As with so much of the material in the UFO field, with no hard evidence, one simply chose which explanation to believe.

In the late 1980s and early 1990s, when huge flying triangles were being sighted over Belgium, the Belgium government finally announced that they were secret government test craft. The commotion died away. Many UFO researchers have asked that if the Phoenix objects were simply flares, why not produce the burned-out flare cylinders or definitive tape of their descent. If the lights were from some secret government test craft, why was it flown through the most populated areas of Arizona? And why didn't the U.S. government simply end the speculation by admitting it was a test craft? Why put out the flares story, which is in severe contrast to videos taken of the event?

// I'm one of the people who are convinced that they were only flares, at least the second major sighting. **//**

While it may never be positively determined what appeared over Phoenix in 1997 and 2008, many residents believe they witnessed something other than flares, something very strange and unusual, perhaps even unearthly.

▶ WERE THE MOON
LANDINGS FAKED?

▽ WHO

▶ The National Aeronautics and Space Administration (NASA)

▽ WHAT

▶ The allegation that NASA, along with elements within the U.S. government, faked the Apollo Moon landings.

▽ WHEN

▶ 1969 to 1972

▽ WHERE

▶ Such claims proliferate on the Internet and have been the subject of several books, television programs, and films.

▽ WHY

▶ If the Moon landings were faked, it was done at the height of the Cold War to demonstrate that the U.S. had significantly surpassed the space program of the former Soviet Union thus proving the United States was the premier nation in space exploration.

additional evidence and commentary:
www.abovetopsecret.com/book/moonlandings

At 4:17 p.m. EST on July 20, 1969, Apollo 11 landed on the surface of our nearest neighbor, the Moon, and man first walked upon another world. Neil Armstrong, the first person to set foot on the Moon, said as he descended the ladder of Apollo 11's lunar module: "One small step for man; one giant leap for mankind."

Five more manned missions to the Moon took place, the last one on December 7, 1972. All together, 24 astronauts traveled to the Moon, with twelve walking on its surface, and three making the trip twice.

The Moon landings were the crowning achievement of a goal that had been set by John F. Kennedy at the height of his presidency, and one largely prompted by the fact that the Soviet Union had trumped the United States by being the first nation to successfully launch a satellite (Sputnik) and a man (Yuri Gagarin) into near-Earth orbit.

As Kennedy stated to NASA Director James E. Webb in 1963, "Everything we do really ought to be tied in to getting on the Moon ahead of the Russians; otherwise we shouldn't be spending that kind of money, because I'm not interested in space. The only justification is because we hope to demonstrate that instead of being behind by a couple of years, by God, we passed them."

The Moon landings were the crowning achievement of the United States if not for all humankind—or were they?

Over the years, there has been a growing controversy concerning whether the historic Moon landings of 1969 to 1972 were all they appeared to be. According to a number of authors, researchers, and investigators—as well as a significant percentage of the American population—the answer is no.

There is a strong undercurrent of belief on the part of many that the Apollo

Moon landings were nothing more than an ingenious and audacious sham—a series of Hollywood-style special effects filmed in secret locations and designed to convince people of the superiority of American technology and ingenuity.

A variation on this theme suggests that the Moon landings occurred in the fashion that we are led to believe but that the photographs and film footage taken on the surface of the Moon were destroyed by intense radiation in outer space. As a result, NASA was forced to recreate footage on Earth to satisfy the natural demand for photographic proof that man walked on the Moon. Of course, such beliefs beg the question: If the government lied about one thing, how can we trust them on anything?

Do such claims have any merit or can the whole controversy be dismissed as mere theories similar to those of the Flat Earth Society?

Early on there was widespread support for the notion that the human race was victim to a huge and elaborate confidence trick. Only twelve months after the first Moon landing was announced, Knight Ridder polled 1,721 Americans and found that no less than 30 percent of them were "suspicious of NASA's trips to the Moon."

> **//**I do not believe the moon landings were faked. Many of the photos were. Much of the information passed to the public was. But not the moon landings themselves. **//**

A 1999 Gallup poll revealed that, thirty years after Apollo 11, an astonishing six percent of the entire American population was convinced that the Moon landings had been faked. A more recent poll—undertaken by Dittmar Associates in 2006—found that 27 percent of all college-educated students between the ages of 18 and 26 "expressed some doubt" that NASA went to the Moon, with a full 10 percent indicating that it was "highly unlikely" that a Moon landing had ever taken place.

Predictably, Moon landing skeptics have been ridiculed and dismissed by both the majority of the public as well as government officials. James Oberg, NBC's "space consultant" who worked on the Space Shuttle program, stated: "It's not just a few crackpots and their new books and Internet conspiracy sites. There are entire subcultures within the U.S. and substantial cultures around the world that strongly believe the landing was faked."

But, how and why did such beliefs begin?

Although, as the Knight Ridder poll revealed, there were deep suspicions on the part of the public as early as 1970 that NASA had faked the Moon landings, it was not until 1974 that the theory began to really take hold.

In that year Bill Kaysing self-published a book entitled *We Never Went to the Moon*. Kaysing was a former employee of Rocketdyne, a division of North American Aviation, later Rockwell International, where NASA's Saturn V rocket engines were built. Kaysing served as the company's head of technical publications.

Kaysing charged that in the years leading up to the Moon landings, and indeed throughout the period when the landing are said to have occurred, NASA completely lacked the technological expertise to undertake such complex missions.

He noted the apparent absence of stars in the photographs of the Moon brought back by the astronauts; he commented on the fact that the high levels of radiation in space should have destroyed the film footage and photographs taken by the various Apollo crews before their return to Earth; and asserted that in one particular piece of film, the American flag planted on the surface of the Moon appeared to move, as if blown by the wind. In a near-vacuum environment, such as on the Moon, there should be no wind.

As a result of Kaysing's research and book, the controversy began to gather momentum. Such conspiracy theories gained further impetus in the wake of Warner Brothers' 1978 conspiracy thriller *Capricorn One*. Starring James Brolin, *Law and Order's* Sam Waterston and none other than O.J. Simpson, the movie tells the story of how NASA is forced to fake its first manned mission to Mars after problems are found in the life-support system of the spacecraft. As a result, the astronauts are secretly flown to an isolated aircraft hangar in a remote desert location that has been turned into a recreation of the Martian surface where they are forced to take part in an ingenious hoax. The movie ends with the conspiracy being blown wide open by Brolin's character and that of Elliot Gould's investigative reporter character, Robert Caulfield.

In recent years, the theories that man has never visited the Moon—or that, at the very least, the film footage and photographs shown to the public are not all that they appear to be—has continued to grow. William Brian, author of the book *Moongate: Suppressed Findings of the U.S. Space Program*, believes that NASA did reach the Moon, but he has problems with some of the film footage and concludes that NASA has distorted the truth about the real nature of the Moon and its environment. He says, "… the Moon's surface gravity is 64 percent of the Earth's surface gravity, not the one-sixth value predicted by Newton's Law of Universal Gravitation."

Brian added: "… the film speed was adjusted to slow down the action to give the impression that the astronauts were lighter than they actually were. With the slow-motion effects, objects would appear to fall more slowly and the public would be convinced of the Moon's weak gravity."

He claimed the Apollo astronauts utilized "a secret zero gravity device" on their flight that was obtained from the study of a "captured extraterrestrial space-ship." In Brian's scenario, NASA was forced to bury this fact—as well as the discovery that the Moon possesses an atmosphere.

David Percy, a member of the Royal Photographic Society and an expert in audio-visual technologies, is the co-author, with Mary Bennett, of *Dark Moon: Apollo and the Whistleblowers*. It is Percy's belief that NASA perpetrated a gigantic hoax on the people of Earth. He believes some errors that can be seen in the photographs, allegedly taken on the Moon, are so patently obvious that they have to be the deliberate work of NASA insiders who were trying to blow the whistle on the fakery.

Marcus Allen, publisher of the British edition of Australia's *Nexus* conspiracy journal is also doubtful of the idea that man visited the Moon. He noted: "Getting to the Moon really isn't much of a problem—the Russians did that in 1959—the big problem is getting people there."

In *Lights on the Moon*, author Philippe Lheureux offers the intriguing theory that the crews on the Apollo missions uncovered scientific data that even to this day has to be protected; and subsequently, NASA decided to present bogus, but less controversial, footage to the world.

It seemed everyone wanted in on the act. Charles K. Johnson, the president of the International Flat Earth Research Society, claimed the Moon landings were "faked in Hollywood studios," but were done so to try and convince people that the world was round, when, according to his beliefs, it is flat. Such theories only confuse the issue.

Researcher and filmmaker Bart Sibrel said, "In my research at NASA I uncovered, deep in the archives, one mislabeled reel from the Apollo 11, first mission, to the Moon. What is on the reel and on the label are completely different. I suspect an editor put the wrong label on the tape 33 years ago and no reporter ever had the motive to be as thorough as I. It contains an hour of rare, unedited, color television footage that is dated by NASA's own atomic clock three days into the flight. Identified on camera are Neil Armstrong, Edwin 'Buzz' Aldrin, and Michael Collins. They are doing multiple takes of a single shot of the mission, from which only about ten seconds was ever broadcast. Because I have uncovered the original unedited version, mistakenly not destroyed, the photography proves to be a clever forgery. Really! It means they did not walk on the Moon!"

// I fully believe that at least the first landing was a hoax but I believe we eventually got there. The reason for the first one being hoaxed, in my opinion, is that we HAD to beat the Russians there. It was a matter of national pride and to fulfill President Kennedy's promise to get there before the end of the decade. //

Critics of Sibrel, who made the documentary *A Funny Thing Happened on the Way to the Moon* in 2001, point out that: "The evidence offered in the reel of footage 'found' by Bart Sibrel is limited and it is important to note that the extracts used have themselves been edited to remove portions that contradict and debunk his theory that the shots of a distant Earth seen by people on TV were faked. This portion of the film is never shown by hoax proponents. The NASA atomic clock referred to is not the same clock as that used during the Apollo missions."

Others who have addressed the theory that NASA conned the world on July 20, 1969 include Charles T. Hawkins, author of *How America Faked the Moon Landings*; film director Aaron Ranen in his production *Did We Go?*; Joe Rogan, comedian and host of the television show *Fear Factor*; and Dr. David Groves.

Groves works for Quantech Image Processing and studied a number of the NASA photographs. He maintains that from studying the NASA imagery, he has been able to pinpoint where artificial lighting has been employed to illuminate the scenes. Of course, the only available light on the Moon should come from the Sun. NASA has insisted that no artificial lighting was taken on the Apollo missions.

Yet Groves has stated that he has been able to determine a light source approximately 24 to 36 centimeters to the right of the camera. If artificial lighting was present, this clearly presents a problem for NASA and its assertions.

NASA had an answer for this apparent anomaly—the Moon's dust both focuses and reflects light in a fashion very similar to that which can be seen in the coating of street signs or dew drops on wet grass, officials explained, so what appears to be a large spotlight close to the camera is nothing of the sort.

But what are we to make of the major claims those proponents of the "We never went to the Moon" scenario present?

//I don't believe people haven't landed on the moon. DUH? I do however believe we are misinformed as a public. The pictures for example have been 'tampered' with as any photo-pro could tell you. Either to make them look better, or for other reasons. Therein lies the gray area to this matter. And, why would we all of a sudden just stop going to the moon? Think about that one? Just food for thought. **//**

Much has been made of the fact that in numerous Moon photographs, the stars are noticeably absent. Supporters of the hoax theory argue that NASA would have been unable to accurately determine the exact position of the stars—and planets—overhead when faking the various films and photographs, so they elected to omit them altogether.

In response this particular issue, NASA maintains that the Sun was shining on the surface of the Moon at the time the relevant footage and photographs were obtained and therefore all the cameras were set for daylight exposure, a setting that completely washed out the stars in the black sky above.

That the astronauts seemingly left almost perfect footprints on the lunar surface is also troublesome. Critics of the official account argue that the lack of moisture and lack of strong gravity should have made any such footprints both light and indistinct. NASA countered this argument by explaining that lunar dust is a silicate, which has special properties in a vacuum allowing it to stick together. Such dust, described as being like "talcum powder or wet sand," would allow for near-perfect footprints.

But one reasonable question followed another. Why did none of the Apollo lunar modules create a blast-crater, or scatter massive amounts of dust when they landed on the Moon? The available film footage and photographs show no widespread disturbances. Skeptics of the Moon landings argued that the lack of any such ground disturbance is evidence that the lunar modules were merely lowered onto a carefully prepared carpet of dust via crane, or lifting-device, in a studio or hangar on Earth.

To counter this argument, NASA officials maintain that as the lunar modules came in for landing, they were traveling both horizontally as well as vertically. Therefore, they were not focused on one particular area of the surface until the very last moment. They also stated that as the lunar modules approached the Moon's surface they were traveling extremely slowly, thus the descent engine had only to support the craft's own weight. They added that the nearly spent propellant fuel coupled with the Moon's lower gravity played a significant role in the lack of a landing crater.

NASA officials also noted that in a vacuum, jet exhaust spreads much wider and is far less focused than in a dense atmosphere, another reason why there was a lack of a crater or widespread disturbance beneath the lunar modules. The Apollo astronauts' testimony that the lunar soil was highly compacted offered support to NASA's explanation for the lack of surface damage.

But then there is the issue of the waving flag. When the Apollo 11 astronauts proudly planted the American flag on the Moon on June 20, 1969, it appeared to move, as if caught in a gust of wind. In a vacuum, of course, this would be utterly impossible. Conspiracy theorists maintain this film of this historic event had to have been shot in an Earth-based studio.

It should be noted, however, that the flag only moves a split second after the astronauts try to position it. On the journey to the Moon, the flag was tightly folded and when it was unwrapped, it took on a "rippled" effect that appeared to some as blowing in the wind. The flag was shown for more than 30 minutes during the televised portion of the landing and at no time did it seem to move. But NASA did little to defuse this issue when in subsequent NASA Moon missions the flags were all encased in a metal frame.

Then it was learned that Apollo 11's telemetry data tapes from the historic flight turned up missing—some say both conveniently and suspiciously—offering further fodder for the conspiracy crowd. That this historic material was indeed missing was confirmed by Dr. David Williams, NASA archivist at the Goddard Space Flight Center, as well as Apollo 11 Flight Director Gene Kranz.

And what of the assertion that deadly space radiation would have either killed the astronauts or at least irradiated them as well as destroying any and all of the photographs and film? It appears obvious that the astronauts were exposed to higher-than-normal levels of radiation while flying to and from the Moon and while walking on its surface. However, dosimeters carried by the crews on each and every flight recorded readings that were comparable with that of a single chest X-ray. NASA asserts that the metal hull of the ship, as well as the containers in which the film was held, protected both crew and cargo.

But then NASA officials have argued that the Van Allen Radiation Belt between the Earth and the Moon extends only about 12,000 miles in depth while Dr. James Van Allen, the belt's namesake, has stated that this area of intense radiation actually extends for more than 64,000 miles. Like all aircraft, weight is an essential consideration in space flight. None of the Apollo mission ships were wholly steel or equipped with lead sheathing. For NASA to argue that their lightweight vehicles would penetrate the Van Allen Belt safely is akin to arguing that if a person runs very fast through a rain storm, they won't get wet.

It is the astronauts themselves who provided evidence that they were exposed to higher than normal levels of radiation. A large number of Apollo astronauts have been diagnosed with early-stage cataracts, which have been shown to be a hazard from high-altitude cosmic ray exposure.

Perhaps the strongest evidence that NASA astronauts did successfully reach the Moon is the 382 kilograms of Moon rocks that were brought back to Earth following the various missions. There is no doubt that the rocks in question did not originate on the Earth. They show evidence of having been subjected to impact events in an air-free environment and one was found to be about 700 million years older than any rock ever found on Earth.

The rock brought back by NASA is also identical to one obtained by the Russians on a later unmanned flight to the Moon. This prompted speculation that earlier unmanned Moon missions gathered the Moon rocks.

// How about that cool dune buggy rover? Where was that stashed? It's huge! And why does the sand shooting out from the tires look exactly like sand on the desert shooting off of car tires. Wouldn't low gravity and lack of atmosphere shoot that stuff like 100 yards into the air? The computing power was less than my wristwatch for crying out loud! Nobody is going to convince me that they flew thousands and thousands of miles, through the Van Allen Belt, entered into the moon's gravitational field and controlled a landing all using a Texas Instruments calculator. //

But significantly, parties outside of the space agency, with no vested interest in reinforcing a hoax, have independently analyzed NASA's Moon material. "Moon rocks are absolutely unique," stated Dr. David McKay, chief scientist for Planetary Science and Exploration at NASA's Johnson Space Center (JSC). McKay is a member of the group that oversees the Lunar Sample Laboratory Facility at JSC where most of the Moon rocks are stored. "They differ from Earth rocks in many respects," he added. "For example," explained Dr. Marc Norman, a lunar geologist at the University of Tasmania, "lunar samples have almost no water trapped in their crystal structure, and common substances such as clay minerals that are ubiquitous on Earth are totally absent in Moon rocks."

If NASA were engaged in wholesale trickery and deceit, one of the biggest questions would be "Who possessed the skills to make the faked footage?" Proponents of the hoax theory point to renowned filmmaker Stanley Kubrick, director of *2001: A Space Odyssey*. Despite the fact that no evidence beyond anonymous hearsay has been offered, an oft-repeated story states that in early 1968, when 2001 was in post-production, NASA officials secretly approached Kubrick to produce films of the first Moon landings. In this version of events, the launches of the Apollo rockets and subsequent splashdowns were real, but the space capsules secretly remained in Earth orbit, rather than journeying on to the Moon.

That Kubrick hired former NASA employees—and major aerospace company employees—Harry Lange and Frederick Ordway to work on *2001*, only added fuel to the fire, as did the 2002 release of a spoof documentary entitled *Dark Side of the Moon*.

> **//**All other expeditions—North Pole, South Pole, Everest, and other far reaches of the globe—are required to have INDEPENDENT VERIFICATION of the event before it is deemed worthy and right to be entered into the record books. Despite many 'landings' on the moon by alleged astronauts, and unmanned vehicles from the U.S. and other countries, guess what one event has never been independently verified? That's right, the Apollo moon landings have NOT been subjected to verification. **//**

Despite the fact that *Dark Side of the Moon* is still lauded in some quarters as the real thing, this production also has been called into question. Aside from those whose existence and identity is proven, such as Kubrick's widow, Christiane, and Dr. Henry Kissinger (both of whose words are reportedly taken out of context), many of the other "interviewees" were simply actors hired to portray completely non-existent characters.

Indeed, one of the program's recurring themes was that those same fictionalized interviewees were given the names of characters that appeared in Kubrick's movies. For example, a man named Dave Bowman appears in *Dark Side of the Moon*. This happened to be the name of one of the astronauts in Kubrick's *2001*. Similarly, another source that appears in *Dark Side of the Moon* is Jack Torrance. This is also the name of the lead character in Stephen King's novel *The Shining*—the 1980 movie version that was directed by Kubrick.

Of course, the whole controversy could be firmly settled once and for all if an Earth-based telescope could focus on the areas of the Moon where NASA maintains its lunar modules landed—and still remain to this day—and photograph them.

Unfortunately, to date, that has not happened, so the controversy rages on.

The largest telescope on Earth can view only approximately 10 meters across. Earth telescopes yet to have even the slightest chance of seeing the flag allegedly planted by the Apollo 11 astronauts. Even the Hubble Space Telescope is incapable of seeing objects on the surface of the Moon that are smaller than 86 meters across—which is far bigger than NASA's lunar modules. It is hoped that NASA's Lunar Reconnaissance Orbiter may be able to resolve this controversy following its planned launch in October 2008.

There have been other occasions when the official world and the scientific community have tried to lay the controversy to rest. In 2002, for example, NASA commissioned James Oberg to write a firm rebuttal of the hoax claims—and came up with a fee of $15,000 in the process. Curiously, however, in that same year NASA withdrew the commission, asserting that the publication of a book on the subject would only dignify the accusations of those who cried "Hoax!"

Two years later, in 2004, Drs. Martin Hendry and Ken Skeldon of Scotland's Glasgow University were awarded a grant by the British-based Particle Physics and Astronomy Research Council to study what were described as "Moon Hoax" proposals. In November of that year they delivered a lecture at the Glasgow Planetarium where the "Top 10" pieces of evidence for a hoax offered by the conspiracy theorists were addressed one-by-one, explained, and summarily dismissed as being groundless.

And while NASA continues to proclaim that it did send astronauts to the Moon—and those who believe that the space agency has been pulling the wool over everyone's eyes for nearly forty years loudly proclaim otherwise—it seems safe to assume that the debate will not die anytime soon. Too many questions remain.

An *Above Top Secret* member offered a simple outlet for Moon landing skeptics, in asking why there was not a NASA forum to ask questions and receive answers on this topic.

But NASA, as one wag put it, must mean "Never A Straight Answer." For example, one ATS member offered this intriguing account of a meeting with the last astronaut on the Moon, Eugene Cernan. He wrote: "I was working as a fishing guide at the time and Mr. Cernan was a client of mine on my boat. A very nice man indeed. However he deflected and/or avoided just about every question anyone asked him related to the Moon landing. My personal opinion is not that he was hiding information, but rather, that he actually didn't know. Even when he was asked if the landing was a hoax, he giggled, but would not say yes or no. His only response was to show pictures he had of the landing."

After admitting that he believed the government has the technology to "wipe" a mind as portrayed in the *Men in Black* films, this member added, "I guess my largest concern is if they [the government] are either just lazy and are using fake landings as disinformation to deflect our attention from what is really happening? Or is it more complicated than that and are there other issues at hand here? Some claim we (humans) have been banned from return trips and landings to the Moon, and that there is an alien presence there ..."

After reviewing all of the claims, counter-claims and evidence both pro and con, the evidence appears to be in NASA's favor—man did set foot on the Moon on six occasions between 1969 and 1972. It would also appear that valid explanations exist for most of the apparent anomalies cited by researchers, such as the waving flag, the lack of stars above the Moon, and the artificial lighting that some maintain can be seen in Apollo photographs.

It could be argued that the NASA-hoaxed-the-Moon-landings theory is a by-product of the innate—and sometimes acutely justified—distrust that has developed due to the distortions and lies found in government scandals such as Watergate, Iran-Contra, 9/11, and the Weapons of Mass Destruction fiasco in Iraq.

But as revealed in comments posted at *Above Top Secret*, the official story of the NASA Moon landings will continue to provoke controversy, debate, and skepticism for some time to come.

// Look at the press conference after the mission. Three very strange acting guys who appear to be embarrassed by the whole thing, and not proud guys returning from the greatest expedition of all time. //

Despite the fact that NASA appears to hold the upper hand in this controversy, the final word does not go to the space agency. Rather, it may go to none other than former President Bill Clinton, who in his 2004 autobiography, *My Life*, wrote: "… Just a month before, Apollo 11 astronauts Buzz Aldrin and Neil Armstrong had … walked on the Moon, beating by five months President Kennedy's goal of putting a man on the Moon before the decade was out. The old carpenter asked me if I really believed it happened. I said sure, I saw it live on television. He disagreed; he said that he didn't believe it for a minute, that 'them television fellers' could make things look real that weren't. Back then, I thought he was a crank. During my eight years in Washington, I saw some things on TV that made me wonder if he wasn't ahead of his time."

Was this just an innocent aside or was former President Bill Clinton trying to tell us something?

▸ WHO PARKED THE MOON?

▽ WHO

▶ Who is the real and unanswered question.

▽ WHAT

▶ The near perfect circular and stationary orbit of the Moon is impossible as a natural occurrence.

▽ WHEN

▶ Since the Moon has been recorded—and worshipped—throughout human history, its inception dates back into pre-history.

▽ WHERE

▶ Earth's only satellite, the Moon orbits from west to east approximately 239,900 miles out in space.

▽ WHY

▶ Another unanswerable question

additional evidence and commentary:
www.abovetopsecret.com/book/moonorigin

Despite six announced visits by U.S. astronauts between 1969 and 1972, the Moon remains a riddle to scientists in many regards. The solutions to these riddles could indicate an alien aspect of our familiar Moon.

Called "the Rosetta Stone of the planets" by Dr. Robert Jastrow, the first chairman of NASA's Lunar Exploration Committee, scientists had hoped by studying the composition of the Moon, to resolve some of the mysteries of how our planet and solar system came into existence.

However, six Moon landings later, science writer Earl Ubell declared, "... the lunar Rosetta Stone remains a mystery. The Moon is more complicated than anyone expected; it is not simply a kind of billiard ball frozen in space and time, as many scientists had believed. Few of the fundamental questions have been answered, but the Apollo rocks and recordings have spawned a score of mysteries, a few truly breath-stopping."

Among these "breath-stopping" mysteries or anomalies as scientists prefer to call them is the fact that the Moon is far older than previously imagined, perhaps even much older than the Earth and Sun. By examining tracks burned into Moon rocks by cosmic rays, scientists have dated them as billions of years old. Some have been dated back 4.5 billion years, far older than the Earth and nearly as old as the solar system.

The Moon has at least three distinct layers of rocks. Contrary to the idea that heavier objects sink, the heavier rocks are found on the surface. And there is a definite disparity in the distribution of minerals. Ubell asked, "If the Earth and Moon were created at the same time, near each other, why has one body got all the iron [the Earth] and the other [the Moon] not much?" asked Ubell. "The differences suggest that Earth and Moon came into being far from each other, an idea that stumbles over the inability of astrophysicists to explain how exactly the Moon became a satellite of the Earth."

The Moon is extremely dry and does not appear to have ever had water in any substantial amounts. None of the Moon rocks, regardless of where they were found, contained free water or even water molecules bound into the minerals. Yet Apollo 16 astronauts found Moon rocks that contained bits of rusted iron. Since oxidation requires oxygen and free hydrogen, this rust indicates there must be water somewhere on the Moon.

> **//** I hate to say it, but if ANY moons were hollow to a significant amount (I am not going to say that there are not some hollow chambers/caves/cavities of some description in these bodies however, but no statistically significant fraction of a body) was indeed hollow, it would adversely affect the known observed densities (derived from orbital calculations) of these bodies. These densities have already been calculated, and none of them are unjustifiably low. Also, we are missing an internal support structure in the event that any significant volume of such a body was missing. Therefore, these bodies would not be able to maintain their structural integrity given the tidal forces imposed by orbiting a larger planet. **//**

Furthermore, instruments left behind by Apollo missions sent a signal to Earth on March 7, 1971, indicating a "wind" of water had crossed the Moon's surface. Since any water on the airless Moon surface vaporizes and behaves like the wind on Earth, the question became where did this water originate? The vapor cloud eruptions lasted 14 hours and covered an area of some 100 square miles, prompting Rice University physicists Dr. John Freeman, Jr. and Dr. H. Ken Hills to pronounce the event one of "the most exciting discoveries yet" indicating water within the Moon. The two physicists claimed the water vapor came from deep inside the Moon, apparently released during a moonquake.

NASA officials offered a more mundane, and questionable, explanation. They speculated that two tanks on Apollo descent stages containing between 60 and 100 pounds of water became stressed and ruptured, releasing their contents. Freeman and Hills declined to accept this explanation, pointing out that the two tanks—from Apollo 12 and 14—were some 180 kilometers apart yet the water vapor was detected with the same flux at both sites although the instruments faced in opposite directions. Skeptics also have understandably questioned the odds of two separate tanks breaking simultaneously and how such a small quantity of water could produce 100 square miles of vapor.

Moon rocks were found to be magnetized—not strong enough to pick up a paper clip, but magnetic nevertheless. However, there is no magnetic field on the Moon itself. So where did the magnetism come from?

The presence of maria, or large seas of smooth solidified molten rock, also presented a mystery. These maria indicate nothing less than a vast outpouring of lava at some distant time. It has now been confirmed that some of the Moon's craters are of internal origin. Yet there is no indication that the Moon has ever been hot enough to produce volcanic eruptions. Another puzzle is that almost all—four-fifths—of the maria are located on the Moon's Earthside hemisphere. Few maria mark the far side of the Moon, often erroneously referred to as the "dark side." Yet the far side contains many more craters and mountainous areas.

In comparison to the rest of the Moon, the maria are relatively free of craters suggesting that craters were covered by lava flow. Adding to this mystery are the mascons—large dense circular masses lying 20 to 40 miles below the center of the Moon's maria. The mascons were discovered because their denseness distorted the orbits of our spacecraft flying over or near them. One scientist proposed that the mascons are heavy iron meteorites that plunged deep into the Moon while it was in a soft, formable stage. This theory has been discounted since meteorites strike with such high velocities, they would vaporize on contact.

Another mundane explanation is that the mascons are nothing more than lava-filled caverns, but skeptics say there isn't enough lava present to accomplish this. It would seem these mascons are huge disk-shaped objects possibly of artificial construction. It is unlikely that large circular disks located directly under the center of the maria like a giant bulls-eye happened by accident or coincidence.

Between 1969 and 1977, Apollo mission seismographic equipment registered up to 3,000 "moonquakes" each year of operation. Most of the vibrations were quite small and were caused by meteorite strikes or falling booster rockets. But many other quakes were detected deep inside the Moon. This internal creaking is believed to be caused by the gravitational pull of our planet as most moonquakes occur when the Moon is closest to the Earth.

An event occurred in 1958 in the Moon's Alphonsus crater, which shook the idea that all internal moonquake activity was simply settling rocks. In November of that year, Soviet astronomer Nikolay A. Kozyrev of the Crimean Astrophysical Observatory startled the scientific world by photographing the first recorded gaseous eruption on the Moon near the crater's peak. Kozyrev attributed this to escaping fluorescent gases. He also detected a reddish glow characteristic of carbon compounds, which "seemed to move and disappeared after an hour."

Some scientists refused to accept Kozyrev's findings until astronomers at the Lowell Observatory also saw reddish glows on the crests of ridges in the Aristarchus region in 1963. Days later, colored lights on the Moon lasting more than an hour were reported at two separate observatories.

Something was going on inside the volcanically dead Moon. And whatever it is, it occurs the same way at the same time. As the Moon moves closer to the Earth, seismic signals from different stations on the lunar surface detect identical vibrations. It is difficult to accept this movement as a natural phenomenon. For example, a broken artificial hull plate could shift exactly the same way each time the Moon passed near the Earth.

There is evidence to indicate the Moon may be hollow. Studies of Moon rocks indicate that the Moon's interior differs from the Earth's mantle in ways suggesting a very small, or even nonexistent, core. As far back as 1962, NASA scientist Dr. Gordon MacDonald stated, "If the astronomical data are reduced, it is found that the data require that the interior of the Moon be less dense than the outer parts. Indeed, it would seem that the Moon is more like a hollow than a homogeneous sphere."

Apollo 14 astronaut Dr. Edgar Mitchell, while scoffing at the possibility of a hollow moon, nevertheless admitted that since heavier materials were on the surface, it is quite possible that giant caverns exist within the Moon. MIT's Dr. Sean C. Solomon wrote, "The Lunar Orbiter experiments vastly improved our knowledge of the Moon's gravitational field ... indicating the frightening possibility that the Moon might be hollow."

Why frightening? The significance was stated by astronomer Carl Sagan way back in his 1966 work *Intelligent Life in the Universe*, "A natural satellite cannot be a hollow object."

// One problem I see with that theory is that numerous species of ancient (and I mean like the oldest) creatures on this planet rely on the tides (i.e. they live in tide pools) to live. Since they have been around for millions of years, that means the Moon has at least been here for the same time. If there are aliens in the Moon, they must've lost their map ... or they need a jump start for their Mooncraft, cuz they've been parked for some time. //

The most startling evidence that the Moon could be hollow came on November 20, 1969, when the Apollo 12 crew, after returning to their command ship, sent the lunar module (LM) ascent stage crashing back onto the Moon creating an artificial moonquake. The LM struck the surface about 40 miles from the Apollo 12 landing site where ultra-sensitive seismic equipment recorded something both unexpected and astounding—the Moon reverberated like a bell for more than an hour. The vibration wave took almost eight minutes to reach a peak, and then decreased in intensity. At a news conference that day, one of the co-directors of the seismic experiment, Maurice Ewing, told reporters that scientists were at a loss to explain the ringing. "As for the meaning of it, I'd rather not make an interpretation right now. But it is as though someone had struck a bell, say, in the belfry of a church a single blow and found that the reverberation from it continued for 30 minutes."

It was later established that small vibrations had continued on the Moon for more than an hour. The phenomenon was repeated when the Apollo 13's third stage was sent crashing onto the Moon by radio command, striking with the equivalent of 11 tons of TNT. According to NASA, this time the Moon "reacted like a gong." Although seismic equipment was more than 108 miles from the crash site, recordings showed reverberations lasted for three hours and 20 minutes and traveled to a depth of 22 to 25 miles.

Subsequent studies of man-made crashes on the Moon yielded similar results. After one impact the Moon reverberated for four hours. This ringing coupled with the density problem on the Moon reinforces the idea of a hollow moon. Scientists hoped to record the impact of a meteor large enough to send shock waves to the Moon's core and back and settle the issue. That opportunity came on May 13, 1972, when a large meteor stuck the Moon with the equivalent force of 200 tons of TNT. After sending shock waves deep into the interior of the Moon, scientists were baffled to find that none returned, confirming that there is something unusual about the Moon's core, or lack thereof.

//...[D]oes a spaceship really have to be able to go somewhere? I mean does everything need to have the meaning we think it should have? //

ATS MEMBER COMMENT

Dr. Farouk El Baz was quoted as saying, "There are many undiscovered caverns suspected to exist beneath the surface of the Moon. Several experiments have been flown to the Moon to see if there actually were such caverns." The results of these experiments have not been made public.

It seems apparent that the Moon has a tough, hard outer shell and a light or nonexistent interior. The Moon's shell contains dense minerals such as titanium, used on Earth in the construction of aircraft and space vehicles.

Many people still recall watching our astronauts on TV as they vainly tried to drill through the crust of a Moon maria. Their specially designed drills could only penetrate a few inches. The puzzle of the Moon's hard surface was compounded by the discovery of what appeared to be processed metals.

Experts were surprised to find lunar rocks bearing brass, mica and amphibole in addition to the near-pure titanium. Uranium 236 and Neptunium 237—elements not previously found in nature—were discovered in Moon rocks, according to the Argone National Laboratory. While still trying to explain the presence of these materials, scientists were further startled to learn of rust-proof iron particles in a soil sample from the Sea of Crisis. In 1976, the Associated Press reported that the Soviets had announced the discovery of iron particles that "do not rust" in samples brought back by an unmanned Moon mission in 1970. Iron that does not rust is unknown in nature and well beyond present Earth technology.

Undoubtedly the greatest mystery concerning our Moon is how it came to be there in the first place. Prior to the Apollo missions, one serious theory as to the Moon's origin was that it broke off of the Earth eons ago. Although no one could positively locate where on Earth it originated, many speculated the loss of material explained the huge gouge in the Earth, which forms the Pacific Ocean. However, this idea was discarded when it was found that there is little similarity between the composition of our world and the Moon.

A more recent theory had the Moon created out of space debris left over from the creation of the Earth. This concept proved untenable in light of current gravitational theory, which indicates that one large object will accumulate all loose material, leaving none for the formation of another large body. It is now generally accepted that the Moon originated elsewhere and entered the Earth's gravitational field at some point in the distant past.

Here theories diverge—one stating that the Moon was originally a planet which collided with the Earth creating debris which combined forming the Moon while another states the Moon, while wandering through our solar system, was captured and pulled into orbit by Earth's gravity. Neither of these theories are especially compelling because of the lack of evidence that neither the Earth nor the Moon seem to have been physically disrupted by a past close encounter. There is no debris in space indicating a past collision and it does not appear that the Earth and the Moon developed during the same time period.

As for the "capture" theory, even scientist Isaac Asimov, well known for his works of fiction, has written, "It's too big to have been captured by the Earth. The chances of such a capture having been effected and the Moon then having taken up nearly circular orbit around our Earth are too small to make such an eventuality credible."

Asimov was right to consider the Moon's orbit—it is not only nearly a perfect circle, but stationary, one side always facing the Earth with only the slightest variation. As far as we know, it's the only natural satellite with such an orbit.

This circular orbit is especially odd considering that the Moon's center of mass lies more than a mile closer to the Earth than its geometric center. This fact alone should produce an unstable, wobbly orbit, much as a ball with its mass off center will not roll in a straight line. Additionally, almost all of the other satellites in our solar system orbit in the plane of their planet's equator. Not so the Moon, whose orbit lies strangely nearer the Earth's orbit around the Sun or inclined to the Earth's ecliptic by more than five degrees. Add to this the fact that the Moon's bulge—located on the side facing away from Earth—thus negating the idea that it was caused by the Earth's gravitational pull—makes for an off-balanced world.

It seems impossible that such an oddity could naturally fall into such a precise and circular orbit. It is a fascinating conundrum as articulated by science writer William Roy Shelton, who wrote, "It is important to remember that something had to put the Moon at or near its present circular pattern around the Earth. Just as an Apollo spacecraft circling the Earth every 90 minutes while 100 miles high has to have a velocity of roughly 18,000 miles per hour to stay in orbit, so something had to give the Moon the precisely required velocity for its weight and altitude ... The point—and it is one seldom noted in considering the origin of the Moon—is that it is extremely unlikely that any object would just stumble into the right combination of factors required to stay in orbit. 'Something' had to put the Moon at its altitude, on its course and at its speed. The question is: what was that 'something'?"

If the precise and stationary orbit of the Moon is seen as sheer coincidence, is it also coincidence that the Moon is at just the right distance from the Earth to completely cover the Sun during an eclipse? While the diameter of the Moon is a mere 2,160 miles against the Sun's gigantic 864,000 miles, it is nevertheless in just the proper position to block out all but the Sun's flaming corona when it moves between the Sun and the Earth. Asimov explained: "There is no astronomical reason why the Moon and the Sun should fit so well. It is the sheerest of coincidences, and only the Earth among all the planets is blessed in this fashion."

Is it merely coincidence? How does one explain this and many other Moon mysteries?

In July 1970, two Russian scientists, Mikhail Vasin and Alexander Shcherbakov, published an article in the Soviet journal *Sputnik* entitled "Is the Moon the Creation of Alien Intelligence?" They advanced the theory that the Moon is not a completely natural world, but a planetoid that was hollowed out eons ago in the far reaches of space by intelligent beings possessing a technology far superior to ours. Huge machines were used to melt rock and form large cavities within the Moon, spewing the molten refuse onto the surface. Protected by a hull-like inner shell plus a reconstructed outer shell of metallic rocky junk, this gigantic craft was steered through the cosmos and finally parked in orbit around the Earth.

//[One radio guest I heard] argued that the Moon was towed into its current orbit by a huge electromagnetic vehicle, and that vehicle can be seen in a photo taken of the moon crater Tsiolkovsky. He also believes that the Moon contains a breathable atmosphere, as evidenced by photos showing smoke or vapor coming from the surface. **//**

In their article Vasin and Shcherbakov wrote, "Abandoning the traditional paths of 'common sense,' we have plunged into what may at first sight seem to be unbridled and irresponsible fantasy. But the more minutely we go into all the information gathered by man about the Moon, the more we are convinced that there is not a single fact to rule out our supposition. Not only that, but many things so far considered to be lunar enigmas are explainable in the light of this new hypothesis."

Outrageous as the spaceship moon theory might first appear, consider how this model reconciles all of the mysteries of the Moon. It would explain why the Moon gives evidence of being much older than the Earth and perhaps even our solar system and why there are three distinct layers within the Moon, with the densest materials in the outside layer, exactly as one would expect of the "hull" of a spacecraft. It could also explain why no sign of water has been found on the Moon's surface, yet there is evidence it exists deep inside. This theory also would explain the strange maria and mascons, perhaps the remnants of the machinery used to hollow out the Moon. The idea of an artificial satellite could explain the odd, rhythmic "moonquakes" as artificial constructs reacting the same way during periods of stress from the Earth's pull. And artificial equipment beneath the Moon's surface might be the source of the gas clouds that have been observed.

Intelligent "terraforming" of the Moon could prove the solution to the argument between "hot moon" and "cold moon" scientists—they are both right! The Moon originally was a cold world, which was transformed into a spacecraft by artificially heating and expelling vast quantities of its interior. This theory also could explain the seeming contradictions over the question of a hollow moon. If the Moon originally was a solid world which was artificially hollowed out, there would be evidence of both phases—exactly what we have with current Moon knowledge.

//There was a great book that devoted a whole chapter to this theory that I read last summer. I forget the name but it was very well researched and the author had plenty of data to back up his claims. //

An artificially hollowed-out Moon would explain why the satellite rings like a bell for hours after struck and why specimens of tough, refractory metals such as titanium, chromium and circonium; "rust-proof" iron; Uranium 236 and Neptunium 237 have been found there.

In fact, the spaceship moon theory may come closer than any other in reconciling the questions over the origin and amazing orbit of the Moon.

But we are not supposed to consider this thesis. The circular logic of modern science regarding the origins of the Moon runs something like this: We know that extraterrestrials don't exist but we do know that the Moon exists and has been mentioned throughout human history. We humans did not create it or place it in Earth's orbit, so it must have been done by extraterrestrials. But since we know they don't exist, we will simply call it an anomaly and will not publicly say anything more about this.

▸ WHAT CRASHED AT ROSWELL?

▽ **WHO**

▸ Four conflicting pronouncements from the U.S. government
claim nothing unusual crashed at Roswell, New Mexico, while
several hundred persons now on the public record claim it was
a spacecraft piloted by non-humans.

▽ **WHAT**

▸ Initially, the Army Air Force announced it had captured a
"flying disc," but this quickly changed to a common weather
balloon, then over the years to a top secret "Mogul" monitoring balloon and finally, to errant crash dummies.

▽ **WHEN**

▸ Something came down from the sky north of Roswell during a
violent thunderstorm over the night of July 3–4, 1947.

▽ **WHERE**

▸ Most serious researchers now believe that there were two
crash sites—the first being a field of crash debris on a ranch
located about 75 miles northwest of Roswell and the second,
involving a damaged spherical object and perhaps even non-
human bodies, some miles to the east southeast of Socorro.

▽ **WHY**

▸ This controversy has been kept alive primarily due to the
wide disparity between official government pronouncements,
supported by little or no hard evidence, versus the immense
amount of witness testimony now available. All sides agree
that the government, which continues to deny it is keeping
anything secret, took physical evidence from the scene.

additional evidence and commentary:
www.abovetopsecret.com/book/roswell

//

Something came from the sky and crashed north of Roswell, New Mexico, on the night of July 3–4, 1947. On that everyone agrees.

But for more than 60 years, both the public and the experts have argued over what exactly came down. Despite being one of the most well documented UFO cases in history, there is no clear public consensus even now on what actually happened. Theories on what was found near Roswell range from extraterrestrial beings and their spaceship to a secret test craft flown by a Japanese crew to a secret spy balloon to a V-2 nose cone filled with dead test monkeys. The U.S. government's most recent pronouncement was that crash test dummies were mistaken for aliens.

All that can be said with certainty is that the military was not honest in its 1947 explanation that the object was a fallen weather balloon.

Many people don't know that the Roswell story actually began days before the crash. Radar installations had been picking up strange and erratic flying objects since June 29 and on Tuesday, July 1, 1947, radar installations in New Mexico began tracking an object zigzagging across the state, exhibiting unconventional speeds and maneuvering ability. On Wednesday July 2, a glowing object was sighted over Roswell. Washington officials flew in to investigate the object on Thursday, but they were too late.

Sometime between Thursday and Friday, July 4, the object was lost from radar scopes and presumed to have crashed.

The next day, after foreman William "Mac" Brazel found debris scattered over an area three-quarters of a mile long and several hundred feet wide on the J.B.

Foster ranch, located about 75 miles northwest of Roswell, the Roswell Volunteer Fire Department was called to the scene. There was so much debris that Brazel's sheep refused to walk through it.

On Sunday, July 6, Brazel drove to town and talked to the sheriff, who suggested that the military be notified. Soon, military units arrived and cordoned off the area. Later in the day, Brazel spoke with Air Intelligence officer Maj. Jesse A. Marcel and showed him a piece of the debris. Marcel returned to Roswell Army Air Field and notified higher authorities that something unusual had occurred. By Monday, July 7, a systematic examination by the military began, including an air search, of the debris field and a site farther east of the Foster ranch.

On Saturday, July 5, soil conservation engineer Grady L. "Barney" Barnett claimed that he and some archeologists who happened to be working north of Roswell discovered a saucer-shaped object with dead bodies around it. These men were soon chased off by the arrival of the military.

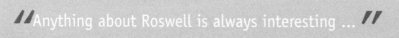

ATS MEMBER COMMENT

//Anything about Roswell is always interesting ... //

The two sightings—one with widely-spread but small pieces of debris and the other with a damaged object and bodies—led to serious speculation that they were parts of the same crash. New evidence even indicated that the object might have struck the ground a second time before coming to rest at the base of a bluff. Lightning or something else may have disrupted the craft causing an explosion which rained debris onto the field below while the object itself flew out of control, hitting the ground once before careening about two miles farther on where it crashed into a bluff. It is also possible the object here was what one government document described as a "damaged escape cylinder."

Returning to his base on Tuesday morning, Marcel stopped by his home and showed the unusual material to his wife and son. The military authorities must have felt the debris did not constitute a serious security problem, for later that morning the information officer of the 509th Bomb Group at Roswell Army Air Field—the only unit armed with atomic weapons at the time—was authorized to issue a press release announcing that the military had recovered a "flying disc." This stirred media interest all over the world. That afternoon, Maj. Marcel was ordered to fly with the debris to Carswell Air Force Base in Fort Worth, Texas.

Meanwhile in Washington, higher military authorities either learned of new developments—some researchers believe they had learned of the discovery of the main body of the UFO and alien bodies from military searchers—or had second thoughts about publicizing the debris. According to the Associated Press, Deputy Chief of the Army Air Forces Lieutenant General Hoyt S. Vandenberg moved to take control of the news out of Roswell.

On Tuesday evening, 8th Air Force commander, Brigadier General Roger Ramey, from his Carswell office told newsmen that Marcel and others had been mistaken and that the "flying disc" actually was nothing more than a weather balloon. Ramey's weather officer, Warrant Officer Irving Newton, was brought in and identified the debris he saw as belonging to a weather balloon. Photographers were allowed to take pictures of the "balloon" wreckage. Today, researchers claim the original debris was replaced by balloon wreckage in Ramey's office minutes before newsmen were ushered inside. James Bond Johnson, who photographed the debris for a Fort Worth newspaper, echoed this charge in later years.

One of the photos taken in Ramey's office depicted the general squatting over the balloon debris holding a telegram in his left hand. Incredibly, thanks to modern computer digital science, many of the words on this telegram can now be discerned. With phrases such as "victims of the wreck," "aviators in the disc," "new find," and "sent out PR [Public Relations] of weather balloons," it is difficult to believe that the message pertained to the recovery of a simple weather balloon.

After Ramey's death in 1963, his wife and a former B-29 crewman both told researchers that the general had admitted that the weather balloon story was "the biggest lie I ever had to tell" and that the Roswell crash involved a "spaceship."

However, following announcement of the balloon explanation, media interest quickly faded. In those security-conscious days following World War II, with fear of a Russian attack becoming a way of life, no one thought to question the official version. There the matter rested until 1978 when Jesse Marcel broke his silence, telling UFO researchers Stanton Friedman and Leonard Stringfield that the object he recovered was not from the Earth. Since then, the story of the Roswell crash has become a focal point of UFO research, spawning dozens of books, TV documentaries, films, and videos.

And the question of what crashed at Roswell remains. This question lies at the center of a clash of conflicting mindsets. One mindset accepts the official explanation that a secret military balloon crashed, somehow was mistaken for a spaceship by otherwise competent intelligence officers, and was hidden away for security's sake for almost a half century, even after the collapse of communism. Another, based on the testimony of several hundred individuals, accepts that a downed spacecraft containing alien bodies was recovered by the military and hidden from the public.

All agree that no spaceship wreckage or alien bodies have been made public. Therefore, the truth seeker is left with only human testimony and official pronouncements.

The basis for accepting the balloon version rests exclusively on government pronouncements that deny any unusual aspect to the Roswell case. A lengthy recitation of past official lies, disinformation and deceit should not be necessary to establish that such pronouncements cannot be accepted at face value. It is also easy to see that the U.S. military, which consumes the lion's share of the yearly national budget, would not want to admit that something was flying in American skies over which they had no control.

The spy balloon theory contends that the wreckage actually was a secret test of a 10-balloon cluster device under "Project Mogul," which was launched July 3 from Alamagordo, NM or a secret Navy "Skyhook" balloon. If it were either of these devices, competent intelligent officers should have been able to distinguish it from a flying saucer. Furthermore, if this theory is correct, a common weather balloon must have been substituted for the Mogul or Skyhook balloon for the news photographers in Fort Worth, substantiating claims that the Air Force deliberately deceived the news media and the public. And if they lied about one thing, it stands to reason they would lie about another.

Apologists for the government's version of the Roswell crash have strenuously argued that it was simply a Mogul balloon and produced a mass of materials relating to that program. A close reading, however, established that while the Mogul mission was classified "Top Secret"—it was intended to monitor the upper atmosphere for any indications that the Russians were testing atomic devices—its components were common-place sensing and balloon materials. About half the Mogul balloon launches were never recovered because no one cared enough to go look for them. Furthermore, it is very difficult to believe that U.S. military men would threaten the lives of American civilians, including children, over some balloon.

It has also been argued that the story of a crashed UFO with alien occupants was concocted to divert the attention of both the public and Soviet spies away from Top Secret experiments being conducted in New Mexico. This explanation falls apart when one considers that according to many separate reports the public was initially galvanized by the reports of a captured disc and foreign spies swarmed into the state to learn what had happened. If the object of the crashed disc story was to divert attention, it failed miserably.

As to the most recent government explanation of crash dummies mistaken for aliens, an official Air Force report on Roswell issued in 1997 and entitled "The Roswell Report: Case Closed," destroyed this thesis by noting that the first crash dummy test took place in 1954.

According to several witnesses, both debris and alien bodies were first taken to Roswell's military hospital then flown to Andrews Air Force Base in Washington and on to Wright Field at Dayton, Ohio. Many people today believe both craft and bodies eventually ended up in a secret government facility in Nevada—Area 51.

Contrasting the lack of documentation to support the official U.S. government pronouncements concerning Roswell, the most credible witnesses on the public record now include:

—**Mother Superior Mary Bernadette**, from the roof of Roswell's St. Mary's Hospital, saw a bright light go to earth north of town and recorded the time as between 11 and 11:30 p.m. in a logbook.

—**Sister Capistrano**, a Franciscan nun standing beside Mother Superior Bernadette at St. Mary's Hospital, also saw the object come down.

—**Corporal E. L. Pyles**, stationed south of Roswell Army Air Field, saw what he first thought was a large shooting star with an orange glow fall through the sky sometime between 11 p.m. and midnight.

—**C. Curry Holden**, one of several field archeologists who stumbled upon the crash site, described a "fat fuselage" without wings. He also said he saw three bodies, two outside the craft, one partially visible inside.

> **"**I don't believe any single person will ever affect disclosure, I believe it will take a huge groundswell of public opinion and demand. The only way to get that public demand is to get the MSM [Mainstream Media] involved. The only way to get the MSM involved is to play the game by their rules ... You see, it is my personal opinion that it's not the public who isn't ready, it's the MSM, the people who have careers and reputations on the line. No serious news person is going to risk their job and credibility on anything that can't be vetted. If you come off the blocks shouting the aliens are among us and the president is a reptile nobody is going to talk to you. **"**

ATS MEMBER COMMENT

—**Dr. C. Bertrand Schultz**, a paleontologist working in the area, heard of the crash and bodies from Holden at the time and encountered the military cordon thrown up around the site.

—**Major Jesse Marcel**, the Roswell intelligence officer who was first on the scene and announced the crash of a "flying disc," took pieces of strange metal that would straighten out after bending home to show his family.

Although Marcel did not contradict the balloon explanation at the time, in later years he said he was correct the first time about a craft from space and that he was muzzled by military authorities. "It was not anything from this Earth. That, I'm quite sure of," Marcel said, "Being in intelligence, I was familiar with all materials used in aircraft and in air travel. This was nothing like this. It could not have been."

—**Dr. Jesse Marcel, Jr.**, Maj. Marcel's son who clearly remembered markings on the metal brought home by his father as consisting of "different geometric shapes, leaves, and circles" akin to hieroglyphics. His father told him the metal came from a flying saucer, then had to explain what a flying saucer was to young Marcel. Today, Marcel, a respected physician with the Veteran's Administration who served in Iraq, said, "Beyond my desire to see my father remembered as a man of integrity and intelligence, I feel that the public has a right to know the answer to one of the biggest questions facing us: Are we alone in the universe? The answer, I believe, is no."

—**Col. William Blanchard**, Roswell Army Air Field commander, visited the crash site and initially indicated to Marcel that the crash involved something highly unusual, perhaps a Soviet secret weapon. He immediately passed the entire matter up to his superiors. Nothing was said about a balloon. Blanchard's authorization to release information to the public concerning a captured disc, whether true or a cover story for some secret operation, should have spelled the end of his military career. Instead, Blanchard, who always declined to discuss the event, went on to become one of the youngest brigadier generals in Army history.

—**Major Edwin Easley**, Blanchard's provost marshal in charge of the Military Police who guarded the crash site, told researchers a large volume of crash debris was loaded onto trucks and taken to the Roswell base where it was placed on an airplane. In recent years, Easley said he promised the president he would not reveal what he saw, but indicated he believed it was an extraterrestrial craft.

—**Sgt. Thomas C. Gonzales**, one of the guards at the site, later confirmed the recovery of "little men" with large heads and eyes.

—**Paul Price**, who with his older brother, visited the crash site before the military swept the area. "There were so many parts for as far as you could see. Some of the pieces just snapped back in your hands when you bent them," he told researchers in later years.

—**Steve MacKenzie**, stationed at Roswell, tracked the object on radar for almost 24 hours and then visited the crash site where he said a major from Washington took charge of the dead bodies, described as small with large heads and eyes. Mackenzie said if the object he tracked had been a weather balloon, secret or not, his superiors would have ordered him to ignore it.

—**Lt. Col. Albert L. Duran**, a member of MacKenzie's unit, has acknowledged seeing the small bodies.

—**Warrant Officer Robert Thomas** flew to Roswell from Washington with a team of experts, including two photographers, early on July 4 after learning of the erratic path of the object tracked by radar. All were on hand at the crash site, according to MacKenzie.

—**Master Sgt. Bill Rickett**, a counterintelligence corps agent, arrived late at the crash site but described what he saw as a curved craft with a bat-like trailing edge which had struck front first into the side of a cliff scattering a great deal of debris. Rickett was assigned to assist University of New Mexico scientist Dr. Lincoln La Paz. According to Rickett, La Paz, apparently unaware of the bodies, concluded the craft was an unmanned probe from another planet.

—**Sgt. Melvin E. Brown** later told family members he helped transport alien bodies from the crash site to a Roswell hanger. He described them as smaller than humans with leathery skin like a reptile.

—**Frank Kaufmann** of the 509th Bomb Group staff told of a single large crate that was placed in a cleared-out hanger at Roswell and protected by armed guards. He said he understood the crate contained bodies recovered at the crash site. In 1994, he told CBS, "They didn't look like they were from Texas."

—**First Lt. Robert J. Shirkey**, former assistant operations officer at Roswell field, described how he participated in an unscheduled flight to Wright-Patterson on July 8, 1947. He described how men in dark suits, "FBI types," carried cardboard boxes of metallic material out to a waiting B-29 aircraft. He still recalled seeing "a small I-beam with hieroglyphic markings on the inner flange, in some kind of weird color, not black, not purple, but a close approximation of the two."

—**W. O. "Pappy" Henderson**, a pilot with the 1st Air Transport Unit, flew the crate and debris in a C-54 transport plane to Andrews Air Field in Washington, then on to Wright Air Field in Ohio, according to Steve MacKenzie. Henderson's widow, Sappho, said he had described the debris as "weird" and nothing he had ever seen before. She added that, following a TV special in 1988, Henderson confirmed the descriptions of small recovered bodies.

—**John Kromschroeder**, a close friend of pilot Henderson with an interest in metallurgy, said he was given a piece of metal by Henderson, who said it was part of the interior of the crashed craft. Kromschroeder said the metal was gray and resembled aluminum but he was unable to cut it even using a variety of tools.

As for Roswell, yes I believe it happened, more so when told by former astronaut Edgar Mitchell that he'd spoken to top officials and was told it was real, not to mention the smoking gun of a discovery, i.e. the bit of paper in Ramsey's hand which details the recovery of bodies from a 'disc'.

—**Major Ellis Boldra**, who may have studied the same piece of metal as Kromschroeder, told his family that the fragment was incredibly strong and did not melt when he subjected it to an acetylene torch but in some way dissipated heat.

—**Sarah Holcomb**, who worked at Wright Field at the time, told researchers she heard from a crew member that a plane had landed with bodies from a flying saucer. Later the base commander came around and said there was no truth to the story but added that anyone mentioning the "rumor" would be subject to 20 years in jail and a $20,000 fine.

—**Helen Wachter** also was at Wright Field and said she overhead the husband of a friend talk excitedly about the arrival of "alien bodies." At first, she thought he meant people from outside the country, but she quickly understood he was referring to extraterrestrials.

—**William W. "Mac" Brazel**, owner of the crash site, said he heard an explosion during a thunderstorm on the night of July 4 and the next day, along with William Proctor, found a field full of scattered debris, described many big pieces of dull gray metal that was unusually lightweight and could not be cut or burned. Four days later, after being held by military authorities and accompanied by military officers, Brazel told the Associated Press the debris consisted of string, paper, some tape, and bits of metal which covered no more than 200 yards in diameter. Oddly enough, he ended this obvious description of some sort of kite or balloon by saying, "I am sure what I found was not any weather observation balloon."

// Don't forget everyone that the flying disk [official news] release was made before his [Roswell base commander Colonel William Blanchard] superiors were there. He may not have known about the cover-up, he was only a colonel. Or do you think every full-bird at every podunk army airfield in the middle of nowhere knows everything about the most top secret things in our Gov.? [Note: By any explanation for the Roswell crash, Col. Blanchard made a mistake in authorizing the 'captured flying disk' news release. Anyone familiar with the U.S. military knows that mistakes like this can cost one's career. Yet, Blanchard went on to a distinguished military career, in fact, becoming one of the youngest brigadier generals in U.S. military history.] //

—**Bill Brazel**, Mac's son, said his father was held for eight days by the military and only released after swearing not to discuss the incident. He told his son he was better off not knowing about it but swore what he saw was not a balloon. Bill Brazel said military authorities muzzled his father. He also said he handled some of the debris found later on his father's ranch and that it resembled aluminum foil but when wadded into a ball, it would straighten itself out smooth. He too said it could not be cut or burned.

—**Floyd and Loretta Proctor**, nearest neighbors of rancher Mac Brazel, recalled that Brazel showed them pieces of the debris that could not be cut or burned.

—**William Proctor**, the Proctor's son, saw a large amount of debris and took some home. Later, according to family members, he was forced to turn it all in to the military.

—**Sallye Tadolini**, the daughter of another of Mac Brazel's neighbors, told researchers that she recalled Bill Brazel showing her a piece of dull-colored metal which he balled up into his fist and, when he opened his hand, returned to its original shape.

—**Frank Joyce**, in 1947 a radio announcer for Roswell station KGFL, confirmed to researchers that Mac Brazel's story after being taken into military custody was "significantly" different from an initial interview during which Brazel mentioned a horrible stench and "little people" that were not human. Joyce said talking to Brazel privately some time later, the rancher admitted that he had changed his story, explaining that military authorities had threatened him and his family. "They told me it would go hard on me if I didn't do what they said," Brazel told Joyce.

—**Robin Adair**, an Associated Press photographer in 1947, was sent by airplane to the debris field on July 8. Although waved off by military authorities, Adair got a bird's eye view of the scene. He said some portions of the ground appeared scorched and that he noticed a discernible "gouge," that left him with the impression that something had struck the ground, then ascended back into the air. "Whatever hit the ground wasn't wood or something soft," he told researchers in recent years. "It looked like it was metal."

—**Glenn Dennis**, then a mortician working for Ballard's Funeral Home in Roswell, said about 1:30 p.m. on July 5, he received a call from the Roswell base mortuary officer asking if the funeral home could provide a number of small caskets that could be hermetically sealed. Dennis said he realized something strange had occurred when the officer called back and asked how to prepare a body, which had been burned or left out in the elements for a period of time. Later that day, Dennis drove to Roswell Field to deliver an injured airman. At the base hospital he saw strange pieces of wreckage in the rear of an ambulance but soon was chased off by an officer, who told him not to talk or "somebody will be picking your bones out of the sand." A few days later, Dennis said a nurse friend told him she was called in to assist in the autopsy of three "foreign bodies" that gave off an overpowering odor. She said the bodies were small with large heads and hands with four fingers ending in pads that looked like suction cups. Dennis is well respected by those who know him, but because he once gave a false name for the nurse in an effort to protect her identity, his whole story has been called into question.

—E. M. Hall, former Roswell police chief, confirmed to researchers that he heard Dennis talking about the base requesting coffins for "the bodies from a flying saucer" within days of the incident.

—George Bush, whose sister Mariam worked as secretary to the base hospital administrator, told researchers he would never forget the day in July 1947 when she came home and told her family she had seen a creature from another world. In obvious emotional distress, she described seeing the bodies of what she first thought were small children in an examination room. But their heads and eyes were too large and their skin was grayish brown. The next day, a more composed, but obviously terrified Mariam Bush, told her family, "I am never to say another word about what I saw. None of you ever heard me say anything about it." She never spoke about the incident again and in 1989 when her body was found in a California hotel room with her head in a plastic bag, her death was ruled a suicide.

—Chaves County Sheriff George A. Wilcox kept a carton of crash debris left by Mac Brazel but was ordered to turn it over to the military. For some time, Wilcox complained how the military usurped his authority, even barring his deputies from the crash site. Wilcox along with his wife, Inez, were told by military police that if he ever talked about the incident, his entire family would be killed.

—Barbara Dugger, the granddaughter of George and Inez, said her grandmother quoted military police as saying if anything was ever said about the incident in any way, "not only would we be killed, but they would get the rest of the family." Years later, Inez Wilcox also confided to her granddaughter that a flying saucer had crashed near Roswell.

—Frankie Rowe was the teenaged daughter of Dan Dwyer, a Roswell fireman who went to the scene on Saturday morning and later told his family he saw the wreckage of a flying craft, two small dead bodies and "a very small being about the size of a 10-year-old child." According to Rowe, military authorities threatened her family and one man told her if she talked about the incident, she would disappear into the desert and would never be seen again.

—Brigadier General Arthur E. Exon was a World War II combat pilot who spent time in a German POW camp and later was stationed with the Air Material Command at Wright-Patterson Air Force Base—as it was known after Wright Field and Patterson Field merged. In recent years, Exon became the highest-ranking officer to confirm that a quantity of material from Roswell arrived at Wright Field for testing by a "special project" team of lab workers. He said the material was "unusual," looked like foil but couldn't be dented even by hammers. According to Exon, the consensus of scientists who studied the Roswell material was that "... the pieces were from space." He also said that he flew over the crash site and was able to see where the craft had come down. Exon added that bodies were found with the main portion of the craft, which ended up in a separate location from the debris.

*//*What is most important is what the ranchers saw. Everything since then has been smoke and mirrors. The government has admitted to lying with two cover stories and is currently on their third. I see no reason to trust them. *//*

The witnesses above represent only a small portion of the total number of people who, by 2008, have spoken out regarding their experiences in Roswell.

At least one politician attempted to get to the truth. In the early 1990s New Mexico Republican Rep. Steven Schiff sent letters requesting information and all files pertaining to the Roswell incident to the secretary of defense, the White House, Pentagon, FBI, CIA, NSA, and all branches of the military. None of his inquiries were answered. Finally, the U.S. General Accounting Office (GAO), responding to a request by Schiff, conducted a document search on records pertaining to the Roswell incident, which only added to the mystery. In July 1995 the GAO reported, "RAAF [Roswell Army Air Field] administrative records (from March 1945, through December 1949) and RAAF outgoing messages (from October 1946 through December 1949) were destroyed." This unusual destruction of documents was done without explanation and apparently without any authority. One of only two documents found by the GOA was an FBI teletype indicating the Bureau may have been monitoring Roswell base telephones and it clearly stated a "disc" was sent to Wright Field. Schiff died of cancer in 1998 at the age of 51.

Without access to physical evidence, the truth of Roswell boils down to whom one trusts—official government pronouncements backed by little to no evidence or several hundred persons who all tell an internally consistent story.

Considering such a clash of belief systems, it is only natural that questions have been raised regarding both the competency and veracity of the Roswell witnesses. But even if half of them are discounted, the remainder, coupled with the missing documents and wreckage, should be more than enough to convince anyone with an open mind that something out of this world occurred at Roswell in the summer of 1947.

> **"** Any foreign technology that would have needed to be covered up at the time is now old news, no reason to cover it up anymore ... Unless whatever tech they recovered has either never been released or it has been released but they need to cover up the origins of that tech. **"**

▶ IS GOD AN ALIEN?

▽ WHO

▶ God

▽ WHAT

▶ The age-old question of who or what is God.

▽ WHEN

▶ Questions as to the nature of God have been around as long as humankind.

▽ WHERE

▶ Questioning the nature of God has permeated the thoughts of humans all around the world.

▽ WHY

▶ To ponder the nature of God appears to be an attribute of all thinking humans.

additional evidence and commentary:
www.abovetopsecret.com/book/god

Is God an alien?

This question is a modern one since people in the past were ignorant of space and the concept of space travel. They did, however, clearly understand that realms of life exist that transcend the three-dimensional material world. And, similar to recent claims of alien abduction, humans throughout recorded history have claimed to have encountered non-human entities.

The understanding that life does not end with our material existence gave rise to religion, the outward manifestation of the inner search for spiritual truth. One must understand the division between spirituality and entrenched religious dogma.

If one believes in the older religious traditions, which portray God as an entity who resides in heaven, separate and apart from this world, then obviously God would be alien to us. But emerging science and philosophies view God as the cohesive and unifying factor of the universe as well as a creative force that encompasses all life.

The basic question concerning God as an alien may come from a basic misunderstanding concerning current literature, which speculates upon an extraterrestrial origin for humankind.

This concept began to take hold in the 1970s when journalist and author Erich Von Daniken aroused much public interest with his books dealing with "ancient astronauts" visiting the Earth. He described a number of anomalistic structures around the world and speculated that they were the result of alien visitation.

Middle East and Bible scholar Zecharia Sitchin added fuel to this speculative fire with his series of books highlighting the "Anunnaki," mentioned in ancient Sumerian tablets and translated as "Those Who from Heaven to Earth Came." Sitchin compares these Anunnaki to the Nephilim of the Old Testament, which in Hebrew translates to "Those Who Have Come Down from the Heavens to the Earth."

In Genesis 6:4, the Bible states, "The Nephilim were on the earth in those days—and also afterward—when the sons of God went to the daughters of men and had children by them. They were the heroes of old, men of renown [*New International*]."

// At the risk of going south when I die, I think that the Bible may prove that god is not a single being, but may be aliens, that used their own DNA to create mankind. //

ATS MEMBER COMMENT

After years of translation and study, Sitchin realized that the biblical *Nephilim* and the Sumerian Anunnaki represented the same concept—that in the Earth's most distant past, beings came down from the stars and founded the world's earliest civilizations. This is a theme that has run through nearly all secret societies, from Freemasonry to the Thule Society.

No one disputes the basic translation of the Sumerian writings, only the interpretation. Conventional encyclopedias have described these writings as mythology. Sitchin and other scholars have simply taken the attitude that perhaps the ancient Sumerians were putting down on their clay tablets their history as they understood it rather than mere myths. After all, the Sumerian descriptions of many of their ancient cities were believed to be fanciful stories until their ruins were discovered and excavated.

Based on Sitchin's work, as well as others including Alan F. Alford, R. A. Boulay, Neil Freer, Dr. Arthur David Horn, Dr. Joe Lewels, C. L. Turnage, Lloyd Pye, Laurence Gardner, and William Bramley, the account of the Anunnaki went something like this: About 450,000 years ago, a group of spacefaring humanoid extraterrestrials arrived at planet Earth. They came from a planet about three times the size of Earth, which the Sumerians called Nibiru. Nibiru was depicted in the ancient

Sumerian literature as the twelfth planet of our solar system. Modern observers have not seen Nibiru because it travels on a lengthy elliptical orbit passing into our solar system only every 3,600 years.

As early as 1981, American scientists were theorizing the existence of a tenth planet in our system based on sightings by an orbiting telescope and studies of irregularities in the orbit of Pluto indicating an additional solar body.

Life on Earth evolved based on its one-year orbit around the Sun, the solar year. Life on Nibiru developed based on its one-year orbit around the Sun—3,600 years to Earthlings. It then stands to reason that life on Nibiru would have evolved somewhat sooner than on Earth. It may also be compared to the normal life span of a human, which would seem to be immortal to the weeks-long life of many insects.

Ancient tablets record that about 450,000 years ago, during Earth's second ice age, the highly developed inhabitants of Nibiru—the Anunnaki—journeyed to Earth as the two planets came into proximity. According to the Sumerians, their initial landings were made in water, just as our own astronauts at first splashed down in the ocean.

Logically, these ancient astronauts would have sought a base camp that provided moderate weather and a good source of water and fuel. The "Fertile Crescent" of Mesopotamia—today known as Iraq—met all these criteria. It is intriguing that today Iraq remains one of the few locations in the world where first world visitors cannot easily visit, thanks to first a boycott after the 1991 Gulf War and the current occupation by American troops.

With the supreme Nibirian ruler, Anu—or An or El, depending on the source—supervising their effort from the home planet, the Anunnaki began a systematic colonization of Earth under the leadership of Anu's two sons, Enlil and Enki. All of these Anunnaki leaders were later to assume the role of "gods," or Nephilim, to their human subjects.

Researchers theorized that these colonists were after Earth's mineral wealth—particularly gold—for use on their home planet. "The Anunnaki sought gold to save their atmosphere, which had apparently sprung leaks similar to those we have created in ours by damaging the Earth's ozone layer with hydrofluorocarbons," explained author Lloyd Pye. "The Anunnaki solution was to disperse extremely tiny flakes of gold into their upper atmosphere to patch holes ... Ironically, modern scientists contend that if we are ever forced to repair our own damaged ozone layer, tiny particulates of gold shot into the upper atmosphere would be the best way to go about it."

Apparently an initial effort to retrieve gold from the Persian Gulf by a water-treatment system proved inadequate for their needs. Anu, along with his heir Enlil, visited the colony and assigned Enki to find more gold. Enlil was placed in overall command of the Earth colony while Enki led a foray to Africa and, eventually, to South America, where gold mining operations were set up. Proof of such early gold mining has come from scientific studies conducted for the Anglo American Corporation, a leading South African mining corporation, in the 1970s. Company scientists discovered evidence of ancient mining operations that were dated as far back as 100,000 BC. Similar ancient mine excavations have been found in Central and South America. This indicated the Anunnaki mining efforts were worldwide and may go far in explaining the early diffusion of humans.

In an effort to ease the increasing rivalry between the half-brothers Enlil and Enki, their father Anu placed Enlil in charge of the Mesopotamian colony E.DIN—perhaps the basis for the biblical Eden—while assigning Enki to AB.ZU or Africa, the "land of the mines."

Further problems for these extraterrestrial colonists arose due to climate changes that caused hardships among the Anunnaki and the unrelenting drudgery of the mining operations. One Sumerian text reported, "When the [Anunnaki], like men, bore the work and suffered the toil—the toil of the gods was great, the work was heavy, the distress was much."

At this point, Enki suggested that a "primitive worker," an *Adamu*, be created that could take over the difficult work. Enki pointed out that a primitive humanoid—what we call *Homo erectus* or a closely related humanoid—was quite prevalent in *Abzu* [Africa] where he worked."

Enki's plan to create a worker race was approved by the Assembly and, according to this story, proved to be the origin of modern man. This explanation also clarifies one of the most puzzling verses in the Bible. After being assured in the Bible that there is only one true God, Genesis 1:26 quoted the singular God as speaking in the plural, "Let us make man in our image, after our likeness ..."

This verse may carry two explanations—first, that the plural *Elohim* of the Old Testament, interpreted as "God" by the monotheists who wrote Genesis, indeed may have referred to the Anunnaki Assembly which approved the creation of man and, second, the idea of creating man "in our image" meant simply genetic manipulation of an existing species, much as humans breed cattle, horses, dogs, cats, and other animals.

Interestingly, according to Sitchin, the Anunnaki had the same ethical debates taking place today over the right of one species to create another. The Anunnaki Assembly, desperately in need of workers, accepted Enki's argument that there was no true creation because they were only tweaking the DNA of existing creatures.

So, the "gods" never created anything new, they merely improved the breed of existing Earth primitives, the same as modern man breeds animals to improve the species.

The Anunnaki Earth mission's medical officer was a female name Ninharsag, also known as Ninti, who had already been working with Enki in genetic experimentation.

The Sumerian account of the creation of the first man—written as LU.LU in the Sumerian or in Hebrew, *Adama*, literally translated as Man of Earth or simply Earthling—is quite clear in light of today's knowledge concerning in vitro fertilization. But up until 25 years ago or so, the whole concept would have been incomprehensible even to the most learned scholar.

According to the Sumerian account, Enki and Ninharsag took the reproductive cell or egg from a primitive African female hominoid and fertilized it with the sperm of a young Anunnaki male. The fertilized ovum was then placed inside an Anunnaki woman—reportedly Enki's own wife Ninki—who carried the child to term. Although a Caesarean section was required at birth, a healthy young male *Adama* hybrid was produced for the first time on Earth, bypassing natural evolution by millions of years.

Several connections between the Sumerian version of man's creation and the Bible are apparent. The Bible speaks of woman being created from Adam's rib. "The great Sumerologist, Samuel N. Kramer, pointed out near the middle of this century that the taking of Eve's origin from Adam's rib probably stemmed from the double meaning of the Sumerian word TI, which means both 'rib' and 'life,'" explained Horn. So, Eve may have received her "life" from Adam without any bone being involved or genetic material may have been extracted from bone marrow.

> **// [T]he Cuna Indians in Panama believe that Adam and Eve came on a spaceship. They could have the only religion on Earth that got it right. //**

ATS MEMBER COMMENT

"Adam was the first test-tube baby," proclaimed Sitchin after the birth of the first modern test-tube baby in 1978. He saw this modern birth as support for his Sumerian translations, especially in light of the fact that modern science only began to conceptualize manipulating our genetic makeup within the twentieth century.

Evidence that the first primitive humans originated in Africa has grown since the 1970s when some of the oldest pre-human remains were found there. The bones of "Lucy" and other *Australopithecus* clearly indicated that early primates lived in that area of Earth more than three million years ago but were not as evolved as even the Neanderthal. Contrary to popular belief, scholars C. P. Groves, Charles E. Oxnard and Louis Leakey have agreed that *Australopithecus* was totally different in morphology from humans. Groves commented that "non-Darwinian" principles would be required to explain any connection between "Lucy" and modern humans. Recent research into mitochondria DNA, the building blocks of the human genetic makeup carried only by females, has been traced to one female primitive in Africa.

According to Sitchin's timeline, the first human—the *Adama*—was produced about 300,000 years ago. After further genetic manipulation, Anunnaki males began interbreeding with human women about 100,000 years ago. Not long after this, a new Ice Age began decimating the human population outside Anunnaki control. Neanderthal disappeared while Cro-Magnon survived only in the Middle East.

By 50,000 years ago, human hybrids fathered by Anunnaki were permitted to rule in selected cities. Thus began the focus on hereditary "bloodlines" so common with all ancient civilizations right up to the modern European royalty and even the Nazis.

Even mainstream researchers who dismiss the story of aliens on Earth concede that life here may have come from space in comets or meteors containing life-bearing chemicals. "Scientists believe that Earth and other planets have been seeded from space with ... potential building blocks of life," stated a *New York Times* article in 1988.

But these new theories of human origins continue to meet stiff resistance from scientific and academic authorities who have so much invested in conventional theories and history, not to mention religious authorities.

Author Dr. Clifford Wilson, who attacked the ancient astronaut theories of von Daniken on Biblical grounds, made clear his belief that UFOs have no connection to God. "To argue that God's heavenly messengers need UFOs to achieve His purposes is to limit God's powers, and His thoughts, to those of men. Much of the modern writing about UFOs and the Bible tends to think of God as little more than a glorified astronaut ... The physical principles by which UFOs operate might well be utilized for the purposes of God, but the Bible certainly does not confine Almighty God to a heavenly 'super-car,'" he wrote.

As every Christian fundamentalist has been taught, Satan is the Great Deceiver. The New Testament's Book of 2 Corinthians 11:14 (*Revised Standard*) states, "... for even Satan disguises himself as an angel of light." "Those who look upon such phenomena as the UFOs, contactees and the occult as benevolent are playing into his hands," warned religious writers John Weldon and Zola Levitt.

Since the UFO researcher is told that from the human perspective he cannot separate angels from demons posing as helpers, he is trapped in a spiritual "hall of mirrors" just as confusing as the one erected about UFOs by government deceit and disinformation. Small wonder so many people chose to ignore the UFO phenomenon rather than deal with all its ramifications.

But questions remain.

For example, even if the Anunnaki or other ETs did produce modern human-kind through genetic manipulation, who created the Anunnaki?

Several persons using the government-tested techniques of psychic remote viewing have seen various visions of life in the universe. All have indicated that intelligent life does not end at the boundaries of Earth. "As best I can, I'd call it the feel of a mantle of some kind," one reported, "like being covered by a bed cover when it's cold or being inside a cocoon of a kind that's everywhere and I mean everywhere. Like this whole universe was full of life just waiting to happen … It's like everything is a humungous pattern and there isn't really one person but rather it's one whole cloth. I'm a seamstress and I can only think of the whole thing as if I were making a gown and the extent of this thing is, well, you can make billions and billions of gowns from it and it would still be endless."

Another viewer said, "I'm sensing that there is what we call God but it's not like we think of God at all. It's more impersonal. It's not a personal thing at all. What is personal is that, well, as best as I can say, it's like people who have gone before us, who are now serving as role models and guides to how things are and how we're supposed to do it while we're here. I'm gonna call them 'people' because they are like me in every conceivable sense of the word, 'cause I don't feel different from them and that's weird in itself. The way I'm getting this is that we are actually all the same, just different casings.

The pattern is the same. It's like a conspiracy for life, all kinds of life forms, that is."

Several remote viewers have told of visiting locations outside of Earth where beings in pyramidal structures worship the "One" or the "All," the sum total of our spirits.

One viewer told of a conversation with a hooded being who patiently tried to explain that each individual being is the eyes and ears of the Creator. The viewer was told, "... when one forgets that, there is separation and separation is unnatural ... regardless of what body form we have, we are also made of something that interfaces with body form. He says we call this the mind, but it's more than that [the soul?] ... He says mind and feelings go together and have always gone together, but that emotions, strong emotions cloud awareness ... to really live simply means to live without fear. Everything is energy and that I must try to understand things in terms of energy exchanged, shared, and not to steal energy from another. He says this is what reality really is—energy and energy exchanges. He's now telling me that what I think the world—no, the universe—is really like, isn't. He says I am relying too much on what others tell me and what I and others agree is."

// Just as we are about to give birth to self-learning AI, we may have started as something similar. Another possibility is that we were on a natural evolutionary path and some beings modified us. It would explain the missing link and how civilization seemingly popped up out of nowhere. They may have also used religion in our past as a way of guiding us ... perhaps even wiped out the first few experiments to start over. //

Mel Riley, one of the original psychic spies for the U.S. Army, told of mentally visiting a distant world where hooded figures worshipped before an unadorned alter in the center of a huge pyramid. He reported feeling a close connection to this unearthly place saying, "It was a very beautiful experience. I felt very calm and secure. I've always had a feeling that there was something I should have remembered about that. That something should come back to me, something relating to that experience. It's almost as if I had been to that place before. It's like I should have remembered that place."

Today, many researchers and philosophers are viewing God as the all-encompassing creative force in the universe, a concept advanced by some extraterrestrials within the UFO literature. This concept is reminiscent of the "Force" mentioned in the *Star Wars* films and falls neatly within Albert Einstein's

Unified Field Theory. This is the idea that the entire universe is one interconnected energy field which encompasses all life—all matter, gas, and energy.

As with any energy, there is a positive and negative pole—a light and dark side, good and evil. At the highest level of this universal energy-mass is self-aware, sentient creative energy from which all else flows. Each human being—as well as alien beings—is an individual unit of this energy-mass, aware of the whole at an intuitive and unconscious level but unaware in the course of the normal material human lifespan.

// I would say that like most ancient writing, we should try to avoid reading any of it literally. These aren't engineering texts or newspapers, and the people who wrote them weren't all that interested in absolutely truthful accuracy. They embellished, they fictionalized, they took information from oral sources that were confused and maybe didn't even make sense to begin with. Dreams and fantasies were just as 'real' to them as anything else. All part of the story. //

The analogy is your computer. The hardware—metal, plastic, and wire—is not the source of the ability to compute. Artificial intelligence lies within the software, which is managed through the billions of tiny bytes of energy moving along the boards. One individual byte is nothing. But collectively, billions of bytes form a certain intelligence that is able to compute numbers and information.

Likewise, science has proven that an electromagnetic energy field surrounds each person. Some call this the aura. Interestingly, science has shown that at the time of death, this energy field does not dissipate but simply moves away, supporting the concept that energy can be neither created nor destroyed. It can only change form. This dictum also would seem to support the idea of life (in the form of self-aware energy) after death.

Like the bytes in a computer, the sum total of energy fields within the universe form a self-aware, sentient creative personality that is omnipotent and omnipresent—a pretty fair description of God.

Several ETs reported by various UFO contactees have acknowledged one supreme force but refused to call it God. "We prefer not to use the word God in speaking of the ultimate creative force of the universe," explained one non-human speaking through an unidentified California woman. "Primarily because the word God in your society has become masculinized and requires the use of the masculine pronoun, thus perpetuating the personification of the universal creative force ... Unfortunately the word God gives rise to anthropomorphic fantasies that have no place in this teaching. For our purposes we shall call this constant creative force the Tao, for it is impossible for the Western mind to construct any visual image around this word."

Several reported quotes by aliens and more than a few New Agers have stated that we are all parts of a greater whole, living in a "pan-dimensional universe." It has been explained that each individual is a bit of sentient energy or soul that is separate from the personality. This soul is "trapped" in a series of physical bodies so it can experience all cycles of life.

"The continuous creative force that is universal casts out entities into physical lifetimes. These entities fragment and become many different personalities. Their integration is the evolutionary pattern for all souls. You do not feel the desire to seek the remaining fragments of your entity until the last physical cycle. Then, at that time, there is almost a compulsion," explained a collection of entities under the name Michael in a popular 1980s book entitled *Messages from Michael*.

"Imagine the Atlantic Ocean as the whole," explained Michael. "Imagine filling ten test tubes, then sealing them so that they are both airtight and watertight, then imagine dropping them back into the ocean. They are part of the whole, yes, but unless some outside force liberates them, they are remote from the source and trapped in an effective prison. This same way the soul is trapped in the body."

Unbelievable as all this sounds to most people, it echoes the basic message of a book first published back in 1955, which has attracted a small but loyal following. *The Urantia Book* is nearly 3,000 pages of an obtuse and overly detailed description of the nature of God and the creation and structure of both Earth and the universe reportedly channeled from a variety of non-human entities, including an entity named Melchizedek.

According to *The Urantia Book*, the original Melchizedek was a direct creation of God who—along with another direct creation, Gabriel—administers our known universe, referred to as Nebadon, which contains 10,000 inhabited systems. Urantia is this book's name for Earth.

The book's authors made it clear that sentient life exits both on other physical worlds as well as in other dimensions. They also stated that humans are spiritual beings of energy living simultaneous existences on many different levels but that most people have lost this knowledge except in regard to religious matters. "We worship God, first, because he is," wrote the authors, "then, because he is in us, and last, because we are in him."

This book agreed with other researchers in stating that a wide variety of non-human life forms—many of them energy beings—visit and work on the Earth for the purpose of assisting in the planet's evolutionary growth. The struggle between good and evil on this world is a physical manifestation of the struggle between those beings who chose to follow their own desires and intellect and those who follow the heartfelt plan of God, the sum total of creative energy.

> **//**I think us going from apes to humans is strong evidence of this [outside interference with human evolution]. According to the evolution theory, we evolved into humans because we started using tools. Our brain grew and we started walking upright ... Well, that's one theory, but apes today are using tools as well, and probably have been forever without evolving into humans. I think an alien genetic upgrade would explain our evolution from apes a lot better. **//**

While words of love, higher consciousness, and the immortality of the spirit are written off by many people as some sort of "New Age" balderdash, there is an intriguing consistency to these messages. Whether this is due to some cosmic truth or simply the result of an evolving mythology among writers of such material who read each other and then add their own interpretation appears to be a matter of individual belief.

The Rev. James A. Wiseman, chairman of the Department of Theology at Catholic University, has stated, "Personally, I've always believed we will find life on other planets." He said those whose faith might be shaken by extraterrestrial life are those who believe in a separate and anthropomorphic God who created life on Earth and Earth alone. He added that changing such "egocentric and ethnocentric mind-set" might require a massive shift in beliefs comparable to Copernicus persuading the public that the Earth actually revolves around the Sun.

▶ WHAT WILL HAPPEN IN 2012?

▽ **WHO**

▸ This question may affect the entire population of the Earth.

▽ **WHAT**

▸ Apocalyptic prophecies aside, a number of sources point to the year 2012 as some sort of major turning point in human history.

▽ **WHEN**

▸ Predictions vary somewhat, but a consensus of sources points to late 2012 with the date December 21 prominently mentioned.

▽ **WHERE**

▸ The solar system containing the Earth.

▽ **WHY**

▸ Here the consensus breaks into two basic possibilities—the astronomical and the spiritual.

additional evidence and commentary:
www.abovetopsecret.com/book/2012

///

There's an old saying that states if everyone tells you that you don't look well, perhaps you ought to lie down.

When ancient prophecies along with recent scientific discoveries tell us that something is changing in our environment and may well culminate in the year 2012, perhaps we'd better start paying attention. As 2012 draws nearer, a growing number of people are speculating on what, if anything, this particular year might portend.

Just as the approach to the millennium year 2000 produced widespread fears and concern over various predictions, such as the much-touted Y2K computer crash, attention has been increasingly focused on the year 2012.

But in this case, there is much more input than a few computer geeks afraid of a time rollover. The idea that 2012 will be the harbinger of new directions for the Earth and humanity goes back thousands of years. Many cultures have prophecies concerning the last days of a "Great Cycle." These include the Mayans, Hopis, Egyptians, Cabbalists, Essenes, the Qero elders of Peru, Navajos, Cherokees, Apaches, Iroquois, the Dogon Tribe in Africa, and Aborigines in Australia.

The most notable of such prophecies concerns the Mayan calendar, based on legends and calculations of this pre-Columbian people in what is now southern Mexico and northern Central America. It is believed by many that the Mayans based their calendar on information from much older cultures such as the Olmecs and Zapotecs. Where this amazing astronomical knowledge originated is open to question but many researchers believe it was handed down from even earlier times.

The winter solstice on December 21, 2012 corresponds with the close conjunction of our Sun with the Galactic Equator or the central belt of our Milky Way galaxy. The Mayans referred to this juncture as the "Sacred Tree" and saw it as the end of the present world and the start of a new 25,000-year cycle of life. The ancient Sumerians, perhaps the world's first great civilization, also recorded a cycle of 25,920 years.

The Mayans with their advanced observatories and knowledge of the constellations used several methods for keeping both terrestrial and celestial time. One primary source was a 260-day calendar called the Tzolkin. Its origins are unknown. The Mayans also had other calendars such as the Haab and the Wayeb. Extended periods of time were measured by the "Long Count," in which one 360-day year was called a "Tun." Twenty Tuns equaled a Katun (7,200 days); 20 Katuns equaled a Baktun (144,000 Tuns); and 13 Baktuns totaled the "Great Cycle" of 1,872,000 days, about 5,125 years.

> **//**Hmmm ... wasn't that supposed to happen in 560 AD, 1348, 1500, 1820, 1928, 2000 ... 2012 ... its just a number and just another year. **//**
>
> ATS MEMBER COMMENT

Many scholars have attempted to compare the Mayan Long Count with contemporary calendars. After much work, our Gregorian calendar was finally reconciled with the Long Count. Correlation with the Mayan calendar showed that the beginning of the Great Cycle was around August 12, 3114 BC with an end date on December 21, 2012. This is the date that our Sun will align with the exact center of the Milky Way galaxy, which the Mayans considered a cosmic womb—a place of death, transformation, regeneration and rebirth.

Dr. Jose Arguelles in his book *Time and The Technosphere* reasoned: "August 13, 3113 BC, is as precise and accurate as one can get for a beginning of history: the first Egyptian dynasty is dated to circa 3100 BC; the first 'city', Uruk, in Mesopotamia, also circa 3100 BC; the Hindu Kali Yuga, 3102 BC; and most interestingly, the division of time into 24 hours of 60 minutes each and each minute into 60 seconds [and the division of the circle into 360 degrees], also around 3100 BC, in Sumer. If the beginning of history was so accurately placed, then must not the end of history, December 21, 2012, also be as accurate?"

According to Mayan legend, dark formations of interstellar dust in our Galaxy known as "dark rifts" or the "Great Cleft," were called the "Black Road" or the "Road to the Underworld." They saw this "road" as a sign pointing to the location where the Sun will align with the center of the Galaxy (the Sacred Tree) and believed it would create a portal to other worlds when sunlight from our Sun enters this rift in 2012 signaling the end of their calendar.

We would do well to remember that scholars differ on their interpretation of the Mayan calendar, and there could still be problems in trying to correlate it with the Gregorian calendar. This means that the precise moment of the end of the Mayan cycle could be off by years or even tens of years. For example, the Islamic calendar ends in 2076 while the Jewish calendar ends in 2240. Nevertheless, most students still pinpoint the year 2012 as an auspicious date.

The foreseen alignment of our Sun with the center of the Galaxy has been acknowledged by science with some fascinating information in the bargain. In 2005, astronomers began detecting strong and unusual radio waves emanating from the center of our Galaxy, about 26,000 light years from Earth. Editors at *National Geographic* wondered if these signals were the last "burping" of energy from a dying star or if they represented something "completely new to science." The normally conventional publication even ventured to state that "the transmission's intriguing characteristics beg the question: Might that source be intelligent?"

"The most spectacular aspect of this is that five bursts occurred at regular intervals of about an hour and a quarter," stated astronomer Scott Hyman of Sweet Briar College in Virginia who aided in the discovery. "They were at a constant intensity ... and each burst had basically the same time profile [about 10 minutes]."

Transient radio emissions are not particularly unusual but, until recently, short-lived radio bursts were rarely detected, because during any given observation radio telescopes could only focus on a relatively small area of the sky.

Subsequent research was conducted by scientists at the Very Large Array (VLA) of radio telescopes, located, interestingly enough, at Socorro, New Mexico, one of the two sites commonly associated with the Roswell crash of 1947. VLA scientists speculated that clashing jets of gases and particles, which formed a cloud of hot gas that emitted radio waves, caused the radio signals. But based on the regular transmissions, others still ponder both the source and the meaning of these signals.

Some 2012 researchers say that the end of the Mayan Great Cycle is the apex of a series of sunspot cycles. They contend that unusual solar activity in 2012 may reverse the Sun's magnetic field, causing earthquakes and flooding on the Earth.

The famous seer Edgar Cayce predicted a shift in the world's magnetic poles sometime after the year 2000. "There will be the upheavals in the Arctic and in the Antarctic that will make for the eruption of volcanoes in the torrid areas, and there will be shifting then of the poles," Cayce stated in 1934. Just such a shift in the Earth's gravitational field was reported in 1998 by NASA's Goddard Space Flight Center. A press release noted that the magnetic poles had moved closer together. The NASA article explained that as the ice on the poles melted, ocean currents moved water toward the equator, promoting this ongoing shift in the Earth's magnetic field.

Some believe the changing magnetic field will alter the endocrine production of the pineal gland, raising human consciousness. In fact, many metaphysical folks think that 2012 will mark a heightening of human awareness, and will include a rebirth of spirituality.

Cayce described an era of enlightenment and peace on the Earth. But before this "kingdom of God" arrives, he foresaw world events that can only be described as apocalyptic—a period involving natural disasters that will dramatically alter the surface of the Earth, wars, economic collapse, and socio-political unrest.

One particularly gifted and tested remote viewer has stated, "2012 is now." He said it is time for those persons with open mind and heart to "step into the light," light generally acknowledged to mean enlightenment, wisdom, or truth. This viewer estimated that only about one in 100,000 persons will move to enlightenment while the others will sink deeper into darkness, chaos, ignorance and despair.

Further corroboration for the idea of a change in magnetic fields came in the summer of 2006 when a small sunspot appeared on the Sun's surface, floated around a bit, and vanished again within a few hours. This particular sunspot was magnetically backwards with a polarization opposite the normal north-south orientation of sunspots. It gained the swift attention of astronomers. David Hathaway, a solar physicist at the George C. Marshall Space Flight Center in Huntsville, Alabama, said, "We've been waiting for this. A backward sunspot is a sign that the next solar cycle is beginning."

One website saw the possibilities in such a cyclic transformation by stating: "Never before has the population of this planet increased by 216,000 people a day! Never before has the Earth's biosphere been in such a precarious state. That which seems like normal lifestyle decisions and behaviors are but precedents set by our modern standards—not necessarily reflecting the most balanced, healthy, or sane way to operate. It is for us to decipher how to live our lives with integrity; to determine what truths empower us to model our lives according to our greatest harmonious potential."

// There's just so much esoteric, spiritual, and religious doctrine converging onto itself. Given this, [along] with the current global geopolitical tension—and it gets far too difficult, for me, to entertain the possibilities that nothing amazingly significant [will be] happening in the next four or so years. //

Whether such a change in the human mind and spirit occurs, it now seems apparent that geophysical changes are taking place on the Earth. Over the past decade, scientists have chronicled some of the greatest hurricanes, tornadoes, tidal waves, and droughts ever recorded. Global warming, so long dismissed by many mainstream scientists, now appears to be a fact.

But it is not just the Earth that seems to be impacted by a changing environment. In 2005, data from NASA's Mars Global Surveyor and Odyssey missions revealed that the carbon dioxide "ice caps" on Mars had been shrinking for three summers in a row. Russian scientist Habibullo Abdussamatov, head of space research at St. Petersburg's Pulkovo Astronomical Observatory, attributed warming on both Mars and the Earth to changes taking place on the Sun. "Man-made greenhouse warming has made a small contribution to the warming seen on Earth in recent years, but it cannot compete with the increase in solar irradiance," stated Abdus-samatov. Mainstream climatologists, who have long been immersed in the politics of global warming, did not readily accept his views. Additionally, the outer planets have become more luminescent, indicating rising temperatures.

Other researchers sincerely believe that all this activity may be due to solar system wide disruption caused by some heavenly object not yet discovered or made public. The ancient Sumerians in their cuneiform stone tablets called this visitor Nibiru, the "Planet of the Crossing," because its orbit crosses the solar system between Mars and Jupiter. They said it proceeds on an elliptical orbit that takes it far outside the solar system before being pulled back by gravitational force. Nibiru has been symbolized in numerous societies—particularly Egyptian—as a "winged disc," a circle with wings stretching to either side.

> **// People upon realizing the reality of 2012 often get fear-filled. They want to run, but there's no place to run to, so they start lying to themselves and think if they can convince others it isn't happening, that makes it somehow more 'real.' It's happening. //**

ATS MEMBER COMMENT

Reports claim that Nibiru can be seen by the naked eye beginning on May 15, 2009, and by Dec. 21, 2012, its arrival will be plain to all. Major earthquakes and other events will begin by Feb. 14, 2013, according to some accounts.

Modern scientists also have suggested that an undiscovered planetary body may be connected with our solar system. As early as 1981, American scientists were theorizing the existence of a tenth planet in our system based on sightings by an orbiting telescope and studies of irregularities in the orbit of Pluto indicating an additional solar body. "If new evidence from the U.S. Naval Observatory of a tenth planet in the solar system is correct, it could prove that the Sumerians ... were far ahead of modern man in astronomy," commented a writer for the *Washington Post News Service*. There is no inconsistency here, as the Sumerians counted the Moon and the Sun as planetary bodies, thus arriving at the number 12, the same number as the pantheon of the Sumerian Anunnaki overlords.

Speculation of an undiscovered body in our solar system goes far back. The astronomer Percival Lowell reported that irregularities in the orbits of Uranus and Neptune led him to conclude that a distant planet, which he called Planet X, must lie beyond Neptune. His search for this planet led to the discovery of Pluto in 1930. However, Pluto's size and mass is not enough to have impacted the orbits of other planets. Something else must be out there.

A 1983 article in the *New York Times* by John Noble Wilford stated, "Something out there beyond the farthest reaches of the known solar system seems to be tugging at Uranus and Neptune ... The force suggests a presence far away and unseen, a large object that may be the long-sought Planet X." The article went on to say: "Recent calculations by the United States Naval Observatory have confirmed the orbital perturbation exhibited by Uranus and Neptune, which Dr. Thomas C. Van Flandern, an astronomer at the observatory, says could be explained by 'a single undiscovered planet.' He and a colleague, Dr. Robert Harrington, calculate that the tenth planet should be two to five times more massive than Earth and have a highly elliptical orbit that takes it some 5 billion miles beyond that of Pluto—hardly next-door but still within the gravitational influence of the Sun." This information apparently was confirmed in a 1992 NASA press release that stated: "Unexplained deviations in the orbits of Uranus and Neptune point to a large outer solar system body of 4 to 8 Earth masses, on a highly tilted orbit, beyond 7 billion miles from the Sun."

On September 10, 1984, *U.S. News & World Report* noted: "Last year, the infrared astronomical satellite (IRAS), circling in a polar orbit 560 miles from the Earth, detected heat from an object about 50 billion miles away that is now the subject of intense speculation." Gerry Neugenbaur, director of the Palomar Observatory for the California Instititute of Technology, said, "All I can say is that we don't know what it is yet."

According to devotees to the subject, Planet X is the cause of the current solar violence, global warming, and other ongoing Earth changes. Researcher Joe Burd noted "numerous events that can't adequately be scientifically explained, that we might even perceive as 'freak accidents,' such as the recent New York City steam pipe explosion, countless mining disasters on the rapid increase, and the Minnesota bridge collapse that happened on August 1, 2007. Statistically speaking, there have been more natural and freak accidents occurring over the past two decades than at any earlier point in modern times. The increased number of structural failure issues are a result of three major factors including a declining global infrastructure, Earth's interaction with other seen and unseen heavenly objects, and frequent low level seismic activity all world."

Some believe the arrival of a new heavenly body was prophesied in the Bible. Jeremiah 48:8 [*Revised Standard*] states, "The Destroyer shall come upon every city, and no city shall escape; the valley shall perish, and the plain shall be destroyed ..." Revelation 8:10–11 foresaw a future when "... a great star fell from heaven, blazing like a torch, and it fell on a third of the rivers and on the fountains of water. The name of the star is Wormwood."

Some scientists and astronomers believe that the object will arrive within our system before, but certainly no later than, 2012. Its arrival, according to some, will precipitate violent solar and electromagnetic storms, huge tsunamis, heat waves, and massive earthquakes.

Strangely, despite all the media attention to a tenth planet in the 1980s and early 1990s, interest from the media quickly faded and very little has been said in recent years. This inattention has caused some researchers to conclude that the arrival of a new solar system body could create havoc on Earth and that governments do not want to panic the population. To prevent such panic, there has been an embargo placed on news concerning Planet X, Nibiru, Wormwood, the Destroyer or whatever you want to call it. It has been reported that NASA, with no explanation, no longer publicly comments on this issue, including its own previous official statements. For a prophetic look at what such a doomsday scenario involving two planets might look like, check out the classic 1951 film *When Worlds Collide*.

Despite any embargo, there are tantalizing clues that some groups are well aware of the its approach and are taking steps to observe and prepare for its arrival. The South Pole Telescope (SPT), a 10-meter diameter sub-millimeter wavelength telescope, designed to sweep large areas of the sky, went into operation at the end of 2006. More than thirty scientists and engineers operate this enormous instrument, located at the U.S. South Pole Station. All researchers and some ancient legends contend that Planet X will first become visible from observatories in the Southern latitudes.

Even more ominously, consider the construction of the Svalbard Global Seed Vault on the Norwegian island of Spitsbergen, one of the Earth's most isolated and inaccessible locations. A venture funded by Microsoft founder Bill Gates, the Rockefeller Foundation, Monsanto Corporation, Syngenta Foundation, and the government of Norway, this project has been nicknamed the "Doomsday Seed Bank." Its purpose is nothing less than to gather and store all known seeds from around the world and to preserve them in the event of a cataclysm such as nuclear war, biological warfare, further global warming, or the arrival of something from outer space. Construction of the vault began in June 2006, and is expected by late 2008 to be completed. Suspicious researchers question: Why this need and why now and why the rush to complete it?

// People often get confused thinking that the GLOBE is the 'WORLD.' It is not. A world map and the world globe has less to do with the planet as a globe rather then the way mankind has cut up the land masses in some aspects of 'control.' The end of the 'world' therefore means the end over governmental control over the land masses ... When I speak about the end of the world, that's what I'm talking about. I'm not talking about the end of human kind, although I do understand the world wide death toll will be upward of 75%. //

Doubters and debunkers might do well to realize how quickly events can reshape the world. To illustrate, simply consider the world in the summer of 1939. Despite a few aggressive moves by foreign dictators like Adolf Hitler and Benito Mussolini, the world was at peace. Europeans were enjoying the pleasant summer weather and Americans were comforted by their isolation from world events. Less than one year later, the world was at war. Britain's back was against the wall while Japan and Germany were at the zenith of their power. Only a year a half after that America was attacked by the Japanese and appeared on the verge of invasion. Just three and a half years later, both Japan and Germany lay in ruins and America found itself the preeminent power in the world.

Many see the convergence of events culminating in 2012 as the impetus for the escalation of efforts to transform the world into a One World government, a New World Order. Although such plans, originating within secret societies, have long been laid, there appears to have been increased efforts since 2001, as if some timetable is being hurried.

> **//** I can not wait to ascend. A shift in realities. Upgrade in dimensions. Mind Blowing Experience Indeed. We are lucky to be a part of this Generation. **//**

ATS MEMBER COMMENT

One thing about the year 2013 seems fairly clear—we will all look back and most probably agree that we are not living in the same world as we did in 2008, just as in 2008 we can all agree that we are not living in the same world that we did in 2000.

WARNING

////////////////////////

CAVEAT LECTOR!

The Internet is a wonderful invention. It has opened new lines of communication for millions all across the planet. But be cautious.

For you see, the upside to the Internet is that everyone and anyone has access to it. The downside is that everyone and anyone has access to it.

The Internet is rife with truths, untruths, half-truths, misinterpretations, exaggerations, and downright hoaxes. One must be most discerning.

For example, one person using the name "GhostRaven" stirred up the *Above Top Secret* community by posting a story about how he or she was recruited to write material designed to prepare both national and local governments for the announcement of a pending attack by aliens. This person then proceeded to explain how this was a hoax and how it had been perpetrated.

Other hoaxes on ATS played themselves out, such as the "Aussie bloke" postings warning that a cloud of comets would destroy the Earth starting on June 18, 2004. This thread went so far that there were claims that someone was covering up the truth and the hoax was itself a hoax. When 2004 came and went with no destruction, the truth became obvious.

Other presumed hoaxes are more difficult to expose, such as a lengthy posting by Timothy S. McNiven, who claimed to be part of a U.S. Army artillery unit in Germany that scripted a war game exercise against the World Trade Center towers during the Jimmy Carter administration. He lambasted 9/11 truth seekers who quite correctly hesitated to disseminate this unsupported story.

Some suspected hoaxes linger on, such as the John Titor—time traveler from the future—story detailed in this book. Most people have written this off as a hoax, yet a few still hold out some thoughts that it might be real.

Likewise, some long-running stories—such as the Billy Meier UFO case and the 12 astronauts of Project Serpo—have continued to cling to life despite compelling arguments to the contrary.

Now that you have become educated to the basics of various mysteries and controversies, you must start to apply critical thinking and learn to separate the wheat from the chaff—the hoax from the genuinely odd.

The quandary of trying to separate the truth from untruth has led me to the creation of my "Huh?" file. When I receive some new bit of information, I neither accept nor reject it out of hand. My world experience has taught me better. I simply say, "Huh?" and file it way in anticipation of further input.

In due time, there usually appears more information which either confirms or repudiates the initial story. From there, the information either goes into other files or into the wastebasket.

Keep your eyes and ears—and your mind—open and maintain a "Huh?" File.

Jim Marrs

For more news and views you won't find in the corporate-controlled mass media, please visit **AboveTopSecret.com** and **JimMarrs.com**.

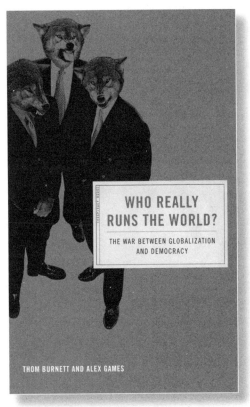

THE TERROR CONSPIRACY:

Provocation, Deception and 9/11

JIM MARRS

Jim Marrs (author of *Rule by Secrecy* and *Crossfire*), as the world's leading conspiracy theorist, unmasks the facts about 9/11 and the New World Order. He presents the official government pronouncement on 9/11 as an obvious conspiracy. The only question is—whose conspiracy was it?

By Jim Marrs
Trade Paperback • 6 x 9 • 504 pages • Current Affairs / Political Science
$16.95   ISBN: 978-1-932857-43-6